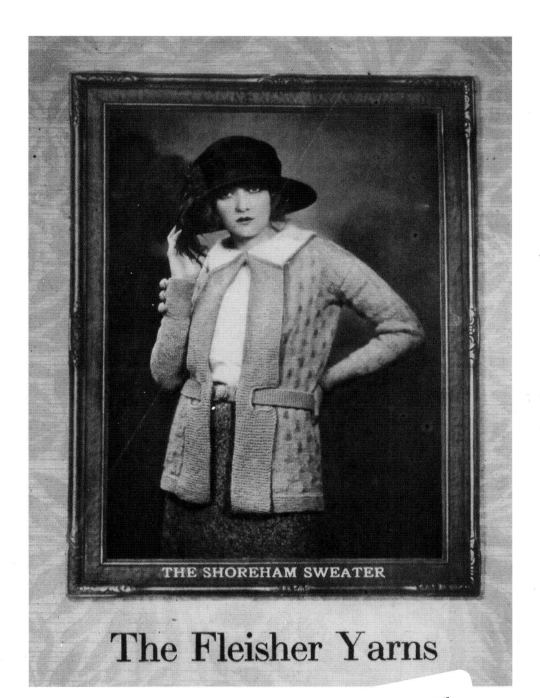

THE SHOREHAM SWEATER

The Fleisher Yarns

Fifth Avenue Fashions

CROCHET... KNITTING

as seen from
the 102 story
EMPIRE STATE
BUILDING

BOOK 51

RETRO

Knits

Cool Vintage Patterns for
Men, Women, and Children
from the 1900s through the 1970s

Kari Cornell and Jean Lampe, Editors

Voyageur Press

cp D?

First published in 2008 by Voyageur Press, an imprint of MBI Publishing Company, 400 1st Avenue North, Suite 300, Minneapolis, MN 55401 USA

Voyageur Press titles are also available at discounts in bulk quantity for industrial or sales-promotional use. For details write to Special Sales Manager at MBI Publishing Company, 400 1st Avenue North, Suite 300, Minneapolis, MN 55401 USA.

To find out more about our books, join us online at www.voyageurpress.com.

Editor: Kari Cornell
Designer: LeAnn Kuhlmann

Printed in Singapore

Library of Congress Cataloging-in-Publication Data
 Retro knits : cool vintage patterns for men, women, and children from the 1900s through the 1970s / edited by Kari Cornell and Jean Lampe.
      p. cm.
  ISBN-13: 978-0-7603-2977-1 (pbk.)
  ISBN-10: 0-7603-2977-X (pbk.)
  1. Knitting—Patterns. 2. Vintage clothing. I. Cornell, Kari A. II. Lampe, Jean. III. Title: Vintage patterns for men, women, and children from the 1900s through the 1970s.
TT825.R427 2008
746.43'2041—dc22
                              2007039572

PERMISSIONS

ACKNOWLEDGMENTS

This great collection of vintage patterns would never have come to exist without the help of many dedicated people. We owe special thanks to those who granted permission for us to use patterns in the book: Catherine Blythe of Spinrite GP Inc., Lynn Brown of Coats & Clark, Ed Hamrick of Caron International, and Dan Musick of Plaid Enterprises, Inc. I would like to personally thank Jean Lampe for offering her knitting expertise, for providing a range of sizes for today's knitter, and for knitting swatch after swatch after swatch to ensure that the recommended yarn weight, needle size, and gauge was correct for each pattern. A special thanks also goes to designer LeAnn Kuhlmann for finessing all of the disparate elements in this book into a cohesive, attractive whole.

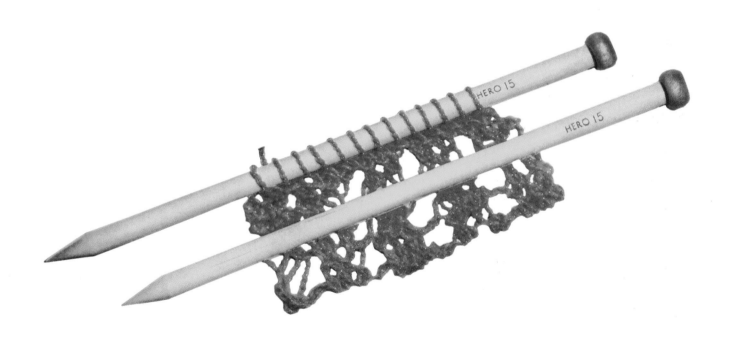

CONTENTS

Cotton Fashions for CROCHET and KNITTING

BOOK 38
TEN CENTS

Happy are those who wear the knits included in this 1930s pattern book!

INTRODUCTION

The design for this classic cable sweater was featured in a 1940s Bernat pattern book.

As long as I can remember, I've adored all things vintage. In high school, I idolized James Dean and Marilyn Monroe, poodle skirts, saddle shoes, and smart sweater sets. For prom, I rented a black gown made in the late 1940s from the community theater's costume shop. In college, I stocked my wardrobe with retro finds from local thrift shops. And when I got married, I found a cream-colored, wool cloche hat at an antique store and had a Minneapolis-based designer make me a simple, pretty wedding gown reminiscent of the 1920s. By the time I started knitting in my early thirties, I was a fan of forties fashion.

It wasn't long before I discovered the hundreds of vintage patterns from the 1940s and beyond available on eBay. Needless to say, a knitter who is a fan of 1940s fashion is very lucky indeed; during the 1940s, a decade often referred to as the Golden Age of Knitting, knitting patterns flooded the market. My stars aligned in another way as well; as an editor at Voyageur Press, I happened to be collecting stories and artwork to fill our first knitting anthology, *For the Love of Knitting*. I spent many hours shopping for vintage patterns and corresponding with top-notch knitters and writers. The book was a labor of love, and the collection of patterns I gathered to use as artwork turned out to be a treasure trove. Once *For the Love of Knitting* was released, readers began to ask where they could find the instructions for the pattern book covers that appeared in the book. And so the idea for *Retro Knits* was born.

With the plethora of magazines, pattern books, and web patterns available to knitters and crocheters today, why the need to dig back into the past? What is it about retro designs that continue to entice knitters?

Knitting from vintage patterns not only evokes fond memories of garments mother, grandmother, or a favorite aunt made for us; it also provides an escape to a time when life seemed less complicated. And retro styles have become classic style.

The women's traditional sweater set, made popular in the 1940s, will always be a wardrobe staple, as will the basic men's V-neck sweater of the 1940s. The fit may be snug or roomy, depending on what is in fashion at any given time, but the sweater design remains essentially the same.

As Jean and I were gathering patterns to include in this collection, we were struck by how similar designs from the 1950s, 1960s, and 1970s are to patterns found in magazines and books published recently. The vintage pattern for the Versatile Shoulderette from the 1950s has made a comeback as today's basic shrug. Our retro version is made in a wonderful fingering-weight yarn that gently drapes over the shoulders. And designs very much like the Hooded Cape and Leg Warmers from our 1970s collection are common in today's fall clothing catalogs. Everything old is indeed new again.

BEFORE YOU BEGIN

Our plan in creating this book was to print a large collection of cool vintage patterns as they were first published, with very few changes. We would include updated yarn and needle suggestions, of course, but otherwise we wanted to retain as much of the wording as possible, and publish the fun photos that accompanied the original patterns. For the most part, we've done just that. But along the way, we made a few discoveries that prompted us to adapt the patterns to make them more useful to the modern knitter. We've added abbreviation explanations, schematics, a glossary of terms used, and, where possible, extra sizes, offering at least three for most projects.

SIZING

The sizes referenced in vintage patterns are quite different from the sizes we are accustomed to today. For example, a women's size 12 of earlier decades would actually fit a size 4 or 6 in current sizes. In the 1940s, a women's size 20 fit a 40″ bust

When they were introduced in the early part of the twentieth century, circular needles revolutionized knitting.

circumference. In a recent Lands' End catalog, a size 20 is listed to fit a 45–1/2″ bust circumference. Using that same bust measurement, we checked the Women's Size Charts listed by the Craft Yarn Council of America (CYCA) Standards and Guidelines for Crochet and Knitting, only to discover that a 40″ bust size was determined to be size 1x. It appears that marketing has played to our vanity over the years because as the population grew larger and heavier, manufacturers gradually began using smaller numbers to designate sizes.

To make the patterns in this book easier to use, project instructions have been revised to fit today's sizes, and additional sizes have been included where possible. The original instructions for many projects were offered only in one size … and not the all-encompassing one size fits many, either. If knitters didn't fit the size 32″ or 34″ bust offered, they surely had to know how to adjust the knitting instructions, or find something else to knit. The vintage instructions we found, especially those dating from the 1910s, 1920s, and 1930s, included very few tips on how to adapt the instructions to make larger sizes.

YARN AND NEEDLE INFORMATION

Many patterns from the 1910s, 1920s, and into the 1930s simply listed the yarn brand with no mention of yardage, fiber content, weight, wraps per inch, or other helpful information. Needle sizes listed in these early patterns were just as vague, with U.S. sizes, old English sizes, or, in later decades, revised English sizes being used interchangeably. It wasn't uncommon to find a combination of both systems listed within a single project. So, to solve the mystery of what yarn weight and needle size to suggest for each project, we turned to the gauge, when it was provided. Some projects, believe it or not, didn't include a gauge.

Making every effort to stay true to each designer's original concept of drape and fluidity, we knit swatch after swatch using a variety of yarns until we found current yarns that provided a similar hand to those displayed in the original pattern photographs. Yarns made from natural fibers always closely matched those projects from earlier decades.

Since the actual yarns and brand names used to make the swatches would not necessarily be available by the time this book went to print, we used the Craft Yarn Council of America's Standard

Yarn Weight System instead. This helpful chart is available for download at http://www.yarnstandards.com. Copies of the CYCA yarn weight table and symbols are also included here, and CYCA yarn weight designations are listed in each set of instructions. We've also included current U.S. and metric sizes for knitting needles and crochet hooks for each project. As with all knitting and crochet projects, use the specified gauge as your guideline, and be prepared to change needle sizes as necessary to obtain it.

CHARTS, SYMBOLS, AND SCHEMATICS

Patterns published in the 1910s, 1920s, 1930s, and 1940s rarely included charts, symbols, or schematics. Patterns from the 1930s or 1940s included instructions for only a single size, but it would provide body measurements and gauge information. It wasn't until the 1950s that basic charts were printed along with some patterns. Although schematics remained rare in patterns of this decade, hints and abbreviation explanations began to appear in a few knitting publications, and multiple sizes were offered with almost every project. By this time, a wider variety of yarns, both natural and synthetic or treated fibers, were available. Although yardage and content information still wasn't included in detail, the terms worsted-, fingering-, and feather-weight were in general use. The word *worsted* was used in earlier decades, as in *knitting worsted*, but that generally referred to how the fibers were prepared and spun, not to yarn weight. From the 1950s onward, the word commonly applied to yarn weight as we know it today.

Standard Yarn Weight System

Categories of yarn, gauge ranges, and recommended needle and hook sizes

Yarn Weight Symbol & Category Names	0 Lace	1 Super Fine	2 Fine	3 Light	4 Medium	5 Bulky	6 Super Bulky
Type of Yarns in Category	Fingering 10 count crochet thread	Sock, Fingering, Baby	Sport, Baby	DK, Light Worsted	Worsted, Afghan, Aran	Chunky, Craft, Rug	Bulky, Roving
Knit Gauge Range* in Stockinette Stitch to 4 inches	33–40** sts	27–32 sts	23–26 sts	21–24 sts	16–20 sts	12–15 sts	6–11 sts
Recommended Needle in Metric Size Range	1.5–2.25 mm	2.25–3.25 mm	3.25–3.75 mm	3.75–4.5 mm	4.5–5.5 mm	5.5–8 mm	8 mm and larger
Recommended Needle U.S. Size Range	000 to 1	1 to 3	3 to 5	5 to 7	7 to 9	9 to 11	11 and larger
Crochet Gauge* Ranges in Single Crochet to 4 inch	32–42 double crochets**	21–32 sts	16–20 sts	12–17 sts	11–14 sts	8–11 sts	5–9 sts
Recommended Hook in Metric Size Range	Steel*** 1.6–1.4mm Regular hook 2.25 mm	2.25–3.5 mm	3.5–4.5 mm	4.5–5.5 mm	5.5–6.5 mm	6.5–9 mm	9 mm and larger
Recommended Hook U.S. Size Range	Steel*** 6, 7, 8 Regular hook B–1	B–1 to E–4	E–4 to 7	7 to I–9	I–9 to K–10½	K–10½ to M–13	M–13 and larger

* GUIDELINES ONLY: The above reflect the most commonly used gauges and needle or hook sizes for specific yarn categories.

** Lace weight yarns are usually knitted or crocheted on larger needles and hooks to create lacy, openwork patterns. Accordingly, a gauge range is difficult to determine. Always follow the gauge stated in your pattern.

*** Steel crochet hooks are sized differently from regular hooks--the higher the number, the smaller the hook, which is the reverse of regular hook sizing.

This Standards & Guidelines booklet and downloadable symbol artwork are available at: **YarnStandards.com**

Most of the charts, symbols, and schematics that accompany the patterns in this book were added at the editing stage to bring the patterns up to date and make them easier to use.

We hope you enjoy this hand-picked selection of vintage patterns and wish you many years of successful retro knitting to come!

1910s

ashion during the early part of the twentieth century, especially women's fashion, reflected a shift from the elaborate designs of the Victorian era to a simpler aesthetic. As women became more active in sports, such as bicycling, tennis, and golf, the puffy sleeves, corseted waistlines, and flared skirts favored in the late 1800s gave way to long, athletic sweaters in simple designs that allowed for ease of movement. The clothing favored by the fashionable set fit snugly and was usually worked in fine yarn on small needles.

Belts, dressy collars, and decorated hems and necklines added style and flair to otherwise plain garments. Many of these athletic sweaters were knit using garter stitch, often combined with large rib-stitch patterns. Most garments were worked in one color, and when a second color was featured, it usually appeared in the collar, cuffs, or trim around edges of sweaters, hats, or scarves.

Winsome Sweater Vest,
published by Monarch, 1910s

This vest from the early twentieth century would be an easy project for a beginning knitter with basic skills. The stitch pattern is simple and provides enough interest to prevent the knitter from becoming bored.

SIZE
Chest: 36–38"

FINISHED MEASUREMENTS
Chest circumference: 40"
Length from shoulder to hem: 24"

MATERIALS
Yarn—CYCA #4 Medium:
 About 600 yds rose (MC);
 75 yds white (CC)
Size 8 [5 mm] knitting needles
2 decorative buttons, about
 3/4" or 1" diameter
Tapestry needle

GAUGE
21 sts = 4–1/2" [11.5 cm]
 and 24 rows = 4" [10 cm]
 in patt st. *Adjust needle size as
 necessary to obtain
 correct gauge.*

BACK

Using CC, CO 93 sts. Work in garter st (knit every row) until border measures 2" from CO. Change to MC and work patt as foll (beg all rows with k3 when working this patt):
Row 1: K3, *yo, k2tog, k1*; rep from * to end of row.
Rep row 1 until work measures 6" from CO
Next 36 rows: K12, work in est patt to last 13 sts, k13.

Underarm Shaping:
When work measures 12" or desired length from CO, beg underarm BO.
Next row: BO 12 sts, work in patt to end of row—81 sts.
Next row: BO 12 sts, work in patt to end of row—69 sts.
Work in patt until back measures 10" from underarm shaping.
Next row: Work 15 sts in patt, BO 39 sts, work in patt to end of row—15 sts each side.

Straps: (make 2)
Working one strap at a time, work in patt on 15 sts for 6" or desired length. Cut yarn leaving 3 yd tail. Place sts on holder. Join yarn to rem 15 sts and work second strap the same. Place sts on holder.

FRONT
Work same as back until both underarm shaping rows are finished. Work in patt until front bib measures 8" from underarm shaping. BO all sts.

FINISHING
With yarn threaded on tapestry needle, sew front and back tog at side seams. Try the vest on, pulling straps over the shoulders until they meet the top edge of the front bib. Pin both straps in place, then decide if you want to make the straps longer or shorter. If more length is needed, remove sts from holder and place on needle, cont working straps in patt until desired length, using the 3 yd yarn tails to complete the extra length. BO all sts when desired length is achieved. If the straps are too long, mark the desired length with a pin, then carefully remove the necessary number of rows until straps are the length you want. BO all sts.

Edging
With CC and crochet hook, work a row of sc (see Glossary) around the edge of neck, straps, and armholes. Fasten off. Use patt st yos at strap ends as buttonholes, align buttons on front bib to match the yos, and sew buttons in place on front bib. Weave in yarn tails to WS of work.

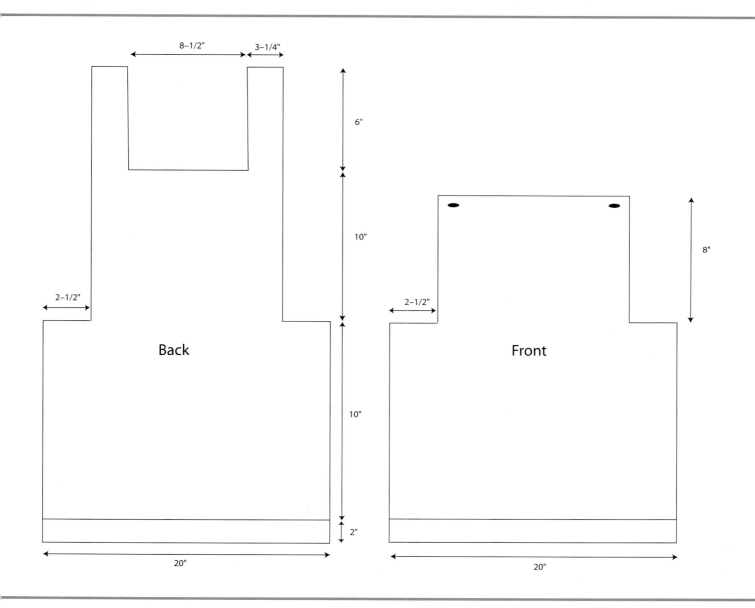

Roseate Sweater, published by Monarch, 1910s

This snug-fitting sweater is worked in two patterns, garter stitch and a wide k8, p8 rib from back to front, with moderate dolman-style sleeves. The collar and cuff trim are knit in a contrasting color.

BACK

With MC and larger needles, CO 104 (104, 120) sts using permanent crochet chain CO (see Glossary).
Row 1 (RS): K4, p8, *k8, p8; rep from * to last 4 sts, k4.
Row 2: P4, k8, *p8, k8; rep from * to last 4 sts, p4.
Rep rows 1 and 2 until front measures 9 (9, 11)", ending with WS row completed.
Change to garter st (knit every row) and beg shaping as foll:

Sizes 38 and 40" only
Inc 1 st at each end of every other row 3 (6) times—110 (116) sts.

Size 42" only
Inc 1 st on next row—121 sts.

All sizes
Work even for 3".
Note: To make a longer body, add more length here before beg sleeve shaping. You'll probably need more yarn.

Sleeve shaping: Cont in garter st, CO 6 sts at beg of next 22 (24, 24) rows—242 (260, 265) sts. Work even in garter st until narrow end of sleeve measures 6 (6, 6–1/2)".

Back neck shaping: Work 102 (111, 112) sts, join new ball of yarn, and BO 38 (38, 41) sts, knit to end of row—102 (111, 112) sts each side of neck.

FRONT

Begin front: Working each side of neck with its own ball of yarn, work even in garter st for 2".

Neck shaping: Inc 1 st each side of neck every other row 7 (7, 8) times—109 (118, 120) sts each side, then CO 2 sts at beg of neck edge rows 3 times—115 (124, 126) sts each side. Work even if necessary until front neck depth measures about 4", ending with WS row completed.

Join front into one piece: Next row (RS): Knit 115 (124, 126), CO 12 (12, 13) sts, knit 115 (124, 126)

sts—242 (260, 265) sts. Cut extra ball of yarn, leaving 4" tail. Work even in garter st until narrow end of sleeve measures 6 (6, 6–1/2)". BO 6 sts at beg of next 22 (24, 24) rows—110 (116, 121) sts. Work even for 3".
Note: If you added extra length on back, add the same amount here.

Sizes 38 and 40" only
Dec 1 st each end every other row 3 (6) times—104 (110) sts.

Size 42" only
Dec 1 st next row—121 sts.
Change to rib patt and work same as back for 9 (9, 11)". BO all sts.

Cuffs
With larger needles, MC, and RS facing, pick up and knit 66 (66, 70) sts.

SIZE
38 (40, 42)"

FINISHED MEASUREMENTS
Chest circumference: 40 (42, 44)"
Length: 20–1/2 (21–3/4, 22–3/4)"
Sleeve length to underarm: 16–1/4 (17–1/4, 18–1/4)"

MATERIALS
Yarn—CYCA #3 Light, 100% wool or blend: About
    1800 (1950, 2100) yds main color (MC); about 100
    (125, 125) yds contrast color (CC)
Size 3 [3.25 mm]; size 7 [4.5 mm] knitting needles
Size D/3 [3.25 mm] crochet hook

Tapestry needle
1 yd smooth cotton waste yarn for provisional CO
    (collar)
Open-ring stitch markers or small coilless pins

GAUGE
22 sts and 44 rows = 4" in garter st on size 7
    [4.5 mm] needles. *Adjust needle size as necessary*
    to obtain correct gauge.

NOTE
Sweater is made in one piece, working from back to
    front and adding sleeves as you work. The collar
    and cuffs are added separately.

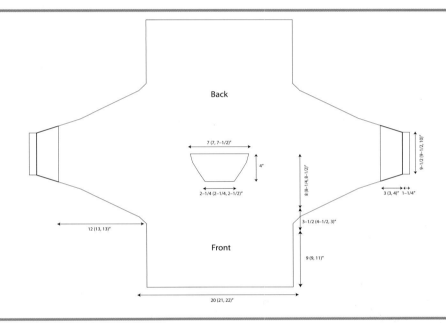

Row 1 (WS): *P2, k2; rep from * to last 2 sts, p2.
Row 2 (RS): *K2, p2; rep from * to last 2 sts, k2.
Rep rows 1 and 2 until cuff measures 1 (1–1/2, 2)"
from pick up row. Change to smaller needles and cont in
rib patt for 2 (1–1/2, 2)". Cont with smaller needles,
change to CC and work 8 rows garter st. BO all sts.
Work second cuff the same.

Collar
With smaller needle, crochet hook, and waste yarn CO
33 sts in provisional crochet chain CO (see Glossary).
Join CC and work back and forth in garter st until collar is
long enough to encircle neckline. Do not BO. Remove
waste yarn from CO and place sts on needle. Align
needles tog so front needle has one end of collar with a
purl row and back needle has the other end with a knit
row (remove yarn from 1 row if necessary to achieve
this), graft both ends tog as foll: cut yarn leaving about

25" tail and thread tapestry needle. Insert needle pwise
into first st on front needle, then pwise into first st on
back needle, draw yarn through. *Insert needle kwise
into first st on front again, draw yarn through. Drop yarn
from needle. Insert needle pwise into the next st on
front needle, draw yarn through. Drop yarn from needle.
Insert needle kwise into the first st on back needle again,
draw yarn through. Insert needle pwise into the next st
on back needle, draw yarn through.
Rep from * across row for each st. When graft is finished,
weave yarn end through several sts on WS to secure.
Pin RS collar to WS of neck. With threaded tapestry
needle, whipstitch (see Glossary) collar around neckline.
Remove pins and fold collar over seam to RS of sweater.

FINISHING
Join sleeve and side seams tog with tapestry needle and
MC using mattress st (see Glossary). Weave ends to WS.

Fairy Bonnet and Sweater, published by Monarch, 1910s

This darling bonnet and sweater set was typical of those popular during the 1910s. This seems to be a convoluted method for constructing a baby's bonnet, but it was popular in the 1910–1920s. It does provide the knitter with several options to easily customize fit. The Fairy sweater is a simple slipover with a sailor-style collar edged with a contrasting color.

METHOD—BONNET

The process begins with the front band, which fits around the face and is worked flat, back and forth. When the depth of this piece is sufficient, extra stitches are cast on to the front of the needle holding the live stitches, and the total stitch count (old and newly cast-on stitches) is divided onto four double pointed needles. The crown is worked in rounds and shaped with decreases. To complete the hat, stitches are then picked up along the lower edge and a neckband is worked. Ribbon or crochet ties are then attached to the front lower edge to secure the hat in place.

FRONT BAND

Using MC, CO 92 sts (if you want to make this section smaller or larger, adjust the CO number). Work in garter st (knit every row) for 18 rows (9 garter ridges).
Row 19: *K1, p1; rep from * to end of row.
Row 20: *P1, k1; rep from * to end of row.
Next 44 rows: Knit.

CROWN

CO 36 sts onto the end of the needle holding the live sts—128 sts. Divide sts onto 4 dpn (32 sts each needle). Join into rnd.
Rnd 1: Knit.
Rnd 2: *K14, k2tog; rep from * to end of last needle—120 sts.
Rnd 3 and all odd-numbered rnds: Purl.
Rnd 4: *K13, k2tog; rep from * to end of last needle—112 sts.
Rnd 6: *K12, k2tog; rep from * to end of last needle—104 sts.
Rnd 8: *K11, k2tog; rep from * to end of last needle—96 sts.

Rnd 10: *K10, k2tog; rep from * to end of last needle—88 sts. Cont decs every other rnd as above, having 1 st fewer between the 8 dec sections until 8 sts rem. Cut yarn, leaving 4" tail. Thread tapestry needle with yarn tail and weave through rem sts twice. Pull gently on yarn tail to draw sts tog and close hat crown. Weave yarn tail to WS and secure.

BAND AROUND NECK

With RS facing, pick up (do not knit) 1 st from each ridge along side edge of front band—22 sts, then 1 st from each of the 36 sts CO at back of crown, then 1 st from each ridge to other side of face band—80 sts.
Row 1: K22, [k2tog] 18 times, k22—44 sts.
Row 2: *K1, p1; rep from * to end of row.
Row 3: *P1, k1; rep from * to end of row.
Rows 4–21: Knit.
BOs all sts.

FINISHING

With crochet hook and CC, work 1 row sc (see Glossary) around face band. Ties: Cut ribbon into two 1 yd sections. With sewing needle and thread, sew one end of each ribbon to end of face band. With rem ribbon, make bows and sew to hat as shown.
If you don't want to use ribbon as ties, with crochet hook and MC (or CC) make two 3/4 yd crochet chains and attach each chain to end of face band using the yarn tail rem after fastening off last ch. Omit ribbon bows.

FAIRY BONNET

SIZE
6 months–1 year

FINISHED MEASUREMENTS
Around face: 11-1/2 (13)"
Depth from front to crown top: 7-1/2 (8)"

MATERIALS
Yarn—CYCA #2 Fine: About 225 yds main color (MC); 3–5 yds contrast color (CC)
Size 2 [2.75 mm] knitting needles; 5 double pointed needles for smaller bonnet
Size 3 [3.25 mm] knitting needles; 5 double pointed needles (dpn) for larger bonnet
Size D/3 [3.25 mm] crochet hook
Optional: 2–3 yds ribbon, about 1" [2.5 cm] wide for ties and bows
Tapestry needle
Sewing needle and matching thread

GAUGE
Smaller size bonnet: 32 sts and 60 rows = 4" [10 cm] using size 2 [2.75 mm] needle in garter st and MC.
Larger size bonnet: 28 sts and 56 rows = 4" [10 cm] using size 3 [3.25 mm] needle in garter st and MC.
Adjust needle size as necessary to obtain correct gauge.

FAIRY SWEATER

SIZE
Chest: 20 (21)"

FINISHED MEASUREMENTS
Chest circumference: 21 (22)"
Length with lower edge turned back: 10-1/2" (12)"
Sleeve length, with cuff: 6-1/2" (7)"

MATERIALS
Yarn—CYCA #3 Light: About 360 (400) yds main color (MC); 90 (100) yds contrast color (CC)
Size 5 [3.75 mm] knitting needles
Tapestry needle
Stitch markers and open-ring stitch markers
Long sewing pins with large heads

GAUGE
22 sts and 40 rows = 4" [10 cm] in garter st. *Adjust needle size as necessary to obtain correct gauge.*

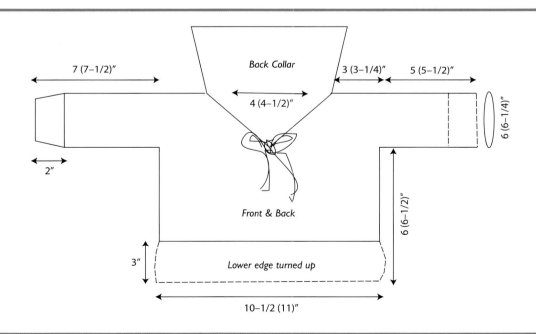

7 (7-1/2)"   Back Collar   3 (3-1/4)"   5 (5-1/2)"
4 (4-1/2)"
6 (6-1/4)"
2"
6 (6-1/2)"
Front & Back
3"   Lower edge turned up
10-1/2 (11)"

METHOD—SWEATER

The body is worked from back cast-on edge to shoulder, over the shoulder, and down the front. The sleeve stitches are added as the body is worked, then the sleeve stitches are bound off once the complete armhole depth is achieved. The sleeve cuff stitches are picked up and added later. This one-piece knitting style was fairly common during this decade.

BODY

Using MC, CO 58 (60) sts for back. Work in garter st (knit every row) until work measures 8 (9)" from CO, ending with WS row completed. Place marker at each end of row. Cont in garter st.

Sleeves:
Next row: CO 28 (30) sts beg of row, then knit these same 28 (30) sts plus rem sts in row—86 (90) sts.
Next row: Rep previous row—114 (120) sts.
Work even on 114 (120) sts until back measures 3–1/2 (4)" from sleeve CO.

Back neck:
Next row: K46 (47) sts, BO center 22 (26) sts, knit to end of row—46 (47) sts each side of neck. **Now work one side of neck at a time.

Shoulders:
Knit 2" in garter st (about 16 rows, 8 ridges).

Front neckline:
Next row: Knit, CO 11 (13) sts at neckline edge—57 (60) sts.
Work even in garter st for 3–1/2 (4)", ending with WS row**. Work other side of neck and shoulders from ** to **.

Join sides of neck:
Next row (RS): Knit 57 (60) sts from first side of neck, then cont across 57 (60) sts from other side of neck—114 (120) sts.
Next row (WS): BO 28 (30) sts from beg of row, knit to end—86 (90) sts.
Next row (RS): BO 28 (30) sts at beg of row, knit to end, sleeve sts completed—58 (60) sts. Place markers at both sides of row.

Finish body:
Work even on 58 (60) body sts in garter st until front measures same as back. BO all sts.

Cuffs

With CC and RS facing, pick up 34 sts across lower edge of sleeve and work in garter st for 1–1/2".
Next row: *K2tog, yo; rep from * across row.
Next row: Knit.

Next row: BO all sts. This cuff will be turned back as shown, but as baby grows it can also be worn straight to add another 2" of sleeve length.
Work second cuff the same.

Collar

With CC, pick up and knit 22 (26) sts across back neck. Work in garter st for 36 rows. BO all sts leaving 4" tail.
Next row: Starting at front, pick up sts (do not knit yet, just pick up the loops) all around neck, beg from the opening in front, around neck, down collar side edge, across collar, along other side edge, around neck, then down second side of front. Do not join work into rnd; cont to work flat in rows.
Next row: Knit, adjusting st count (inc or dec) so you have even number of sts and all sides of neck and collar have an equal number of sts. Make sure all sides lie flat and smooth. Insert open-ring st ms into corner st at both corners of collar.
Next row: Sl 1, [yo, k2tog] to end of row, end sl 1.
Next row: Knit, working yo, k1, yo in each corner st of back collar.
Next row: Knit without incs.
Next 2 rows: Rep last 2 rows.
Remove open-ring ms, BO all sts.
With threaded tapestry needle, sew 2 front edges of borders tog. Smooth back both sides of front opening lightly. Block to shape and smooth. Block back collar.

Front Bow

With CC, cast on 11 sts, work in garter st for about 12" or desired length. BO all sts. Tie garter strip into bow and stitch to front V.

FINISHING

Align sleeve ms so both sides of sleeve tops are even. Pin in place. With threaded tapestry needle, sew front and back tog at side, sleeve, and cuff seams using invisible weaving for garter st (see Glossary). Rem all ms and pins. Weave in ends to WS. Fold sleeve cuffs back about 2" and lightly tack in place. Optional: Fold lower body edge upward about 3" as shown.

Tam,
published by Monarch, 1910s

Here is a sweet ladies tam, knit in garter stitch, stockinette stitch, and block stitch. The hat is worked flat from crown to lower edge.

SIZE
Adult women

FINISHED MEASUREMENTS
Crown diameter: 8–1/2"
Band circumference: 21–1/2"

MATERIALS
Yarn—CYCA #3 Light, washable wool, or blends: About 200 yards main color (MC); 30 yards contrast color (CC); optional—few yards CC #2 for sewing trim.
Size 5 [3.75 mm] knitting needles
Tapestry needle
8 stitch holders
Stitch markers

GAUGE
24 sts and 48 rows = 4" [10 cm] in garter st on size 5 [3.75 mm] needles. *Adjust needle size as necessary to obtain correct gauge.*

TAM 3

CROWN
With MC and beginning at center of crown CO 8 sts.
Work in garter st (knit every row) as follows:
Rows 1, 3, 5, 7: Knit.
Row 2: K1f&b (see Glossary) in every stitch—16 sts.
Row 4: [K1f&b, k1] 8 times—24 sts.
Row 6: [K1f&b, k2] 8 times—32 sts.
Place marker at beg of row; place marker beg of next 7 sections (8 ms total).
Row 8: Inc 1 st at beg of each section—40 sts.
Row 9: Knit.
Rep last 2 rows until there are 22 sts in each section—176 sts. Do not remove stitch markers.

Begin block pattern
Rows 1–4: *K4, p4; rep from * to end of row.
Rows 5–8: *P4, k4; rep from * to end of row.
Rows 9–12: Rep rows 1–4.

Begin garter stitch and decreases
Work in garter st dec 1 st at beg of each section (after the marker) until there are 128 sts remaining (or until this section fits head). Remove markers.

Begin block pattern
Work 12 rows of block patt as before, then rep rows 5–8 of block patt (16 rows total).

Begin stockinette stitch:
With RS facing change to CC and work in St st (knit 1 row, purl 1 row) for 1–1/2". BO tightly. The lower edge should roll forward to expose the purl side.

FINISHING
Thread tapestry needle and close back seam with invisible weaving for garter st (see Glossary), weave in tails to WS to secure. Attach tassel (see Glossary) to top of hat. Optional: Thread tapestry needle with CC#2 (yellow, as shown in photo), work line of backstitch (see Glossary) around hat band after row 16 of second block pattern and first row of final St st.

MINERVA
KNITTING BOOK

VOLUME XXIII   PRICE 25¢

1920s

In the Roaring Twenties, a more refined version of the long, lean sweater favored by sporting women a decade earlier made its way into the everyday wardrobe. Under the influence of designers like Coco Channel, openwork, multicolor, and Art Deco–inspired geometric intarsia designs added interest and beauty to the straight-cut garments. Women typically topped off the look with a knit or crocheted cloche. In children's clothing, intarsia motifs or scenes, stripes, and colorful trims were popular.

Although most garments knit in the 1920s were worked in garter stitch, projects that called for simple stitch patterns and stockinette stitch became more common. Duplicate stitch was often used to add color designs in both adult and children's clothing after the project was completed. The overall garment fit for adults and children loosened somewhat in this decade, and sweater and jacket lengths were longer. Women's suits, complete with shells, vests, matching cloche hats in knit or crochet, and scarves, became stylish during the 1920s.

Lady's Bow Sweater, published by Minerva, 1928

This design is similar to those offered in knitting magazines and books in the past couple of decades, except in its construction. When the garment is finished, there are only two side and two sleeve seams to sew. The decorative bow and contrast color border around the neck are worked in duplicate stitch after the sweater is finished. We've updated the sizing and added two extra sizes.

METHOD

The sweater beg at lower back and is worked upward to shoulders; after separating sts for neckline, work cont on same sts over shoulders and down front. After completing the neckline and joining both sides of neck tog, work then cont as one piece again to the lower edge of front. After picking up sts around the armholes, sleeves are worked down to the cuffs. Because back and front are worked as one piece, we suggest you use the permanent crochet chain CO (see Glossary) to CO sts for the back, a method that will match a standard BO, so that both edges appear the same when finished.

BACK

With MC and smaller needles, CO 106 (110, 116) sts. Work in garter st (knit every row) for 1–1/2". Change to larger needles and work in St st (knit 1 row, purl 1 row), until back measures 16 (16–1/2, 17)" from CO edge, ending with WS row completed.

Underarm shaping:
Next row (RS): K7, place these sts on holder for underarm, knit to end of row—99 (103, 109) sts.
Next row (WS): P7, place these sts on holder for underarm, purl to end of row—92 (96, 102) sts. Work even in St st on these 92 (96, 102) sts until back measures 26 (27, 28)" from CO, ending with WS row completed.

Neck and shoulders:
Next row (RS): K28 (29, 31), place these sts on holder for right shoulder; BO 36 (38, 40) sts for back neck; knit to end of row—28 (29, 31) sts.
Place marker in last st at end of row to indicate shoulder.

Front neck:
Cont in St st on these 28 (29, 31) sts, work left front neck (as worn) as foll:
Working one st in from neck edge, inc 1 st at neck every 4th row 14 (14, 16) times—42 (43, 47) sts, then every other row 4 (5, 4) times—46 (48, 51) sts.
Cut yarn leaving 4" tail and place these sts on holder.

Remove right shoulder sts from holder; join yarn. Place marker in last st at armhole edge to denote shoulder and work right neck the same as left neck. When both neckline sides are equal length, with same number of sts, remove left neck sts from holder and join all sts into 1 row—92 (96, 102) sts.
Work even in St st as necessary until front armhole measures same as back armhole, about 70 (73, 77) rows from shoulder ms.

Underarm shaping:
CO 7 sts at end of next 2 rows—106 (110, 116) sts. Work even in St st until front measures same as back to garter st border. Change to smaller needles and work in garter st for 1–1/2". BO all sts.

SLEEVES

With MC and RS facing, pick up and knit 50 (53, 55) sts from underarms to shoulder ms, then the same number of sts from shoulder to underarms—100 (106, 110) sts. Beg with WS row, work 14 rows in St st, joining sleeves to underarm sts on holders by working last st of row and one st from holder with k2tog on RS, and p2tog on WS rows.

Sleeve shaping:
When sleeve caps are joined to underarm sts, beg sleeve shaping.
Dec 1 st each side of next row—98 (104, 108) sts, then dec 1 st each side every 4th row 19 (24, 25) times—60 (56, 58) sts, then every 6th row 6 (3, 3) times—48 (50, 52) sts. Work even until sleeve measures 16–1/2 (17, 17–1/2)" from first row of shaping; end with WS row completed. Change to smaller needles, dec 5 sts evenly

SIZE
40 (42, 44)"

FINISHED MEASUREMENTS
Chest circumference: 42 (44, 46)"
Length: 26 (27, 28)"
Sleeve length to underarm: 18 (18–1/2, 19)"

MATERIALS
Yarn—CYCA #3 or #4 Light or Medium, 100% wool or blend: About 1500 (1625, 1750) yds main color (MC); about 75 yds contrast color (CC) for duplicate st
Note: Some light-worsted or DK yarns will achieve correct gauge. If not, try a standard worsted-weight yarn.
Size 4 [3.5 mm] knitting needles; 16" circular needle for neckline
Size 7 [4.5 mm] knitting needles
Tapestry needle
Stitch holders, or several strands of smooth cotton yarn to use as holders
Open-ring stitch markers or small coilless pins

GAUGE
20 sts and 28 rows = 4" in St st on size 7 [4.5 mm] needles. *Adjust needle size as necessary to obtain correct gauge.*

spaced across row—43 (45, 47) sts. Work in garter st for 1–1/2". BO all sts.
Work second sleeve the same.

Neck Border
With RS facing, MC, and circular needle, pick up and knit 35 (38, 39) sts across back neck, pick up and knit 52 (55, 58) sts along left neck edge, pm to denote center front, pick up and knit 52 (55, 58) sts along right neck edge, pm to denote beg of rnd—139 (148, 155) sts.
Rnd 1: Purl to 2 sts before center front m, p2tog, sl m, ssp (see Glossary), purl to end of rnd—137 (146, 153) sts.

Rnd 2: Knit to 2 sts before center front m, k2tog, sl m, ssk (see Glossary), knit to end of rnd—135 (144, 151) sts. Rep rnds 1 and 2 until border measures about 1–1 1/4" from first purl rnd. BO all sts.

FINISHING
Sew side seams and sleeves using mattress st (see Glossary) and MC. Weave in ends to WS and secure.

Bow and Band
With tapestry needle and CC, work bow and band in duplicate st (see Glossary) around neck as shown in photo.

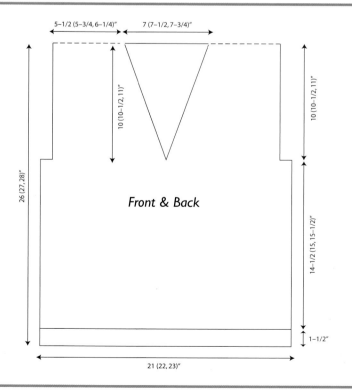

Front & Back

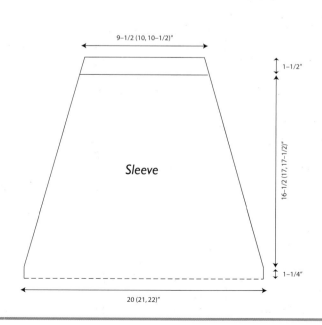

Sleeve

Men's Checked Cardigan, published by Pictorial Review, 1924

This comfortable cardigan for him is great for relaxing on weekends, running errands, or playing a round of golf. The check pattern is worked in k6, p6 and reverses to p6, k6 after six rows. The original design began at the lower back then worked upward to the shoulder line, where stitches were divided for neck and center fronts, then continued on down the two fronts. We decided to modify this project by working three separate pieces and adding shoulder seams in order to support the garment weight and prevent drooping shoulders and stretched neckline—and maintain the pattern sequence at the side edges. We also added extra sizes and worked the front band by picking up stitches along both fronts and around the back neck, instead of working a very long single band and later stitching same to the garment, as shown in the photo. The new front bands also include six buttons/buttonholes to accommodate the updated sizes.

Extremely Serviceable Is This Men's Checked Sweater

No. 355—Knitted Sweater

SIZE
Chest: 36–38 (40–42, 44–46)"

FINISHED MEASUREMENTS
Chest circumference: 40 (44, 48)"
   with front band buttoned
Length: 26 (27, 28–1/2)"
Sleeve length from underarm to
   cuff: 19 (19–1/2, 20–1/2)"

MATERIALS
Yarn—CYCA #2 Fine, 100% wool
   or blend: About 1830 (2030,
   2330) yds
Size 3 [3.25 mm]; size 5 [3.75
   mm] knitting needles
6 buttons, about 3/4" diameter
Sewing needle and matching
   thread to attach buttons
Tapestry needle
Stitch holders
Long sewing pins with large,
   colored heads
Stitch markers

GAUGE
24 sts and 32 rows = 4" [10 cm]
   in St st on size 4 [3.5 mm]
   needles. *Adjust needle size as
   necessary to obtain correct
   gauge.*

BACK

With smaller needles, CO 106 (118, 130) sts.
Row 1: *K2, p2; rep from * to last 2 sts, k2.
Row 2: *P2, k2; rep from * to last 2 sts, p2.
Rep rows 1 and 2 until work measures 3" from CO edge.
Next row: Cont in rib, inc 14 sts evenly spaced across row—120 (132, 144) sts.
Rows 1–6: Change to larger needles, *k6, p6; rep from * to end of row.
Rows 7–12: *P6, k6; rep from * to end of row.
Rep these 12 rows until work measures 15–1/2 (16, 16–1/2)" or desired length from CO. Place markers at each end of row to denote underarms.
Cont in patt until back measures 26 (27, 28–1/2)" from CO. Work 37 (43, 48) sts in patt, place sts on st holder, BO center 46 (46, 48) sts, work rem shoulder sts and place on holder—37 (43, 48) sts on each shoulder.

RIGHT FRONT (AS WORN)

With smaller needles, CO 54 (58, 66) sts. Work in k2, p2 rib patt same as back for 3".
Next row: Cont in rib, inc 6 (8, 6) sts evenly spaced across row—60 (66, 72) sts, ending with WS row completed. Change to larger needles and main patt. Work as foll:

Sizes 36–38" and 44–46" only

Row 1 (RS): *K6, p6; rep from * to end.
Row 2 (WS): *P6, k6; rep from * to end.
Rep rows 1 and 2 twice more (6 rows total).
Row 7 (RS): *P6, k6; rep from * to end.
Row 8 (WS): *K6, p6; rep from * to end.
Rep rows 7 and 8 twice more (6 rows total).
Rep these 12 rows for patt.

Size 40–42" only

Row 1 (RS): *P6, k6; rep from * to last 6 sts, p6.
Row 2 (WS): *K6, p6; rep from * to last 6 sts, k6.
Rep rows 1 and 2 twice more (6 rows total).
Row 7 (RS): *K6, p6; rep from * to last 6 sts, k6.
Row 8 (WS): *P6, k6; rep from * to last 6 sts, p6.
Rep rows 7 and 8 twice more (6 rows total).
Rep these 12 rows for patt.

All sizes

Work in est patt until front measures 15–1/2 (16, 16–1/2)" from CO edge. Place marker at side edge to denote underarms. At the same time, place marker at other edge to denote beg of neckline.

Neckline shaping:

Dec 1 st at neck edge every other row 9 (7, 5) times—51 (59, 67) sts. Then dec 1 st at neck edge every 4th row 14 (16, 19) times—37 (43, 48) sts. Place shoulder sts on holder.

LEFT FRONT (AS WORN)

With smaller needles, CO 54 (58, 66) sts. Work in k2, p2 rib patt same as back for 3".
Next row: Cont in rib, inc 6 (8, 6) sts evenly spaced across row—60 (66, 72) sts, ending with RS row completed. Change to larger needles and main patt. Work as foll:

Sizes 36–38" and 44–46" only

Row 1 (WS): *P6, k6; rep from * to end.
Row 2 (RS): *K6, p6; rep from * to end.
Rep rows 1 and 2 twice more (6 rows total)
Row 7 (RS): *K6, p6; rep from * to end.
Row 8 (WS): *P6, k6; rep from * to end.
Rep rows 7 and 8 twice more (6 rows total).
Rep these 12 rows for patt.

Size 40–42" only

Row 1 (WS): *K6, p6; rep from * to last 6 sts, k6.
Row 2 (RS): *P6, k6; rep from * to last 6 sts, p6.
Rep rows 1 and 2 twice more (6 rows total).
Row 7 (WS): *P6, k6; rep from * to last 6 sts, p6.
Row 8 (RS): *K6, p6; rep from * to last 6 sts, k6.
Rep rows 7 and 8 twice more (6 rows total).
Rep these 12 rows for patt.

All sizes

Work as for right front.

Pockets (make 2)

With smaller needles, CO 36 sts. Work in main patt for 36 rows, change to smaller needles and work in k1, p1 rib for 8 rows. BO in rib patt. Work second pocket the same. Place pockets above rib on fronts as shown in photo and pin in place. With threaded tapestry needle, whipstitch (see Glossary) pockets in place, leaving ribbed top edge open. Remove pins.

Shoulders

Remove shoulder sts from holders and place on dpn. With RS tog, align needles, holding front and back shoulders tog. Attach yarn and join one set of shoulder sts tog using the three-needle BO (see Glossary). Rep for other set of shoulder sts.

SLEEVES

Note: Sleeves are worked from top down to wrist.
With larger needles and RS facing, beg at one underarm marker, pick up and knit 126 (132, 144) sts around the armhole and ending at the other underarm marker. Work in main patt, same as body.

Sleeve shaping:

Maintaining patt, dec 1 st on each side every other row 8 (10, 12) times—110 (112, 120) sts. Then dec 1 st on each side every 4th row 26 (26, 27) times—58 (60, 66) sts. Work even in patt until sleeve measures 16 (16–1/2, 17–1/2)″ from pick up row.

Cuff:

Next row (RS): Change to smaller needles, knit row, dec 8 (6, 8) sts evenly spaced across row—50 (54, 58) sts.
Row 1 (WS): *P2, k2; rep from * to last 2 sts, p2.
Row 2 (RS): *K2, p2; rep from * to last 2 sts, k2.
Rep rows 1 and 2 until cuff measures 3″ from beg of rib. BO in rib.
Work second sleeve the same.

Front Band

Note: The original design had a front band worked separately, then stitched to the fronts later. We're suggesting another method. The band sts are picked up around the center front edges, worked in rib, then BO, so there is no sewing to do after the band is completed.
With RS facing, pick up and knit 99 (103, 107) sts from lower edge of right front to first m (beg of neckline shaping), then pick up and knit 65 (69, 76) sts along right side of neck, pick up and knit 46 (46, 48) back neck sts from holder, pick up and knit 65 (69, 76) sts along left neck edge to second m, then pick up and knit 99 (103, 107) sts to lower left edge—374 (390, 414) sts.
Row 1 (WS): *P2, k2; rep from * to last 2 sts, p2.
Row 2 (RS): *K2, p2; rep from * to last 2 sts, k2.
Rep these 2 rows once more, then rep row 1.
Next row (RS) buttonholes: Work in rib to second m (left front), sl m, work 3 sts in rib patt, BO next 2 sts, [work 16 (17, 18) sts, BO 2 sts] 5 times, work in est rib patt to end.
Next row (WS) close buttonholes: *Work in rib patt to BO st, CO 2 sts; rep from * 5 times more to m, sl m, complete row in patt—5 buttonholes made.
Next 3 rows: Work even in rib patt. BO all sts loosely.

FINISHING

Block all pieces and air-dry completely. Join side and sleeve seams. Weave in ends to WS. With sewing thread and needle, attach buttons to right front band, aligning with buttonholes along left band.

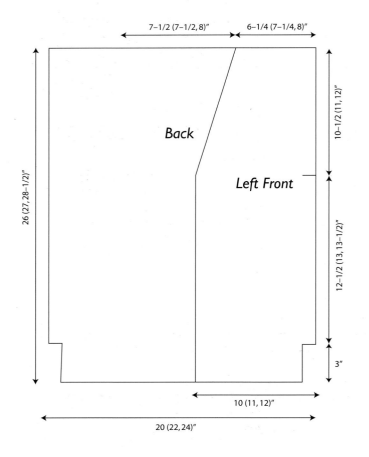

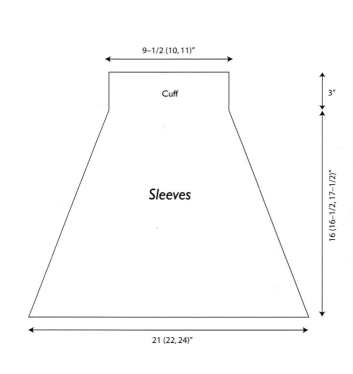

Mildred Scarf,
Published by Fleisher's, 1920s

This scarf from the 1920s is another easy project for the advanced beginning knitter. The Indian Cross Stitch pattern is relatively simple to master. The scarf can be made in two sections, each worked from the cast-on row upward, then grafted together at the halfway point using invisible weaving for garter stitch (often referred to as Kitchener stitch for garter stitch). It can also be worked as one piece, from one short end to the other.

CO 72 sts. Knit 16 rows (8 garter st ridges).
Row 1 of Indian Cross St patt: *Wrapping the yarn around the needle 3 times, k1; rep from * across row.
Row 2 of patt: *Sl first 6 sts on to right-hand needle, dropping the extra wraps as you do so, making 6 elongated sts, insert left-hand needle in the first 3 sts and draw these 3 loops over the last 3 loops to form a cross. Place all 6 loops back on left-hand needle, purl these 6 sts; rep from * across row—12 sets of crosses.
Next 6 rows: Knit (3 garter st ridges)

Rep rows 1–8 twice more until there are 3 bands of Indian Cross St patt. Cont working in garter st until scarf measures about 30" from CO edge; this is one-half of scarf. Place live sts on holder. Rep instructions from CO row until second half of scarf measures 30". Remove sts from holder and place on needle. Thread tapestry needle with a length of yarn about 25". Join both halves of scarf tog through live sts using Invisible weaving for garter st (see Glossary). Weave in all loose ends.

Note: If preferred, you may also reverse the patt after the first 30" is completed and cont in garter st until the Indian Cross St patt beg; complete those rows, then work 16 rows of garter st, BO all sts.

SIZE
Width: 14–1/2"
Length: 60"

MATERIALS
Yarn—CYCA #4 Medium, 100% wool or blend:
    About 720 yds
Size 9 [5.5 mm] knitting needles

Tapestry needle
Large stitch holder or about 20" of smooth cotton
    waste yarn to use as holder

GAUGE
5 sts and 10 rows = 1" on size 9 [5.5 mm] needles in
    garter st. *Adjust needle size as necessary to
    obtain correct gauge.*

Winnifred Negligee,
published by Fleisher's, 1920s

Although this garment is called a "negligee," a word normally associated with a robe, housecoat, or dressing gown, we see the project as an updated oversized, loosely-knit sweater with drop shoulders and a charming V-shape "sleeve" knit from the shoulder down . . .
with no sleeve seams! We've lengthened the body several inches, so it will fit pretty much as shown in the photo. Remember, most women were shorter in the 1920s.

BACK
With CC, CO 67 sts, work 5 rows in garter st (knit each row). Join MC and work in St st (knit 1 row, purl 1 row) until back measures 26" from CO edge, ending with WS row completed.

Make neckline opening:
Next RS row: K18, BO 31, knit to end of row (18 sts each shoulder).
Next WS row: P18, CO 31, P18.
Cont with MC, work front same as back, ending with CC and 5 rows of garter st. BO all sts loosely, so tension for CO and BO have the same elasticity.

SLEEVES
Measure down along each front side edge about 7–1/2" from neckline row, place open-ring m in end of row sts, then measure 7–1/2" down along the back from neck-line row, pm in end of row sts. With MC and RS facing, pick up and knit 45 sts as foll: 22 sts from m to neckline row, 1 st at neckline row, 22 sts from neckline to m.
Work 3 rows in St st beg with WS row.
Next RS row: K1, k2tog, knit across row to last 3 sts, ssk, k1—43 sts.
Next WS row: Purl
Rep last 2 rows until 3 sts rem.
BO all sts.
With CC, pick up and knit about 67 sts around edge of sleeve, adjust sts on next row by inc or dec as necessary to create a smooth edge, knit 3 rows even, inc 1 st at sleeve point every row.
Loosely BO all sts on WS. Remove ms.
Work second sleeve the same.

Back Neck Roll
With CC, pick up and knit 31 sts across back of neck only. Knit 4 more rows. BO on WS row.
Note: If you're not making this as a negligee, the roll across the back neck isn't necessary. Feel free to omit it and proceed to *Finishing.*

FINISHING
Sew side seams from CO edge to armhole using mattress st (see Glossary) and MC.
Finish neck: With MC and crochet hook, work 1 rnd of sc (see Glossary) around entire neckline. Fasten off.
Belt: With 4 strands of CC, make a crochet chain about 72" long. Finish ends with tassels.
Tassels (make 2): Wind CC 28 times around a 4" piece of cardboard, remove from cardboard and tie another strand of CC (about 12") around one end of folded loops, about 1/2" down from top, sew tassel to belt end with threaded tapestry needle. Cut through loops at opposite end of tassel and fluff ends. Weave in all loose ends to WS of work.

SIZE
Chest: 38–42"

FINISHED MEASUREMENTS
Chest: 44–1/2"
Length from shoulder to hem: 26"

MATERIALS
Yarn—CYCA #3 Light, 100% wool or blend: About 600
**   yds rose (MC)**
CYCA #2 Fine, 100% angora or angora/wool blend:
About 90 yds pink (CC)

Size 9 [5.5 mm] knitting needles
Size F/8 [5 mm] crochet hook
Tapestry needle
Cardboard, about 4" length for making tassels
2 open-ring stitch markers

GAUGE
12 sts and 20 rows = 4" in St st on size 9 [5.5 mm]
**   needles. The needle size is slightly larger than**
**   normal for the yarn weight specified in order to**
**   create a drapey, loosely knit fabric.** *Adjust needle*
size as necessary to obtain correct gauge.

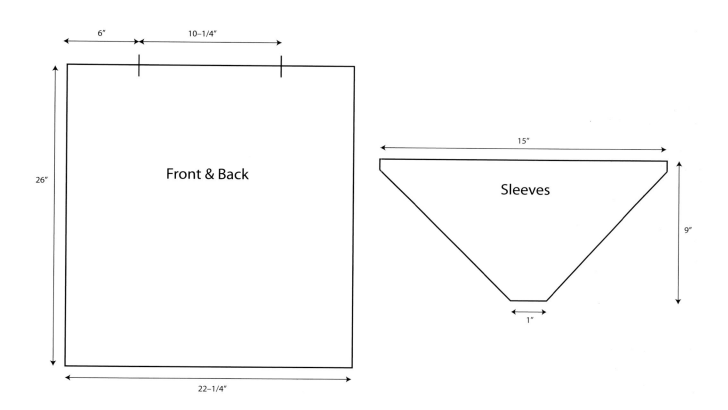

BEAR BRAND ★ BUCILLA

Manual of Yarncraft

VOL. 310 ★ 35¢ (IN U.S.A.)

1930s

During the Great Depression years of the 1930s, Americans turned to knitting as a way to wear the latest styles at an affordable cost. Styles changed dramatically in this decade, as the straight, lean look of the 1920s gave way to curve-hugging sweaters and skirts. Knitters were inundated with new and exciting patterns in a wide variety of fitted and semi-fitted styles. This was the decade of the Sweater Girl, as fashionable young women tried to capture the look made famous by Lana Turner in the movie *They Won't Forget*. The sweaters of the 1930s tended to be shorter than those common in the 1920s, usually falling to the upper hip. Slim-fitting sweaters featuring puff or fitted sleeves were available in pullover or cardigan twin sets. Boleros, swimsuits, and fitted below-the-knee skirts were all the rage. Women's knitted suits remained fashionable as well but were worn with hats other than the cloche, tailored scarves, and gloves. Angora was the hot new yarn for knitting smart hat, scarf, and glove sets.

The men of the 1930s looked dapper in cardigans with zipper fronts and close-fitting V-neck vests worked in lightweight yarns, which fit comfortably under suit jackets or sports coats. Adorable patterns for babies were abundant. Three- or four-piece pram sets included hats with earflaps, coats, mitts, and nicely fitted pull-ups with knit-in booties. School and dress sweaters were favorite knits for the kids, and some knitters even stitched sweaters for the family pooch.

Women's Classic Cardigan, published by Bear Brand, 1939

This basic cardigan with modified drop shoulder and sleeves worked from top to cuff is not much different from what we'd expect to see for a basic cardigan today. However, the original pattern was offered in one size only (35″ chest) in a fingering-weight yarn with a gauge of 8 stitches/10 rows per inch. With recalculated numbers and a slightly larger gauge, we now offer three sizes. The increased amount of ease brings the project into twenty-first century fit while maintaining the designer's basic concept. Note that the grosgrain ribbon is placed on the right side of the work along the center front edges. Normally, we'd expect the ribbon to be attached on the wrong side of a front band, but here its use is both functional and decorative.

SIZE
Chest: 38 (40, 42)″

FINISHED MEASUREMENTS
Chest: 42 (44, 46)″, including front underlap
Length: 24 (25–1/2, 27)″
Sleeve length from underarm to cuff: 18–1/2
   (19, 19–1/2)″

MATERIALS
Yarn—CYCA #2 Fine, 100% wool or wool/angora
   blend: About 1464 (1666, 1868) yds
Note: You may be able to obtain a similar fabric
   weight, drape, and gauge using DK weight
   (CYCA #3) in fine merino wool Size 4 [3.5 mm];
   size 6 [4 mm] knitting needles
7 buttons, about 1/2″ diameter
1–3/4 yds grosgrain ribbon, 1″ wide, in color to
   match yarn (pre-wash the ribbon to prevent
   shrinkage if you plan to wash the sweater later)
1 spool silk buttonhole thread (silk twist) in color
   to match grosgrain ribbon
Sewing thread to match ribbon, sewing needle
Tapestry needle
2 stitch holders

GAUGE
24 sts and 32 rows = 4″ [10 cm] in St st on size 6
   [4 mm] needles. *Adjust needle size as
   necessary to obtain correct gauge.*

BACK

With smaller needles, CO 114 (118, 122) sts.
Row 1 (RS): *K2, p2; rep from * to last 2 sts, k2.
Row 2 (WS): *P2, k2; rep from * to last 2 sts, p2.
Rep last 2 rows until rib measures 2–1/2" from CO, inc 12 (14, 16) sts evenly spaced across last row of rib—126 (132, 138) sts.
Change to larger needles. Beg with knit row, work in St st until back measures 16 (16–1/2, 17)" from CO.

Underarm shaping:

BO 6 (9, 9) sts at beg of next 2 rows.
Work even in St st until back measures 23 (24–1/2, 26)" from CO, change to smaller needles and work 1" in garter st (knit all rows). When back measures 24 (25–1/2, 27)" from CO, knit 36 (36, 37) sts for shoulder, BO 42 (42, 46) sts for back neck, then knit rem sts for other shoulder. Place both sets of shoulder sts on separate st holders. Cut yarn leaving 4" tails.

LEFT FRONT (AS WORN)

With smaller needles, CO 58 (58, 62) sts. Work in k2, p2 rib patt same as back for 2–1/2", inc 5 (8, 7) sts evenly spaced across last row of rib—63 (66, 69) sts.
Change to larger needles. Beg with knit row, work in St st until front measures 16 (16–1/2, 17)" from CO, ending with WS row completed.

Underarm shaping:

Next row (RS): BO 6 (9, 9) sts beg of row, knit across row to end (center front)—57 (57, 60) sts. Work even in St st until left front measures 21 (22–1/2, 24)" from CO, ending with RS row completed.

Neckline shaping:

Next row (WS): BO 11 (11, 12) sts at neck edge, purl rem sts—46 (46, 48) sts.
Next row (RS): Knit.
Next row (WS): P1, dec 1 st, purl across row—45 (45, 47) sts.
Rep last 2 rows 9 (9, 10) times more. *At the same time*, when work measures 23 (24–1/2, 26)", change to smaller needles and working rem rows in garter st (same as back), complete decs—36 (36, 37) shoulder sts.

Mark for buttons:

Working along the center front edge, about 2 sts from the edge, mark the first button placement 3 rows above the last row of rib (no buttons/buttonholes placed in lower rib). Evenly space 5 more buttons along the center front edge and mark their position with thread. The 7th button will be attached to the neck rib, so make sure you allow for that in the spacing.

RIGHT FRONT (AS WORN)

With smaller needles, CO 58 (58, 62) sts. Work in k2, p2 rib patt same as left front for 2–1/2", inc 5 (8, 7) sts evenly spaced across last row of rib—63 (66, 69) sts.
Change to larger needles. Beg with knit row, work in St st. *At the same time,* on the 3rd row of St st, beg buttonholes to align with 6 button positions marked on left front.

Buttonholes:

RS row: K2, BO 3, knit to end.
Next row (WS): Purl to BO sts, CO 3 sts using backward loop CO (see Glossary), p2.
Cont in St st and making buttonholes to align with button ms until front measures 16 (16–1/2, 17)" from CO, with RS row completed.

Underarm shaping:

Next row (WS): BO 6 (9, 9) sts beg of row, purl across row to end (center front)—57 (57, 60) sts. Work even in St st, cont with buttonholes along center front edge until right front measures 21 (22–1/2, 24)" from CO, ending with WS row completed.

Neckline shaping:

Next row (RS): BO 11 (11, 12) sts at neck edge, knit rem sts—46 (46, 48) sts.
Next row (WS): Purl.
Next row (RS): K1, dec 1, knit across row—45 (45, 47) sts.
Rep last 2 rows 9 (9, 10) times more. *At the same time*, when work measures 23 (24–1/2, 26)", change to smaller needles and working rem rows in garter st (same as back), complete decs—36 (36, 37) shoulder sts.

Join shoulder stitches:

Remove shoulder sts from holders and place on needles. With tapestry needle threaded with about 36" strand of yarn, align left front shoulder sts with left back shoulder sts, WS tog, and weave shoulder sts tog using invisible weaving for garter st (see Glossary). Join right front shoulder sts to right back shoulder sts the same. Re-thread tapestry needle as necessary.

SLEEVES

With RS facing, pick up and knit 96 (108, 120) sts beg at left front underarm and ending at left back underarm; when you reach the first BO underarm st, *insert right needle into BO, wrap yarn around as if to knit and pull up a loop (1 new st on needle). Turn work to WS, pass the new st over the first st on left needle and drop the new st, purl across all sts to end; insert right needle into first BO st as if to purl, wrap yarn around pwise and pull up a loop (1 new st on needle). Turn work to RS, pass new st over the first st on left needle and drop the new st, knit across all sts to end. Rep from * joining BO sts to sleeve sts as you work. When all BO sts are joined to sleeve, cont in St st as foll:

Sleeve shaping:

Cont in St st, dec 1 st each side (make dec 1 st in from

edges), every 6th (4th, 4th) row 16 (13, 28) times, then every 8th (6th, 6th) row 3 (12, 2) times—58 (58, 60) sts. Work even until sleeve measures about 15 (15–1/2, 15–1/2)" from last row of underarm join, ending with RS row completed.

Next row (WS): Change to smaller needles and purl 1 row, dec 4 (4, 6) sts evenly spaced across row—54 sts.

Cuff:
Row 1 (RS): *K2, p2; rep from * to last 2 sts, k2.
Row 2 (WS): *P2, k2; rep from * to last 2 sts, p2.
Rep last 2 rows until cuff measures 3" from beg of rib patt. BO in rib patt.
Work second sleeve and cuff the same.

Neck Ribbing
With smaller needles and RS facing, pick up and knit 11 (11, 12) sts from right front BO, 18 sts from side neck, 42 (42, 46) sts across back neck BO, 18 sts from left side neck, 11 (11, 12) sts from left front BO sts—100 (100, 106) sts. Inc or dec 2 sts on first row of rib to balance patt for sizes 38 and 40" only, to obtain a multiple of 4 + 2 sts.
Row 1 (WS): *P2, k2; rep from * to last 2 sts, p2.

Row 2 (RS): *K2, p2; rep from * to last 2 sts, k2.
Work 3 rows total in rib patt. On next RS row, make buttonhole at right front edge as foll: K2 sts, BO 3 sts, work in est rib patt to end of row.
Next row: Work in rib to BO sts, CO 3 sts, p2. Cont in rib patt for 3 rows more. BO in patt.

FINISHING
Join body side seams with mattress st (see Glossary), working 1 st in from each side edge to maintain k2, p2 rib patt. Work underarm sleeve seams the same. Cut grosgrain ribbon into two lengths, each length the same as the center front length (including neck rib), plus 1/2". Turn under 1/4" at top and bottom of each length; baste, then using sewing thread and needle, sew one length of ribbon to right side of each center front, from neck edge to CO edge. The ribbon should cover the first 6 sts at each front edge. Carefully cut buttonhole slits in ribbon over buttonholes made in knitted right front, and using buttonhole st (see Glossary), work around buttonholes with silk twist, joining both layers of fabric (knitted and ribbon) tog. Sew buttons to left front edge opposite buttonholes, remove marking thread. Weave in loose yarn tails to WS of work. Block to size.

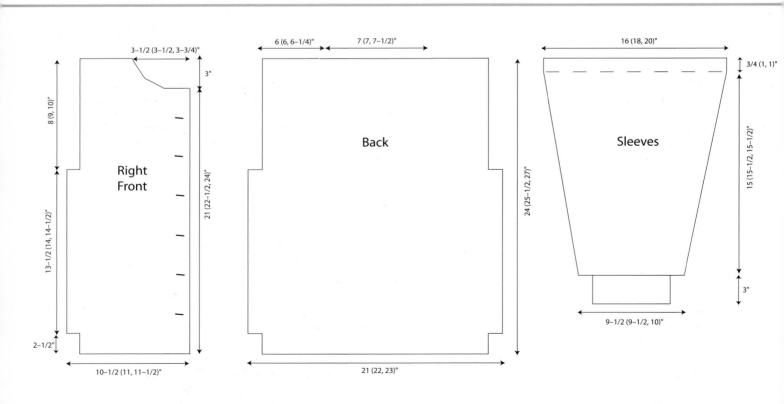

Women's Ruffle Edge Cardigan, published by Lux, 1939

This cardigan is one piece of a three-piece ensemble of cardigan, vestee, and skirt. Only the cardigan is included here, worked in super-fine yarn at 9 stitches per inch.

BACK

With smaller needles, CO 150 sts.
Row 1 (RS): *K2, p1; rep from * to end.
Row 2 (WS): *K1, p2; rep from * to end.
Rep last 2 rows until rib measures 3–1/2" from CO, ending with WS row completed.
Next row (RS): Change to larger needles and work in St st, beg with knit row. *At the same time,* inc 25 sts evenly spaced across row—175 sts.
Next row (WS): Purl.
Work even in St st until back measures 12–1/2" from CO edge.

Underarm shaping:
BO 7 sts at beg of next 2 rows—161 sts.
BO 3 sts beg of next 2 rows—155 sts.
BO 2 sts beg of next 4 rows—147 sts.
Row 9: K2tog, knit to end of row—146 sts.
Row 10: P2tog, purl to end of row—145 sts.
Next 2 rows: Rep rows 9 and 10—143 sts.
Next 2 rows: Work even.
Next 2 rows: Rep rows 9 and 10—141 sts.
Next 2 rows: Work even.
Next 2 rows: Rep rows 9 and 10—139 sts.
Work even in St st until back measures 20–1/2" from CO, ending with WS row completed.

Left side of neck and shoulder shaping:
Row 1 (RS): BO 11 sts, knit to end of row—128 sts.
Row 2 (WS): BO 11 sts, purl to end of row—117 sts.
Row 3: BO 11 sts, knit until there are 29 sts on right needle, BO 37, knit to end (40 sts on each shoulder). Cont work on last 40 sts only for left shoulder.
Row 4: BO 11 sts, p29.
Row 5: BO 3 sts, k26.

SIZE
Chest: 38"

FINISHED MEASUREMENTS
Chest: 40"
Length: 21"
Sleeve length to underarm: 18"

MATERIALS
Yarn—CYCA #1 Super Fine, 100% wool or blend: About 2300 yds
Size 0 [2 mm]; size 1 [2.25 mm] knitting needles

Size B/1 [2.25 mm] crochet hook
4 buttons, about 1/2" diameter; 4 smaller buttons for cuffs
Sewing thread to match ribbon, sewing needle
Tapestry needle
2 stitch holders

GAUGE
36 sts and 48 rows = 4" [10 cm] in St st on size 1 [2.25 mm] needles. *Adjust needle size as necessary to obtain correct gauge.*

Row 6: BO 11 sts, p15.
Row 7: BO 2 sts, k13. BO rem 13 sts for shoulder.

Right side of neck and shoulder shaping:
Join yarn at neck edge of rem 29 sts.
Row 4: BO 3 sts, p26.
Row 5: BO 11 sts, k15.
Row 6: BO 2 sts, p13.
Row 7: BO 13 sts.

RIGHT FRONT (AS WORN)
With smaller needles, CO 75 sts.
Row 1(RS): *K2, p1; rep from * to end of row.
Row 2 (WS): *K1, p2; rep from * to end of row.
Rep last 2 rows until rib measures 3–1/2" from CO. End with WS row completed.
Next row (RS): Change to larger needles and work in St st, beg with knit row. *At the same time,* inc 15 sts evenly spaced across row—90 sts.
Next row: Purl.
Work even in St st until front measures 5–1/2" from CO, ending with WS row completed.

Front shaping:
Row 1 (RS): K2tog, knit across row until 4 sts rem, turn work.
Row 2 and every WS row: Purl.
Row 3: Knit until 8 sts rem, turn work.
Row 5: Knit until 12 sts rem, turn work.
Row 7: K2tog, knit until 16 sts rem, turn work.
Row 9: Knit until 20 sts rem, turn work.
Row 11: Knit until 24 sts rem, turn work.
Row 13: K2tog, knit to end of row.
Next 5 rows: Work even across row in St st.
Rep last 6 rows until side edge is 12–1/2" from CO, ending with RS row completed.

Underarm shaping:
Row 1 (WS): BO 7 sts, purl to end of row.
Row 2 and every RS row: Knit, cont to k2tog every 6th row at front edge.
Row 3: BO 3 sts, purl to end.
Row 5: BO 2 sts, purl to end.
Row 7: BO 2 sts, purl to end.
Row 9: P2tog, purl to end.
Rows 11 and 15: Rep row 9.
Rows 13 and 17: Purl.
Row 19: Rep row 9.
From this point on, work in St st, cont to k2tog every 6th row on front edge until 46 sts rem.
Work even in St st until front measures 20–1/2" from CO, ending with RS row completed.

Shoulder shaping:
Row 1 (WS): BO 11 sts, purl to end of row—35 sts.
Row 2: Knit.
Rep last 2 rows twice—13 sts. BO 13 sts.

LEFT FRONT (AS WORN)
Work as for right front until piece measures 5–1/2", ending with RS row completed.
From this point on, work as right front but substitute purl sts for knit sts and vice versa.

LEFT SLEEVE
With larger needles, CO 45 sts.
Beg with WS row, work 5 rows in St st.
Row 6 (RS): Knit to last st, k1f&b (see Glossary)—46 sts.
Rep these 6 rows 3 times more—49 sts.
Row 25: Purl. Cut yarn and sl 49 sts onto holder.
Using same needle, CO 25 sts.
Beg with WS row, work 5 rows in St st.
Row 6 (RS): K1f&b, knit to end of row—26 sts.
Rep these 6 rows 3 times more—29 sts.
Row 25: Purl.

Sleeve opening:
Row 1 (RS): Knit the 29 sts, CO 6 sts, sl the 49 sts from holder onto needle and knit them, joining this piece to the 35 sts—84 sts.
Row 2: Purl.
Work 2 rows in St st.
Row 5: K1f&b, knit across row until 1 st rem, k1f&b—86 sts.
Work even for 5 rows in St st.
Rep last 6 rows until there are 128 sts on needle.
Work even in St st until sleeve measures 18" from CO, ending with WS row completed.

Cap shaping:
Row 1 (RS): BO 2 sts, knit to end of row—126 sts.
Row 2: BO 2 sts, purl to end of row—124 sts.
Row 3: K2tog, knit to last 2 sts, k2tog—122 sts.
Row 4: Purl.
Rep last 2 rows 33 times—56 sts .
Row 71: K2tog, knit until 2 sts rem, k2tog—54 sts.
Row 72: P2tog, purl until 2 sts rem, p2tog—52 sts.
Rep last 2 rows until 24 sts rem. BO 24 sts.

RIGHT SLEEVE
Work as for left sleeve, substituting purl sts for knit sts and vice versa.

Right Band and Frill
With larger needles, CO 200 sts.
Row 1 (RS): Knit.
Row 2: Purl.
Rep rows 1 and 2 once more.
Note: When BO within the row, don't forget that the st rem on the right needle after the last BO counts as the first st in the next instruction within the same row.
Row 5: K139, BO 5 sts, *K12, BO 5 sts; rep from * twice more, k5—180 sts.
Row 6: P5, CO 5 sts, *p12, CO 5; rep from * twice more, p139—200 sts.

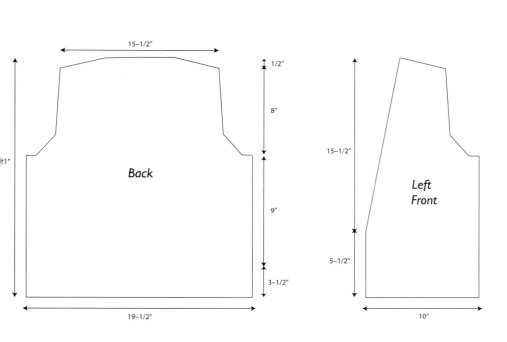

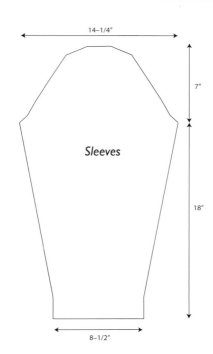

Rep rows 1 and 2 twice more.
Row 11 (RS): Purl (turning ridge).
Row 12: Purl.
Row 13: Knit.
Rep last 2 rows once more.
Row 16: P5, BO 5 sts, *p12, BO 5; rep from * twice, p139.
Row 17: K139, CO 5 sts; *k12, CO 5 sts; rep from * twice.
Rows 18 and 20: Purl.
Row 19: Knit.
Row 21: K1f&b in every st across row—400 sts.
Row 22: Purl.
Row 23: Knit.
Rep last 2 rows twice.
Row 28: Knit.
Row 29: K1, *yo, k2tog; rep from * until 1 st rem, yo, k1. BO all sts.

Left Band
Make same as right band, omitting buttonholes on left front.

Sleeve Plackets with Buttonholes (make 2)
With larger needles, CO 18 sts.
Work first 4 rows same as right band and frill.
Row 5: K3, BO 3, k6, BO 3, k3—12 sts.
Row 6: P3, CO 3, p6, CO 3, p3—18 sts.

Work same as right band with frill from row 7 to row 15.
Row 16: P3, BO 3, p6, BO 3, p3—12 sts.
Row 17: K3, CO 3, k6, CO 3, k3—18 sts.
Beg with Row 18, finish plackets same as right band and frill.

Sleeve Plackets without Buttonholes (make 2)
Work same as other plackets, omitting buttonholes in lower plackets.

FINISHING
Block all pieces and air-dry completely. Join shoulders with backstitch (see Glossary). Join side and sleeve seams using mattress st (see Glossary). Join ends of right and left bands at back of neck with backstitch. Beg with buttonhole end, pin in place as you fit the CO edge of band along right front, around neck and along left front. Whipstitch (see Glossary) in place. Remove pins. Fold band along turning ridge and match up buttonholes. Whipstitch down at beg of frill, sew around buttonholes to join tog. Fit and sew the plackets with buttonholes to front of sleeve openings in same manner, sewing end of each band to the 6 CO sts. Fit and sew sleeve plackets without buttonholes the same, sewing end of each band under first placket. Work 1 row sc (see Glossary) around cuffs. Fit and sew in sleeves. With sewing needle and thread, sew on buttons to correspond with buttonholes. Weave in all ends to WS.

Ear Cosy Baby Hat,
published by Patons Beehive, 1930s

Stockinette stitch and a simplified fisherman's knit pattern are used to make this warm, snuggly hat for baby. The ear cosies ("cozies" for U.S. readers) are just the thing for keeping baby warm, and the attached ties will help keep the hat in place!

SPECIAL ABBREVIATIONS
k1B—knit 1 in row below st on left needle, allow existing st to drop from needle (this is not an inc).
M1k—make 1 kwise. Insert left needle from front to back under the running strand between st on right needle and st on left needle. Knit into back strand, thereby twisting st to close hole.
M1p—make 1 pwise. Bring yarn to front, insert left needle from back to front under the running strand between st on right needle and st on left needle. Purl into front strand, thereby twisting st to close hole.
k1f,b,&f—Inc 2 sts by knitting into the front loop, back loop, then front loop again.

EAR PIECES (MAKE 2)
CO 3 sts.
Row 1: K1, k1f,b&f, k1 (5 sts).
Row 2: Sl 1, k1, p1, k2.
Row 3: Sl 1, k1B, M1p, p1, M1p, k1B, k1—7 sts.
Row 4: Sl 1, k1, p3, k2.
Row 5: Sl 1, k1B, [p1, M1k] twice, p1, k1B, k1—9 sts.
Row 6: Sl 1, *k1, p1; rep from * to last 2 sts, k2,
Row 7: Sl 1, k1B, p1, k1B, M1p, p1, M1p, k1B, p1, k1B, k1—11 sts.
Row 8: Sl 1, [k1, p1] twice, p1, [p1, k1] twice, k1.
Row 9: Sl 1, [k1B, p1] twice, M1k, p1, M1k, [p1, k1B] twice, k1—13 sts.
Row 10: Same as row 6.
Row 11: Sl 1, *k1B, p1; rep from * to last 2 sts, k1B, k1.
Rows 12 through 17: Rep rows 10 and 11.
Cut yarn leaving 4" tail. Sl all sts to holder.
Make second ear cosy the same.

HAT
CO 8 sts. With WS facing, work across 13 sts of one ear cosy, CO 21 sts, work across 13 sts of second ear cosy (WS facing), CO 8 sts—63 sts.
Row 1: Sl 1 [k1, p1] 3 times, k1, work across 13 sts of ear cosy in est patt, [k1, p1] 10 times, k1, work across 13 sts of second ear cosy, [k1, p1] 3 times, k2.
Row 2: Sl 1, *k1, p1; rep from * to last 2 sts, k2.
Row 3: Sl 1, *k1B, p1; rep from * to last 2 sts, k1B, k1.
Work 10 rows more in patt.
Next row (WS): K1, purl to last st, k1.

Next row (RS): *K2, M1k, k3, M1k, k2; rep from * to end of row—81 sts.
Working the first and last st as k1 every row (edge sts), work in St st until work measures 4" from CO, finishing with a purl row completed.

SIZE
6–12 months

FINISHED MEASUREMENTS
Opening: 15"; hat stretches to fit head snuggly
Depth from crown to forehead: 6"

MATERIALS
Yarn—CYCA #3 Light, washable wool or blend: About
    125–150 yds (exact amount will depend on the
    size of pom-pom)

Size 6 [4 mm] knitting needles
Size G/6 [4 mm] crochet hook
Tapestry needle
2 stitch holders
Pom-pom maker, or 2 circles of cardboard roughly
    the circumference of pom-pom

GAUGE
22 sts and 28 rows = 4" [10 cm] in St st on size 6
[4 mm] needles. *Adjust needle size as necessary
to obtain correct gauge.*

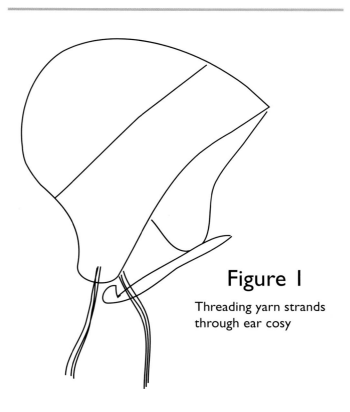

Figure 1

Threading yarn strands
through ear cosy

Crown shaping:
Row 1: [K6, k2tog] 10 times, k1—71 sts.
Row 2 and every WS row: K1, purl to last st, k1.
Row 3: [K5, k2tog] 10 times, k1—61 sts.
Row 5: [K4, k2tog] 10 times, k1—51 sts.
Row 7: [K3, k2tog] 10 times, k1—41 sts.
Row 9: [K2, k2tog] 10 times, k1—31 sts.
Row 11: [K1, k2tog] 10 times, k1—21 sts.
Next row (WS): [K1, p2tog] 10 times—11 sts.
Cut yarn leaving 4" tail, thread through rem sts, and
gently pull tail to close sts and top of hat. Weave tail to
WS to secure.

FINISHING
Thread tapestry needle and close back seam with
mattress st (see Glossary), weave in tails to WS to
secure.

Ties (make 2): Cut 4 strands of yarn, each about 30"
in length. With crochet hook, pull strands through to
halfway point at beg of ear cosy (see Figure 1). Divide
strands into 2 groups and tightly twist each group
clockwise, then allow them to twist around each other
counter-clockwise. Secure twist with overhand knot about
1" from ends. See Glossary for instructions on how to
make tassels or pom-poms.

Women's Bathing Suit, published by Wolsey, 1930s

Swimsuits for men and women were fairly popular items to knit in the 1930s and 1940s. What fiber to use? Wool has plenty of elasticity, and very soft wools like merino or Rambouillet are easy to wear next to the skin. However, wool holds about 30 to 40 percent of its weight in moisture when wet, so the yarn would need to be lightweight. A 100 percent fine cotton is a possibility, although cotton has no elasticity, so it's not a perfect choice. A blend of cotton and synthetic might work well. The project shown here was made with Wolsey "Sea Pride" 4-ply bathing wool. Unfortunately, we couldn't find any information about this yarn. The manufacturer specified that it was bathing wool, which may have meant it was blended or plied with something else, or was perhaps pre-shrunk. It's possible that current sock yarns would work, especially those made with elastic.

PATTERN STITCH

Rows 1, 3, and 5: P3, *k6, p3; rep from * to end of row.
Rows 2, 4, and 6: Purl.
Rows 7, 9, and 11: K3, *p3, k6; rep from * to end of row.
Rows 8, 10, and 12: Purl.
Cont patt st this way, moving the patt 3 sts to the left on every 6th row thereafter.

UNDERPANTS (WORKED ENTIRELY IN ST ST)
Back

With MC, CO 2 sts.
Row 1 (WS): Purl
Row 2 (RS): K1f&b (see Glossary), k1—3sts.
Row 3: P1, p1f&b (see Glossary), p1—4 sts.
Cont to inc 1 st on every row this edge, keeping other edge straight until 54 sts are on needle.
Next row (RS): (At inc edge) CO 3 sts, knit to end—57 sts.
Next row (WS): Purl, making inc at end of row—58 sts.
Rep these 2 rows once more.
Next row: CO 3 sts, knit to end—65 sts.

Leave these sts on holder and make another piece; only work the incs at the opposite end of the needle until 53 sts are on needle.
Next row: CO 3 sts, purl to end—56 sts.
Next row: Knit, inc 1 st at end of row—57 sts.
Rep last 2 rows twice more—65 sts.
Next row (WS): Purl to end, join on first piece and purl to end—130 sts total.
Next row: Knit to end. Work another 5 rows in St st, then k2tog at both sides of next row and every 6th row thereafter until 4 dec have been made at each side, then k2tog at both ends of every 4th row until 96 sts rem. Work 3 rows in St st after last dec.

Short row shaping:

Short row 1: K90, turn work
Short row 2: Sl 1, p83, turn work
Short row 3: Sl 1, k77, turn work
Short row 4: Sl 1, p71, turn work
Cont to work 6 sts fewer after each turn until 12 sts rem in center. Sl these sts onto spare needle or holder.

SIZE
Chest: 32–34″

FINISHED MEASUREMENTS
Chest circumference: 32–34″

MATERIALS
Yarn—CYCA #1 Super Fine or #2 Fine: About 1200 yds main color (MC); about 60 yds white (CC 1); about 60 yds red (CC 2)
Note: 4-ply is an English yarn weight designation. It's slightly thicker than fingering-weight, but finer than sport-weight yarns.
Size 2 [2.75 mm] knitting needles
Size C/2 [2.75 mm] crochet hook
Tapestry needle
Stitch holders

GAUGE
34 sts and 48 rows = 4″ [10 cm] in St st. *Adjust needle size as necessary to obtain correct gauge.*

Wolsey

No. 299

VIENNESE DESIGN

using 10 ounces of

"SEA PRIDE" 4-PLY

★

PRICE 2d

Front

Beg same as back, inc on every row on one edge until 35 sts are on needle. Make second piece, inc on opposite edge. Now join both pieces tog with the straight edges to the center, and inc 1 st at both ends of row until 80 sts on needle.

Next row: CO 3 sts, work to last st, inc in this st—84 sts.
Rep this last row 9 times—120 sts.
K2tog at both sides every 6th row—96 sts.
Work 9 rows after last dec, then sl sts on holder.

SKIRT
Back

With MC CO 147 sts and knit 10 rows.
Next row: Purl.
Work in patt st and k2tog at both sides of every 10th row until125 sts remain. K2tog at both sides of every 4th row until105 sts remain.
Next row (WS): Join underpants to skirt as foll: hold underpants to the front of work with the WS facing you, purl tog 1 st from underpants and 1 st from skirt 4 times, *p1 st from skirt only, then purl tog 1 st from each piece 11 times; rep from * to last 5 sts, p1 st from skirt, then purl tog 1 st from each piece 4 times.
Work even in patt without dec until work measures 16" from CO.
Next row (WS): P37, BO 31, purl to end. Working on these last sts 37 sts as foll:
Next row (RS) Work to last 2 sts, k2tog.
Next row: BO 2 sts, purl to end.
Rep last 2 rows until all sts are dec. Join yarn to rem sts and work in the same way.

Front

Work same as back, joining the underpants, etc., until work measures 15".

Front V:

Next row (RS): Work 51 sts, k2tog, turn work, purl back to beg of row.
Working on these 52 sts, cont as foll:
Next row (RS): Work to last 2 sts, k2tog—51 sts
Next row (WS): Rep last 2 rows 9 times more—42 sts.
Work next 7 rows without dec.
Next row: Work to last 2 sts, k1f&b, k1—43 sts.
Work even for 3 rows.
Next row: K2tog, work to end—42 sts.
Next row: Purl.
Rep last 2 rows once more—41 sts.
Next row: K2tog, work to last 2 sts, k1f&b, k1
Next row: Purl.
Next row: K2tog, knit to last 2 sts, k2tog—39 sts.
Next row: Purl.
Rep last 2 rows until all sts are dec. Join yarn to rem sts and work to match first side.

Front insertion:

CO 3 sts.
Row 1: Purl.
Now working in patt, inc 1 st at both ends of next row, and every 4th row until 45 sts are on needle.
Work even another 3 rows.
BO loosely.
Sew this piece into front V opening.

Straps (make 2)

CO 14 sts and work 18" in k1, p1 rib. BO in rib.
Work second strap the same.

Gusset

With MC CO 2 sts.
Row 1 (WS): Purl
Row 2 (RS): K1f&b, k1—3 sts.
Cont in St st and inc 1 st at both ends of every row until 7 sts on needle, then inc at both ends of every knit row until 35 sts on needles.
Work 13 rows without inc, then k2tog at both ends of next and every 4th row until 9 sts rem.
K2tog at both ends of every row until all sts are dec.
Cut yarn leaving 3" tail and fasten off rem st.

Sailing Boat

With CC 2, CO 12 sts and knit 1 row.
Working in garter st, inc 1 st at beg of the 2nd and 4th rows only—14 sts.
Work even until piece measures 2–1/2"; on shaped edge k2tog every other row—4 sts. BO all sts.

Sail

With CC 1, CO 20 sts and working in garter st, k2tog at both ends of every 4th row until all sts are dec. Cut yarn leaving 3" tail and fasten off rem st.

FINISHING

Stitch the boat into position as shown in photo image, making a few waves by *twisting CC 1 around the darning needle about 26 times (same as making French knots), then anchor yarn through another st in same row several sts away; rep from * 2 or 3 times to make each group of waves. Set gusset in underpants, putting short-shaped end to front and long shape to back, leaving the straight edges between legs.

With crochet hook, work 2 rows of double crochet (see Glossary) around top of suit and the legs. Press on WS of work with a warm iron over a damp cloth. Sew up seams and press. Set shoulder straps into position, crossing them at the back. Try on suit to determine desired strap length and mark sewing position. Join straps to back with whipstitch (see Glossary), spacing straps about 2" apart.

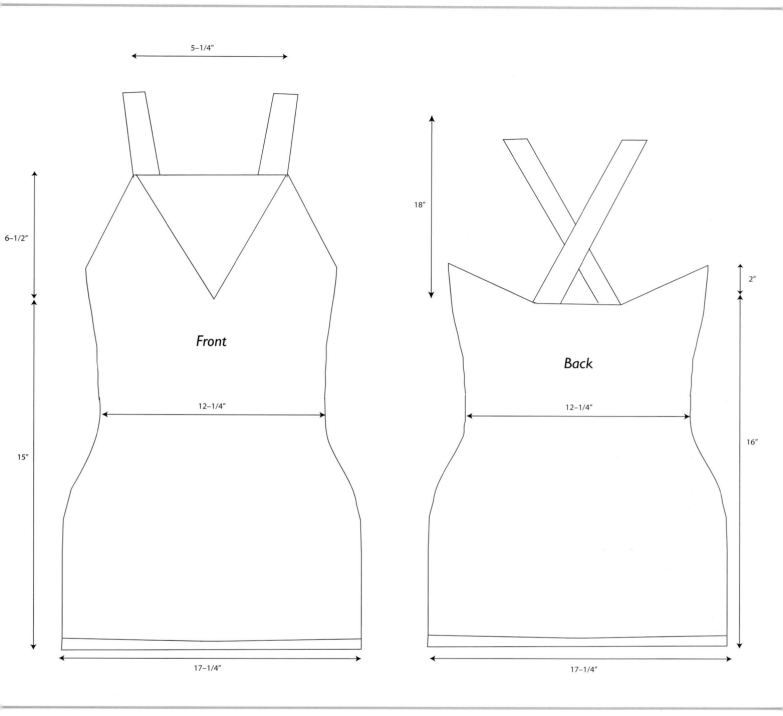

5–1/4"

6–1/2"

15"

Front

12–1/4"

17–1/4"

18"

2"

16"

Back

12–1/4"

17–1/4"

FOR A GREATER MEASURE OF KNITTING PLEASURE

No. 1599
See Page 49

VOL·314
25¢ (IN U.S.A.)

SMART STYLES OF BEAR BRAND *and* BUCILLA YARNS

1940s

The 1940s, often referred to as the Golden Age of Knitting, offered more patterns than any other decade in the first part of the twentieth century. The 1940s were a time to knit practical items, since involvement in World War II dominated life on the homefront and clothing was rationed in many parts of the world. Knitters banded together to make socks, gloves, and helmet-style headwear for men in service.

At the same time, knitters conserved resources by knitting sweaters, vests, cardigans, gloves, scarves, socks, and even underwear for every family member. Much of the knitwear made during this period was worked in a single color, although some items, such as gloves and children's wear, had contrasting color trims. Projects using two colors became more popular during the war, since yarn wasn't readily available, and knitters began using recycled yarns from older knits and garments that had fallen out of fashion or were simply outgrown. Stitch patterns, such as cables in every shape and form, were very popular for men and women, young and old, and military-style rib patterns became commonplace in men's wear. Gloves and mitts were offered in a variety of patterns and styles for every member of the family and were knit using two needles or double pointed needles.

Wartime rationing made an impact on fashion, as hemlines grew shorter and embellishments like wide lapels and bows disappeared in an effort to conserve resources. Knitting was the one way women could express their individual sense of style. Simple, handknit dress sets became an important part of every fashionable woman's wardrobe.

Bunny Hugger Cardigan,
published by Bear Brand, 1940

A simple short-sleeved, button-front blouse worked in garter stitch. With a delicate pattern worked along the front bands and collar for contrast, the fingering-weight angora/wool blend yarn creates a blouse suitable for daytime functions, work, or an evening out on the town. In the updated version, we've maintained the short sleeve with its gathered cap and the upper hip-bone length, increased the measurements to those more in line with what is worn today, and added two extra sizes. You'll need a few more buttons than shown in the photo to accommodate the added body length.

BACK

CO 153 (159, 167) sts.

Row 1 (RS): *K1, p1; rep from * to last st, k1.

Row 2 (WS): *P1, k1; rep from * to last st, p1.

Rep last 2 rows until rib measures 3–1/2" from CO, inc 17 (19, 20) sts evenly spaced across last row of rib—170 (178, 187) sts.

Change to garter st and work even until back measures 14 (14–1/2, 15)" from CO.

Underarm shaping:

BO 9 (11, 11) sts at beg of next 2 rows, working in garter st across rem sts to end—152 (156, 165) sts.

Dec 1 st each side every other row 8 (10, 10) times—136 (136, 145) sts.

Work even in garter st until back measures 22 (23, 24)" from CO.

Shoulder shaping:

BO 12 (12, 13) sts beg of next 2 rows—112 (112, 119) sts.

BO 13 sts beg of next 2 rows—86 (86, 93) sts.

BO 13 (13, 14) sts beg of next 2 rows—60 (60, 65) sts.

BO rem sts.

LEFT FRONT (AS WORN)

CO 77 (79, 83) sts. Work in k1, p1 rib patt same as back for 3–1/2", inc 8 (10, 10) sts evenly spaced across last row of rib—85 (89, 93) sts.

Work even in garter st until front measures 14 (14–1/2, 15)" from CO, ending with WS row completed.

Underarm shaping:

Next row (RS): BO 9 (11, 11) sts beg of row, knit across row to end (center front)—76 (78, 82) sts.

Next row (WS): Knit.

Beg with next row, dec 1 st at armhole edge every RS row 8 (10, 10) times—68 (68, 72) sts. Work even in garter st until left front measures 19–1/2 (20–1/2, 21–1/2)" from CO, ending with RS row completed.

Neckline shaping:

Next row (WS): BO 15 (15, 16) sts at neck edge, knit rem sts—53 (53, 56) sts.

Next row (RS): Knit.

Next row (WS): K1, dec 1 st, knit across row—52 (52, 55) sts.

Rep last 2 rows 14 (14, 15) times more. *At the same time,* when work measures 22 (23, 24)" and there are 38 (38, 40) sts rem, ending with WS row completed, beg shoulder shaping.

SIZE
Chest: 38 (40, 42)"

FINISHED MEASUREMENTS
Chest: 40 (42, 44)", not including front bands
Length: 22–1/2 (23–1/2, 24–1/2)"
Sleeve length to underarm: 6–1/2 (7, 7–1/2)"

MATERIALS
Yarn—CYCA #1 Super Fine, 100% angora or angora/wool blend: About 1800 (1960, 2120) yds
Size 2 [2.75 mm] knitting needles

Size 3 [2.1 mm] steel crochet hook
15 (16, 17) buttons, about 3/8" diameter
Sewing needle to sew on buttons
Tapestry needle
2 stitch holders
Long sewing pins with large heads

GAUGE
34 sts and 56 rows = 4" [10 cm] in garter st on size 2 [2.75 mm] needles. *Adjust needle size as necessary to obtain correct gauge.*

Shoulder shaping:
Next row (RS): BO 12 (12, 13) sts, knit to end—26 (26, 27) sts.
Next row (WS): Knit.
Next row: BO 13 sts, knit to end—13 (13, 14) sts.
Next row: Knit.
Next row: BO rem sts.

RIGHT FRONT (AS WORN)
Work same as left front until front measures 14 (14-1/2, 15)" from CO, ending with RS row completed.

Underarm shaping:
Next row (WS): BO 9 (11, 11) sts beg of row, knit across row to end (center front)—76 (78, 82) sts.
Next row (RS): Knit.
Beg with next row, dec 1 st at armhole edge every WS row 8 (10, 10) times—68 (68, 72) sts. Work even in garter st until right front measures 19-1/2 (20-1/2, 21-1/2)" from CO, ending with WS completed.

Neckline shaping:
Next row (RS): BO 15 (15, 16) sts at neck edge, knit rem sts—53 (53, 56) sts.
Next row (WS): Knit.
Next row (RS): K1, dec 1, knit across row—52 (52, 55) sts.
Rep last 2 rows 14 (14, 15) times more. *At the same time,* when work measures 22 (23, 24)", and there are 38 (38, 40) sts, ending with RS row completed, begin shoulder shaping.

Shoulder shaping:
Next row (WS): BO 12 (12, 13) sts, knit to end—26 (26, 27) sts.
Next row (RS): Knit.
Next row: BO 13 sts, knit to end—13 (13, 14) sts.
Next row: BO rem sts.

Join shoulders:
*With RS tog, align left front shoulder BO with left back shoulder BO and pin in place. Thread tapestry needle with about 20" strand of yarn and sew shoulders tog using backstitch (see Glossary). Re-thread tapestry needle as necessary. Rep from * for right front and back shoulders. Remove pins.

Right Front Band
CO 13 sts. [Knit 1 row. Purl 1 row] 2 (3, 4) times—4 (6, 8) rows.

Begin pattern:
*First row (RS): K2, p4, yo, k1, yo, p4, k2—15 sts.
Row 2 (WS): K6, yo, p3, yo, k6—17 sts.
Row 3: K1, p5, yo, k5, yo, p5, k1—19 sts.
Row 4: K6, yo, p7, yo, k6—21 sts.
Row 5: K1, p5, ssk, k5, k2tog, p5, k1—19 sts.
Row 6: K6, p2tog, p3, p2tog, k6—17 sts.

Row 7: K1, p5, ssk, k1, k2tog, p5, k1—15 sts.
Row 8: K6, p3tog, k6—13 sts.
Row 9 (buttonhole row): K6, yo (for buttonhole), k2tog, k5—13 sts.
Rows 10–14: [Purl 1 row. Knit 1 row] 2 times. Purl 1 row*.
The 14 rows from * to * form the patt; rep patt 14 (15, 16) times more. BO all sts.
Pin band along right front center edge, easing where necessary. With threaded tapestry needle, whipstitch (see Glossary) band in place.

Left Front Band
CO 13 sts. *Knit 1 row, purl 1 row. Rep from * 1 (2, 3) times more—4 (6, 8) rows.
[Purl 1 row. Knit 1 row] 4 times. [Knit 1 row. Purl 1 row] 3 times.
Rep from ** to ** 14 (15, 16) times more. BO all sts.
Pin band along left front center edge, easing where necessary. With threaded tapestry needle, whipstitch band in place.

COLLAR
With RS facing, skip first 6 sts of right front band sts, pick up and knit 47 (47, 48) sts along right front neck, then 59 (59, 64) sts along back neck, then 47 (47, 48) sts along Left Front Neck (don't include last 6 sts of left front band sts)—153 (153, 160) sts. Beg with WS row, work in St st for 13 rows more.
Row 1 (RS): *P6, yo, k1, yo; rep from * to last 6 sts, p6—195 (195, 204) sts.
Row 2 (WS): *K6, yo, p3, yo; rep from * to last 6 sts, k6—237 (237, 248) sts.
Row 3: *P6, yo, k5, yo; rep from * to last 6 sts, p6—279 (279, 292) sts.
Row 4: *K6, yo, p7, yo; rep from * to last 6 sts, k6—321 (321, 336) sts.
Row 5: *P6, ssk, k5, k2tog; rep from * to last 6 sts, p6—279 (279, 292) sts.
Row 6: *K6, p2tog, p3, p2tog; rep from * to last 6 sts, k6—237 (237, 248) sts.
Row 7: *P6, ssk, k1, k2tog; rep from * to last 6 sts, p6—195 (195, 204) sts.
Row 8: *K6, p3tog; rep from * to last 6 sts, k6—153 (153, 160) sts.
Next 5 rows: [Purl 1 row. Knit 1 row] 2 times. Purl 1 row. BO all sts

SLEEVES
CO 77 (85, 91) sts. Work rib patt same as body for 1-1/2", inc 9 (9, 11) sts evenly spaced across last row of rib—86 (94, 102) sts.

Sleeve shaping:
Inc 1 st each side every 4th row 1 (6, 15) time(s)—88 (106, 132) sts, then every 6th row 11 (9, 4) times—110 (124, 140) sts. Work even in garter st until sleeve measures 6-1/2 (7, 7-1/2)" from CO edge.

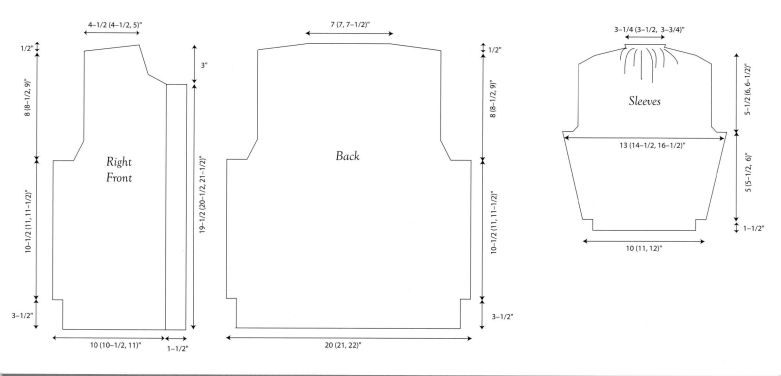

Cap shaping:
BO 9 (11, 11) sts beg of next 2 rows—92 (102, 118) sts. Dec 1 st each side every other row 10 (12, 14) times—72 (78, 90) sts. Work even in garter st until cap measures about 5 (5-1/2, 5-3/4)" from BO edge. BO 2 (2, 3) sts beg of next 4 rows—64 (70, 78) sts. Next row: K3, *k3tog; rep from * to last 3 sts, k3—28 (30, 32) sts.
BO rem sts.
Work second sleeve the same.

FINISHING
Join body side seams with mattress st (see Glossary), working 1/2 st in from each side edge to maintain k1, p1 rib patt. Work underarm sleeve seams the same.

With RS tog, pin sleeve into armhole opening, matching underarm body and sleeve seams and easing-in extra fullness to each side shoulder seam to evenly distribute upper sleeve gathers. Sew sleeve to body using backstitch. Rep for other sleeve. Sew buttons in center of left front band opposite buttonholes of right front band. With crochet hook and yarn, beg at lower edge of right front (RS facing), sc (see Glossary) along outer edge of band, keeping work flat, work 3 sc in corner st at neck edge, then 1 sc in each st to beg of collar, sc around collar outer edge to left front, working 3 sc in corners, then 1 sc in each st from end of collar to neck edge of front band, 3 sc in corner st, then sc along outer edge of left band to lower edge. Fasten off. Weave in loose yarn tails to WS of work. Block to size.

Men's Vest,
published by Bear Brand, 1940

This is an easy-to-make classic vest for him that will move along quickly despite the gauge. The vest features a simple wide-rib body pattern bordered with bands of traditional cables. This project is uncomplicated, take-along knitting, with enough interest to prevent it from becoming another UFO. Find the perfect yarn and color and in no time at all, you'll mark off another completed holiday gift! We've added two additional sizes.

BACK

With smaller needles, CO 126 (138, 150) sts.
Row 1 (RS): *K2, p2; rep from * to last 2 sts, k2.
Row 2 (WS): *P2, k2; rep from * to last 2 sts, p2.
Rep last 2 rows until rib measures 4″ from CO, inc 14 (16, 18) sts evenly spaced across last row of rib—140 (154,168) sts. Change to larger needles and beg main patt as foll:.

Pattern stitch:
Row 1 (RS): K4, p6, *k8, p6; rep from * to last 4 sts, k4.
Row 2 (WS): P4, k6, *p8, k6; rep from * to last 4 sts, p4.
Rep the last 2 rows until back measures 14–1/2 (16, 17–1/2)″ or desired length from CO, ending with WS row completed.

Underarm shaping:
BO 8 (11, 13) sts at beg of next 2 rows—124 (132,142) sts. Dec 1 st each side every other row 9 (10, 13) times—106 (112, 116) sts.
Work even in est patt until back measures 24 (26, 28)″ or desired length from CO, ending with WS row completed.

Shoulder shaping:
BO 9 (9, 10) sts beg of next 4 (4, 6) rows—70 (76, 56) sts.
BO 10 (10, 0) sts beg of next 2 (2, 0) rows—50 (56, 56) sts.
BO rem sts for back neck.

FRONT

Work same as back, including all shaping, until front measures 15–1/4 (16–3/4, 18–1/4)″ from CO edge, ending with WS row completed.

Neck shaping:
Next row (RS): Work to center of row, drop yarn and attach a second ball, complete row in est patt with second ball. Turn work to WS, maintaining est patt. Work both sides of neck at same time, each with its own ball of yarn (remember to cont armhole shaping at armhole edges).

Dec 1 st at each neck edge every 2nd row 15 (19, 17) times, then every 4th row 10 (9, 11) times—28 (28, 30) sts on each shoulder.
When front measures 24 (26, 28)″ or desired length from CO, end with WS row completed—28 (28, 30) sts each shoulder.

Shoulder shaping:
Row 1 (RS): BO 9 (9, 10) sts at beg of left shoulder (as worn), work in est patt to neck, drop yarn. Pick up second ball of yarn and work across right shoulder in patt.
Row 2 (WS): BO 9 (9, 10) sts at beg of right shoulder (as worn), work in est patt to neck, drop yarn. Pick up

SIZE
Chest: 38 (42, 44)"

FINISHED MEASUREMENTS
Chest circumference: 40 (44, 48)"
Length: 24-3/4 (26-3/4, 28-3/4)"

MATERIALS
Yarn—CYCA #1 Super Fine, 100% wool or blend:
   About 1050 (1250, 1450) yds

Size 1 [2.25 mm]; size 3 [3.25 mm] knitting needles
Cable needle
Tapestry needle
Long sewing pins with large, colored heads

GAUGE
28 sts and 36 rows = 4" [10 cm] in wide rib patt on
   size 3 [3.25 mm] needles. *Adjust needle size as
   necessary to obtain correct gauge.*

second ball of yarn and work across left shoulder in
est patt.
Rows 3 and 4: Rep rows 1 and 2.
Row 5: BO 10 (10, 10) sts at beg of left shoulder,
work same as row 1.
Row 6: BO 10 (10, 10) sts at beg of right shoulder,
work same as row 2.

FINISHING
Block front and back pieces to measurements. With
RS tog and threaded tapestry needle, sew shoulders
using backstitch (see Glossary). Join body side seams
with mattress st (see Glossary), working 1 st in from
each side edge to maintain k2, p2 rib patt at lower
rib. Weave in ends to WS and secure.

Cable-stitch Neckband
With smaller needles, CO 10 sts.
Rows 1, 3, and 5 (RS): Knit.
Rows 2, 4, and 6 (WS): K2, p6, k2.
Row 7 (RS): K2, sl next 3 sts to cable needle and
hold in front of work, k3 sts from left needle, k3 sts
from cable needle, k2.
Row 8 (WS): K2, p6, k2.
Rows 9–12: Rep rows 1–4.
Rep rows 7 through 12 for cable patt until band is
about 26 (28, 29)", or long enough to fit completely
around neckline, slightly stretched. Do not BO sts. Slip
10 neckband sts onto safety pin, and beg at center
back neck, pin each half of neckband to vest neckline,
pinning in place and working toward the center front
V. Overlap the left side of band (as worn) over the
right side. If band fits smoothly around neckline when
slightly stretched, replace 10 sts from safety pin and
BO. If not, adjust band length as necessary, either by
cont to work cable st or removing any extra row.
Sew band neatly to neck edge with whipstitch (see
Glossary), taking care that seam does not draw up
(seam must be as elastic as neck band); sew ends of
band in place with left end overlapping right. Remove
pins, weave ends to WS and secure.

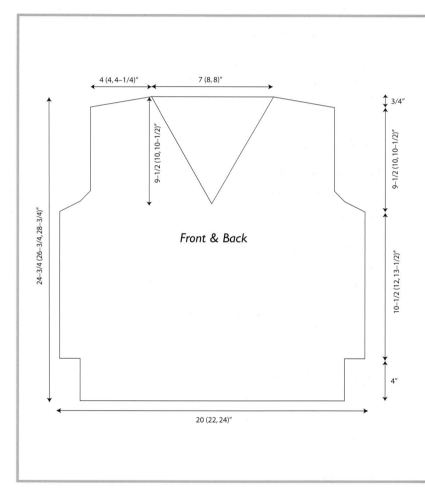

Front & Back

4 (4, 4–1/4)"
7 (8, 8)"
3/4"
9-1/2 (10, 10-1/2)"
9-1/2 (10, 10-1/2)"
24-3/4 (26-3/4, 28-3/4)"
10-1/2 (12, 13-1/2)"
4"
20 (22, 24)"

ARMHOLE BANDS (MAKE 2)
CO 10 sts and work armhole band same as neck band for
19 (20, 21)", when slightly stretched. BO not BO, Beg at
underarm seam, pin band in place around armhole edge.
When band fits smoothly, BO sts. Sew band to armhole.
Remove pins, weave in ends to WS and secure. Make
second armhole band the same.

Seasider Cardigan,
published by Bear Brand, 1940

A smart, button-front, short-sleeved cardigan (or blouse) in stockinette stitch with front bands worked in single crochet, the Seasider promises to be a favorite part of your wardrobe. Made with a soft, lightweight angora yarn, this top is perfect to wear for any function, day or evening. We've updated the sizes (the original pattern indicates that a 38″ bust equals size 18. Ahem!). This project would look great in a variety of yarns. For summertime, try yarns in linen, cotton/blend, or silk.

BACK
With smaller needles, CO 86 (90, 94) sts.
Row 1 (RS): *K2, p2; rep from * to last 2 sts, k2.
Row 2 (WS): *P2, k2; rep from * to last 2 sts, p2.
Rep last 2 rows until rib measures 4″ from CO, inc 8 (9, 10) sts evenly spaced across last row of rib—94 (99, 104) sts.
Change to larger needle and St st, work even until back measures 14–1/4 (16–1/4, 16–3/4)″ from CO.

Underarm shaping:
BO 5 (6, 7) sts at beg of next 2 rows, working in St st across rem sts to end—84 (87, 90) sts.
Dec 1 st each side every other row 5 (6, 6) times—74 (75, 78) sts.
Work even in St st until armhole measures 7–1/2 (8, 8–1/2)″ from BO.

Shoulder shaping:
BO 6 (6, 7) sts beg of next 4 rows—50 (51, 50) sts.
BO 7 (7, 6) sts beg of next 2 rows—36 (37, 38) sts.
BO rem sts for back neck.

LEFT FRONT (AS WORN)
With smaller needles, CO 42 (46, 46) sts. Work in k2, p2 rib patt same as back for 4″, inc 5 (3, 6) sts evenly spaced across last row of rib—47 (49, 52) sts.
Change to larger needles and St st, work even until front measures 14–1/4 (16–1/4, 16–3/4)″ from CO, ending with WS row completed.

Underarm shaping:
Row 1 (RS): BO 5 (6, 7) sts beg of row, knit across row to end (center front)—42 (43, 45) sts.
Row 2 (WS): Purl.
Row 3 (RS): K1, dec 1, knit to end (center front)—41 (42, 44) sts.
Rep last 2 rows 4 (5, 5) times more—37 (37, 39) sts.
Work even in St st until left front measures 20–1/4 (22–3/4, 23–1/4)″ from CO, ending with RS row completed.

Neckline shaping:
Next row (WS): BO 11 (11, 9) sts at neck edge, purl

rem sts—26 (26, 30) sts.
Next row (RS): Knit.
Next row (WS): P1, dec 1 st, purl across row—25 (25, 29) sts.
Rep last 2 rows 6 (6, 9) times more, *at the same time,* when work measures 21–3/4 (24–1/4, 25–1/4)″ from CO, ending with WS row completed, beg shoulder shaping.

FINISHED MEASUREMENTS
Chest: 34 (36, 38)", including buttoned front bands
Length: 22–1/4 (24–3/4, 25–3/4)"
Sleeve length to underarm: 5"

MATERIALS
Yarn—CYCA #3 Light, 100% angora or any yarn that
knits to gauge: About 775 (800, 975) yds

Size 3 [3.25 mm] knitting needles
Size 4 [3.5 mm] crochet hook
7 buttons, about 1/2" diameter
Sewing needle to sew on buttons
Tapestry needle
2 stitch holders
Long sewing pins with large heads

GAUGE
22 sts and 30 rows = 4" [10 cm] in St st on size 6
[4 mm] needles. *Adjust needle size as necessary to
obtain correct gauge.*

Shoulder shaping:
Next row (RS): BO 6 (6, 7) sts, knit to end.
Next row (WS): Purl.
Next row: BO 6 (6, 7) sts, knit to end.
Next row: Purl.
Next row: BO rem 7 (7, 6) sts.

RIGHT FRONT (AS WORN)
Work same as left front until front measures 14–1/4
(16–1/4, 16–3/4)" from CO, ending with RS row
completed.

Underarm shaping:
Row 1 (WS): BO 5 (6, 7) sts beg of row, purl across row
to end (center front)—42 (43, 45) sts.
Row 2 (RS): Knit.
Row 3 (WS): P1, dec 1, purl to end (center front)—41
(42, 44) sts.
Rep last 2 rows 4 (5, 5) times more—37 (37, 39) sts.
Work even in St st until right front measures 20–1/4
(22–3/4, 23–1/4)" from CO, ending with WS row
completed.

Neckline shaping:
Next row (RS): BO 11 (11, 9) sts at neck edge, knit rem
sts—26 (26, 30) sts.
Next row (WS): Purl.
Next row (RS): K1, dec 1, knit across row—25 (25, 29)
sts.
Rep last 2 rows 6 (6, 9) times more. *At the same time,*
when work measures 21–3/4 (24–1/4, 25–1/4)" from
CO, ending with RS row completed, beg shoulder
shaping.

Shoulder shaping:
Next row (WS): BO 6 (6, 7) sts, purl to end.
Next row (RS): Knit.
Next row: BO 6 (6, 7) sts, purl to end.
Next row: Knit.
Next row: BO rem 7 (7, 6) sts.

SLEEVES
With smaller needles, CO 50 (50, 54) sts. Work k2, p2
rib patt same as body for 1", inc 6 (8, 6) sts evenly
spaced across last row of rib—56 (58, 60) sts. Change to
larger needle and St st.

Sleeve shaping:
Inc 1 st each side every 4th (4th, 2nd) row 6 (6, 3)
times—68 (70, 66) sts, then every 6th (6th, 4th) row 1
(1, 6) time(s)—70 (72, 78) sts. Work even in St st until
sleeve measures 5" from CO edge.

Cap shaping:
BO 5 (6, 7) sts beg of next 2 rows—60 (60, 64) sts.
Dec 1 st each side every other row 13 (11, 11) times—
34 (38, 42) sts. Dec 1 st each side every 3rd row 4 (6,
7) times—26 (26, 28) sts. Work even in St st until cap
measures about 5–3/4 (6, 6–1/4)" from BO edge. BO
3 sts beg of next 4 rows—14 (14, 16) sts.
BO rem sts.
Work second sleeve the same.

Join shoulders:
*With RS tog, align left front shoulder BO with left back
shoulder BO and pin in place. Thread tapestry needle
with about 20" strand of yarn and sew shoulders tog
using backstitch. Re-thread tapestry needle as necessary.
Rep from * for right front and back shoulders. Remove
pins.

NECK RIBBING
Establish neck ribbing:
With smaller needles and RS facing, beg at right front
edge, pick up and knit 11 (11, 9) sts from BO, 11 (11,
14) sts from right neck edge, 36 (37, 38) sts from back
neck BO, 11 (11, 14) sts from left neck edge, 11 (11,
9) sts from left front edge BO—80 (81, 84) sts.
Row 1 (WS): *P2, k2; rep from * across row. *At the
same time,* inc 2 (1, 2) sts evenly spaced across row,
ending row with p2—82 (82, 86) sts.

Row 2 (RS): *K2, p2; rep from * to last 2 sts, k2.
Row 3: *P2, k2; rep from * to last 2 sts, p2.
Rep rows 2 and 3 until rib measures 1″ from pick up row. BO in patt.

FINISHING

Join body side seams with mattress st (see Glossary), working 1 st in from each side edge to maintain k2, p2 rib patt. Work underarm sleeve seams the same. With RS tog, pin sleeve into armhole opening, matching underarm body and sleeve seams and easing-in any extra fullness each side shoulder seam. Sew sleeve to body using backstitch. Rep for other sleeve.

Right Front Band: With crochet hook and RS facing, beg at lower right front corner, work 1 row sc along right front edge, spacing sc evenly to keep work flat, without puckers. Turn work.

Row 2: Ch 1, 1 sc in each sc to end of row. Turn work.
Row 3: Ch 1, 1 sc in each of next 2 sc, ch 2, skip next 2 sts for buttonhole, cont sc in each sc and making 6 more buttonholes, evenly spaced, same as first buttonhole; complete last buttonhole 2 sc from neck edge. Turn work. Work 2 more rows sc. Fasten off.

Left Front Band: With RS facing, beg at upper left front corner, work 6 rows sc (this band has one more row than right front band) along left front edge, omitting buttonholes. With sewing needle and thread, attach buttons to left front matching buttonholes on right front. Weave in loose yarn tails to WS of work. Block to size.

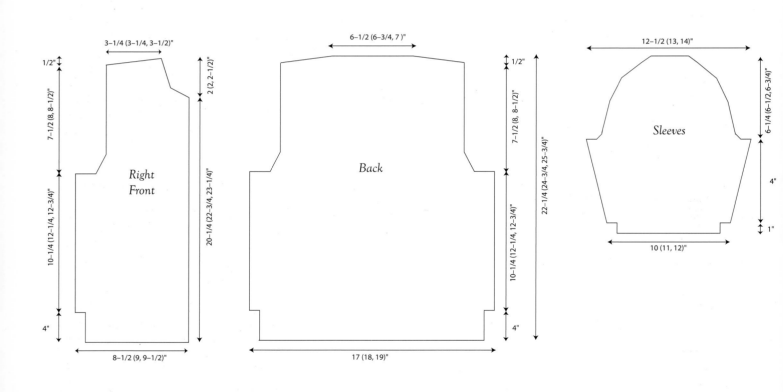

Men's Cardigan, published by Coats & Clark, 1947

Looking for a good basic cardigan for him? With set-in sleeves and front bands that are worked along with the two fronts, this project offers lots of easy stockinette stitch knitting. Make this your take along knitting, in the car, to meetings, to the doctor's office, or to the kids' ball games. The original pattern actually contained four (count 'em) sizes, but it was necessary to amend the measurements in order to fit today's male. If basic colors of gray, navy, or maroon aren't to your liking why not try a multicolor yarn? A simple classic knit like this provides a perfect canvas for exciting yarns and never goes out of style.

SIZE
Chest: 38 (40, 42, 44)"

FINISHED MEASUREMENTS
Chest circumference: 40 (42, 44, 46)", not including front bands
Length: 25-1/2 (26, 27, 27-1/2)"
Sleeve length from underarm to cuff: 18-1/2 (19, 20, 21)"

MATERIALS
Yarn—CYCA #3 Light, 100% wool or blend: About 1464 (1666, 1868) yds
Size 3 [3.25 mm] knitting needles

Size 5 [3.75 mm] knitting needles; 2 double pointed needles (dpn) (or size 3 [3.25 mm] dpn) to use as holders for back neck band grafting.
7 buttons, about 3/4" diameter
Sewing thread and needle to attach buttons
Tapestry needle
2 stitch holders
Long sewing pins with large, colored heads
Coilless pins

GAUGE
22 sts and 28 rows = 4" [10 cm] in St st on size 5 [3.75 mm] needles. Adjust needle size as necessary to obtain correct gauge.

BACK

With smaller needles, CO 99 (103, 109, 113) sts.
Row 1 (RS): *K1, p1; rep from * to last st, k1.
Row 2 (WS): *P1, k1; rep from * to last st, p1.
Rep last 2 rows until rib measures 2-1/2" from CO, inc 11 (13, 12, 13) sts evenly spaced across last row of rib—110 (116, 121, 126) sts.
Change to larger needles, beg with knit row, work in St st until back measures 15 (15-1/2, 16, 16)" or desired length from CO, ending with WS row completed.

Underarm shaping:
BO 5 (6, 6, 7) sts at beg of next 2 rows—100 (104, 109, 112) sts. Dec 1 st each side every other row 4 (5, 6, 6) times—92 (94, 97, 100) sts.
Work even in St st until back measures 24-1/2 (25, 26, 26-1/2)" or desired length from CO, ending with WS row completed,

Shoulder shaping:
BO 8 (8, 8, 9) sts beg of next 4 (2, 2, 4) rows—60 (78, 81, 64) sts.
BO 0 (9, 9, 0) sts beg of next 0 (4, 4, 0) rows—60 (42, 45, 64) sts.

small safety pins, then use these ms as your guide for buttonhole placement when you work the left front.

With smaller needles, CO 57 (59, 63, 65) sts. Work in k1, p1 rib patt same as back for 2–1/2", inc 6 (7, 5, 6) sts evenly spaced across last row of rib—63 (66, 68, 71) sts, ending with WS row completed. Change to larger needles; beg with knit row work in St st and front band rib as foll:
Row 1 (RS): [K1, p1] 4 times, knit across rem of row.
Row 2 (WS): Purl to last 8 sts, [k1, p1] 4 times.
Rep the last 2 rows until front measures 15 (15–1/2, 16, 16)" from CO edge, ending with RS row completed.

Underarm shaping:
Row 1 (WS): BO 5 (6, 6, 7) sts, purl to last 8 sts, work 8 sts in est rib patt—58 (60, 62, 64) sts.
Row 2 (RS): Work 8 sts in rib, knit to end of row.
Dec 1 st at armhole edge (WS rows) every other row 4 (5, 6, 6) times.
When front measures 16 (16–1/2, 17, 17)", end with WS row completed.

Neck shaping:
Next row (RS): Work 8 sts in rib, dec 1 st, knit to end of row.
Next row (WS): Purl (work rem underarm shaping at beg of row as necessary).
Cont neck shaping, working inside the 8 rib sts, dec 1 st at neck edge every other row 15 (15, 15, 13) times more, then every 4th row 5 (5, 6, 8) times—33 (34, 34, 36) sts, includes 8 st rib band.
When front measures 24–1/2 (25, 26, 26–1/2)" or desired length from CO, ending with RS row completed, beg shoulder shaping

Shoulder shaping:
Row 1 (WS): BO 8 (8, 8, 9) sts, purl to last 8 sts, work in est rib patt.
Row 2 (RS): Rib 8, (work neckline dec as est if necessary) knit to end.
Row 3: BO 8 (9, 9, 9) sts, purl to last 8 sts, rib 8.
Row 4: Rib 8, knit to end.
Row 5: BO 9 (9, 9, 10) sts, purl to last 8 sts, rib 8.
Row 6: Rib 8. Place these sts on holder.

Mark for buttons:
Working upward along the front band and about 2 sts in from center front edge, place button ms (coilless pins), inserting first m about 1/2" from lower edge and last m at beg of neck shaping. Place rem button ms evenly spaced between these two ms.

LEFT FRONT (AS WORN)
Work same as right front, reversing shaping by working underarm shaping beg with RS row, and neckline decs

on WS rows after the 8 rib band sts. Work shoulder shaping beg of RS rows. Make buttonholes as you work left front after carefully aligning placement with coilless pin button ms on right front.

Buttonholes:
RS row: Knit across row to rib patt, work 3 sts in rib, BO 3 sts, rib to end.
WS row: Rib 2 sts, CO 3 sts to replace BO sts, rib 3 sts, purl to end.
Rep these 2 rows for each buttonhole made. When left front is completed, place rem 8 rib band sts on holder.

SLEEVES
With smaller needles, CO 47 (49, 51, 53) sts.

Cuff:
Work in k1, p1 rib patt same as back until cuff measures 4" from CO, inc 5 (7, 8, 7) sts evenly spaced across last row of rib—52 (56, 58, 60) sts.

Sleeve shaping:
Change to larger needles and St st. Dec 1 st each side (make decs 1 st in from edges) every 2nd (4th, 4th, 4th) row 4 (22, 25, 27) times—60 (100, 108, 114) sts, then every 4th (6th, 6th, 6th) row 22 (2, 1, 1) time(s)—104 (104, 110, 116) sts.
Work even in St st until sleeve measures 18–1/2 (19, 20, 21)" from CO, ending with WS row completed.

Cap shaping:
BO 5 (6, 6, 7) sts beg of next 2 rows—94 (92, 98, 102) sts.
Dec 1 st each side every other row 4 (5, 6, 6) times—86 (82, 86, 90) sts.
Dec 1 st each side every row 16 (14, 17, 17) times—54 (54, 52, 56) sts
Dec 1 st each side every other row 10 (10, 9, 10) times—34 (34, 34, 36) sts.
BO 4 sts at beg of next 4 rows—18 (18, 18, 20) sts.
BO rem sts.
Work second sleeve the same.

FINISHING
With RS tog and threaded tapestry needle, sew shoulders (not including 8 rib sts from each front band) using backstitch (see Glossary). Join body side seams with mattress st (see Glossary), working 1/2 st in from each side edge to maintain k1, p1 rib patt. Work underarm sleeve seams the same. Pin sleeves to body, matching underarm seams. With threaded tapestry needle, sew sleeve to body with backstitch. Remove pins. Attach second sleeve the same. Sew buttons in place at the coilless pin ms on right front band, making sure buttons align with buttonholes on left front band. Remove coilless pin ms.

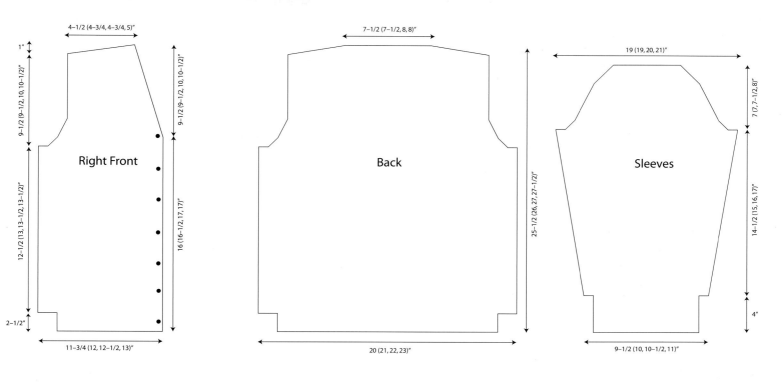

Right Front

Back

Sleeves

Neck Ribbing

Sl 8 right front band sts from holder onto larger needles, cont working in est rib patt for about 3–3/4 (3–3/4, 4, 4)", or until rib band (slightly stretched) meets center of back neck. Place sts on dpn. Sl 8 left front band sts from holder to larger needles and work same as right front, minus 1 row. Thread tapestry needle and join bands tog using knit grafting for ribs in opposite directions (such as cardigan bands meeting at the back neck) as foll: With RS facing, sl knit sts of one band onto a dpn, then place purl sts of same band onto a holder. Rep for other band. Graft the 2 sets of knit sts tog with Kitchener st (see

Glossary). Turn the bands over, sl the rem sts (they were the purl sts, but they're now knit sts on this side of the bands), and join them tog with Kitchener st. Thread tapestry needle with yarn and whipstitch along the inside band edge to back neck.

Note: If you haven't tried this method of joining rib bands before, work up 2 small rib samples and practice before grafting the cardigan bands together. Weave in loose yarn tails to WS of work. Block to size.

Men's Argyle Socks, published by Bernat, 1945

Argyle socks are a wonderful introduction to intarsia knitting. Each color is worked from its own bobbin or yarn butterfly. Intarsia produces a single-layer fabric regardless of the number of colors used, unlike Fair Isle knitting, which produces a double layer by stranding colors not in use across the back of the work. Intarsia is also worked flat, back and forth, on straight needles (or circular needles used as straight needles). This project offers two sock lengths, the "regulation" length and a shorter anklet-style sock.

ADULT SIZES
To fit shoe sizes 7–8 (9–10, 11–12)
Size variations will depend on foot lengths.

MATERIALS
Yarn—CYCA #1 Super Fine, 100% wool or wool blend:
   About 215 yds per 50 g skein
215 yds gray (main color—MC); 100 yds each of navy
   (color A) and medium blue (color B); about 5 yds
   each of Yellow (color C) and Red (color D)
Size 1 [2.25 mm] knitting needles; set of double
   pointed needles (dpn) for anklets.
Size 2 [2.75 mm] knitting needles; set of dpn for
   regulation and anklets.
Tapestry needle
Yarn bobbins (optional)
Stitch holders

GAUGE
30 sts and 42 rows = 4" on size 2 [2.75 mm] needles
   in St st. *Adjust needle size as necessary to obtain
   correct gauge.*

NOTES

1: Wind 2 balls each MC, color A, and color B. Wind about 4 yds each of color C and color D.

2: Always twist yarns around each other when changing colors to prevent making holes between colors.

REGULATION SOCK

With MC and larger needles, CO 58 (66, 74) sts.
Row 1: *K2, p2; rep from * to last 2 sts, k2.
Row 2: *P2, k2; rep from * to last 2 sts, p2.
Rep rows 1 and 2 until work measures 3", dec 4 sts evenly spaced across last row—54 (62, 70) sts.

Establish diamonds:

Row 1 (RS): Join A, k2, with MC k11 (13, 15) sts, with C k1, with D k1, with MC k11 (13, 15), join B k2, join second ball of MC, k11 (13, 15), with D k1, with C k1, with MC k11 (13, 15), with A k2.

Row 2: With A p3, MC p9 (11, 13), C p1, MC p2, D p1, MC p9 (11, 13), B p4, MC p9 (11, 13), D p1, MC p2, C p1, MC p9 (11, 13), A p3.

Row 3: With A k4, MC 7 (9, 11), C 1, MC 4, D 1, MC 7 (9, 11), B 6, MC 7 (9, 11), D 1, MC 4, C 1, MC 7 (9, 11), A 4.

Cont in St st in this way, knitting or purling 1 st more on each half of A side diamonds and 1 more st on each side of B diamond, moving the C diagonal line 1 st toward the outside and the D diagonal line 1 st toward the center every row until sts are on the needle as foll:
With A work 7 (8, 9) sts, MC 1, C 1, MC 10 (12, 14), D 1, MC 1, B 12 (14, 16), MC 1, D1, MC 10 (12, 14), C 1, MC 1, A 7 (8, 9).

Next row: for first cross of diagonals with diamonds, cont as follows:
With A work 7 (8, 9) sts, C 1, MC 12 (14, 16), D 1, B 12 (14, 16), D 1, MC 12 (14, 16), C 1, A 7 (8, 9).

Next row: With A work 6 (7, 8) sts, C 1, A 2, MC 10 (12, 14), B 2, D 1, with B 10 (12, 14), D 1, B 2, MC 10 (12, 14), A 2, C 1, A 6 (7, 8).

Cont in patt until sts are on needle as foll:
A 2, C 1, A 10 (12, 14), MC 2, B 10 (12, 14), D 1, B 2, D 1, B 10 (12, 14), MC 2, A 10 (12, 14), C 1, A 2.

Next row: With A work 1 st, C 1, A 12 (14, 16), B 12 (14, 16), D 2, B 12 (14, 16), A 12 (14, 16), C 1, A 1.

Next row: With A work 2 sts, C 1, A 10 (12, 14), MC 2, B 10 (12, 14), D 1, B 2, D 1, B 10 (12, 14), MC 2, A 10 (12, 14), C 1, A 2.

Cont in patt until sts are on needle as foll:
A 7 (8, 9), C 1, MC 12 (14, 16), D 1, B 12 (14, 16), D 1, MC 12 (14, 16), C 1, A 7 (8, 9).

Next row: With A work 6 (7, 8) sts, MC 2, C 1, MC 10 (12, 14), D 1, MC 2, B 10 (12, 14), MC 2, D 1, MC 10 (12, 14), C 1, MC 2, A 6 (7, 8).

Next row: With A work 5 (6, 7) sts, MC 4, C 1, MC 8 (10, 12), D 1, MC 4, B 8 (10, 12), MC 4, D 1, MC 8 (10, 12), C 1, MC 4, A 5 (6, 7).

Cont in patt to just before the end of A and B diamonds, when sts are on the needle as foll: A 3, MC 8 (10, 12), C 1, MC 4, D 1, MC 8 (10, 12), B 4, MC 8 (10, 12), D 1, MC 4, C 1, MC 8 (10, 12), A 3.

Next row: With A work 2 sts, MC 10 (12, 14), C 1, MC 2, D 1, MC 10 (12, 14), B 2, MC 10 (12, 14), D 1, MC 2, C 1, MC 10 (12, 14), A 2.

Break off A and B balls, join B at each end and A at center of next row.

Next row: With B work 2 sts, MC 11 (13, 15), C 1, D 1, MC 11 (13, 15), A 2, MC 11 (13, 15), D 1, C 1, MC 11 (13, 15), B 2.

Next row: With B work 3 sts, MC 9 (11, 13), D 1, MC 2, C 1, MC 9 (11, 13), A 4, MC 9 (11, 13), C 1, MC 2, D 1, MC 9 (11, 13), B 3.

Cont in this manner until there are 3 complete diamonds at seam of sock and the sts are on the needle same as row 1. Break off A balls at each end and B ball at center, and the C and D nearest the ends of the needle.

Sl center 26 (30, 34) sts on holder for instep. Shape heel on first and last 14 (16, 18) sts as foll:

Heel flap:

Sl these 28 (32, 36) sts onto needle and join. Be sure that seam or joining of heel sts from each end of needle is in center of your work. With MC, work even in St st or heel st for 2–1/2 (2–3/4, 3)", ending with **a purl** (WS) row completed.

Heel turn (short rows):

K16 (18, 20) sts, k2tog, k1, turn work to WS, leaving rem sts unworked.
Short row 1: Sl 1, p5, p2tog, p1, turn
Short row 2: Sl 1, k6, k2tog, k1, turn
Short row 3: Sl 1, p7, p2tog, p1, turn.
Cont in this manner, always having 1 st more before the dec, until 16 (18, 20) sts rem on needle. With knit side (RS) of work facing you, pick up 14 (16, 18) sts along side edge of heel flap. Purl back across 30 (34, 38) sts and pick up 14 (16, 18) sts along other side of heel flap—44 (50, 56) sts.

Heel gusset shaping:

Next row (RS): K1, ssk, knit to within last 3 sts, k2tog, k1.
Next row (WS): Purl across.
Rep these last 2 rows until 26 (30, 34) sts rem on needle. Work even in St st until foot measures 6 (8, 10)" or desired length, allowing 2" for shaping toes.

Instep:

Sl 26 (30, 34) instep sts from holder onto needle, continue in est patt until there are 5 or 6 complete diamonds from beg. This piece should fit with ease the heel-to-toe sole piece just completed; if not, work even with MC until it does fit snugly rather than loosely, to the heel/sole piece.

Toe shaping (join sock stitches and work in rounds):

Divide sole sts in half and sl each half onto dpn. With instep needle referred to as Needle #2 (this needle holds all the instep sts), and heel needle to the right of instep needle as Needle #1 (with half the sole sts), and heel needle to the left as Needle #3 (with the other half of sole sts), work in rnds to shape toe as foll:
Rnd 1: With MC, knit across all needles.
Rnd 2: Needle #1: Knit to within last 3 sts, k2tog, k1.
Needle #2 (instep sts): K1, ssk, knit to last 3 sts, k2tog, k1.
Needle #3: K1, ssk, knit to end of needle (end of rnd 2).
Rep rnds 1 and 2 until 8 (10, 12) sts on Needle #2. Sl sts from Needle #3 onto Needle #1 and align parallel with sts on Needle #2. You should have the same number of sts on both needles. With threaded tapestry needle, weave toe sts tog with Kitchener st (see Glossary). With threaded needle and MC, seam back leg length tog with mattress st (see Glossary), taking in 1 full st on each edge to maintain the k2, p2 rib patt. Cont with mattress st and MC to join the instep and sole pieces tog. Weave in all loose ends to WS of work.

ANKLETS

With smaller needles and MC, CO 58 (66, 74) sts. Work in k2, p2 rib same as regulation sock, ending RS row with k2, and WS row with p2, for 1–1/2". Dec 4 sts evenly across last row—54 (62, 70) sts. Change to size 2 [2.75 mm] needles and work in argyle patt same as for regulation sock until 1 diamond has been completed. Shape heel and sole same as for regulation sock. Cont in patt on instep sts for 2 or 3 diamonds, as desired. Work even until piece is desired length (see regulation sock). Shape toe same as regulation sock.

Baby Bonnet and Jacket, published by Beehive, 1940s

"The jacket of this little set has been the knitter's favorite for many years, and in response to so many requests, a matching bonnet has been added." This sentence was the intro to the sweater and bonnet set we've included here. The set is a wonderful gift to make for a new baby, and if worked in superwash wool or a washable blend it's sure to get lots of wear. The jacket and bonnet are knit in stockinette stitch with a simple eyelet lace border pattern and picot edges. If you need something for a baby boy, this set will still work. Make the entire jacket and hat in stockinette stitch, omitting the eyelet lace borders but keeping the picot edge borders. Drop the ribbon rosettes on the hat and add I-cord ties instead, and you're all set to go for the new baby boy!

BORDER PATTERN

Row 1 (RS): K1, *yo, k2tog; rep from * to last st, k1.
Row 2 and all WS rows: K1, purl to last st, k1.
Row 3: K5, *yo, k2tog, k9; rep from * to last 7 sts, yo, k2tog, k5.
Row 5: K3, *k2tog, yo, k1, yo, ssk, k6; rep from * to last 9 sts, k2tog, yo, k1, yo, ssk, k4.
Row 7: K2, *k2tog, yo, k3, yo, ssk, k4; rep from * to last 10 sts, k2tog, yo, k3, yo, ssk, k3.
Row 9: K1, *k2tog, yo, k5, yo, ssk; rep from * to last st, k1.
Row 11: *K2tog, yo, k7, yo, ssk; rep from * to last st, k1.
Row 13: Knit.
Row 15: Rep row 1.
Row 16: Rep row 2.
Work these 16 rows for border patt.

SIZE
3–6 months

FINISHED MEASUREMENTS
JACKET
Chest: 18"
Length: 10"
Sleeve length to underarm: 6"

BONNET
Width around face edge: 11–1/2" (back seam rem open for 3" at lower edge)
Depth: 6"

MATERIALS
Yarn—CYCA #1 Super Fine, washable wool or blend: About 500 yds
Size 3 [3.25 mm] knitting needles
Size 1 [2.75 mm] steel crochet hook
4 yds ribbon, about 1/2" wide
Tapestry needle
Spare knitting needle, same size as project needle or one size smaller
5 large safety pins

GAUGE
32 sts and 40 rows = 4" [10 cm] in St st on size 3 [3.25 mm] needles. *Adjust needle size as necessary to obtain correct gauge.*

JACKET

Note: Jacket is worked in one piece to armholes.

CO 144 sts.

Row 1 (RS): Knit

Row 2: K1f&b (see Glossary), purl to last 2 sts, p1f&b, k1—146 sts.

Rep rows 1 and 2 twice more—150 sts.

Row 7: K1, *yo, k2tog; rep from * to last st, k1.

Row 8: K2tog, purl to last 2 sts, k2tog—148 sts.

Row 9: Knit.

Rep rows 8 and 9 twice more—144 sts.

Row 14: K1, purl to last st, k1.

These 14 rows complete hem, which is turned under to the WS on 7th row to make the picot edge.

Work the 16 border patt rows once. Change to St st until piece measures 6–1/2" from CO edge, ending with a WS row completed.

Right Front

K34, k2tog for armhole—35 sts. Turn work, leaving rem sts on spare needle.

Working on the 35 sts, dec 1 st at armhole edge every row 14 times—21 sts.

Dec 1 st at armhole edge every other row until 8 sts rem, ending with a knit row completed. Cut yarn leaving 4" tail; sl these 8 sts on safety pin to hold.

Back

With RS of work facing, join wool to sts on spare needle. K2tog, k68, k2tog—70 sts. Leave rem sts on spare needle for left front. Working on these 70 sts, dec 1 st each end of needle every row 14 times—42 sts.

Dec 1 st each end of needle every other row until 16 sts rem, ending with knit (RS) row completed. Cut yarn leaving 4" tail; sl these 16 sts on another safety pin to hold.

Left Front

With RS of work facing, join yarn to sts on spare needle, k2tog, k34—35 sts. Working on these 35 sts, work same as right front, being careful to work armhole dec on opposite side.

Right Sleeve

CO 42 sts, work 6 rows St st, ending with purl (WS) row completed.

Row 7 (RS): K1, *yo, k2tog; rep from * to last st, k1.

Rows 8–15: Beg with purl row, work 8 rows in St st.

Row 16: K1, p4, p1f&b, *p5, p1f&b; rep from * to last 6 sts, p4, p1f&b—49 sts.

Row 17: K1, *yo, k2tog; rep from * to end of row.

Row 18: K1, p4, p1f&b, *p5, p1f&b; rep from * to last 7 sts, p6, k1—56 sts.

Next 9 rows: Work rows 3 to 11 of border patt.

Row 28 (WS): K1f&b, purl to last 2 sts, p1f&b, k1—58 sts.

Row 29: Knit

Row 30: Rep row 28—60 sts.

Row 31: K1, *yo, k2tog; rep from * to last st, k1.

Beg with purl row, work even in St st until sleeve measures 6–1/2" from CO edge, ending with purl (WS) row completed.

Cap:

Row 1 (RS): K1, k2tog, knit to last 3 sts, k2tog, k1—58 sts.

Row 2: Purl.

Rep these last 2 rows until 18 sts rem, ending with knit (RS) row completed.

Next row (WS): K1, p9, turn work, k10. Cut yarn leaving 4" tail, sl rem 18 sts on safety pin.

Left Sleeve

Work same as right sleeve to 18 sts on needle, but end with purl row completed.

Next row: K10, turn work, p9, k1. Cut yarn leaving 4" tail, sl rem 18 sts on safety pin.

Neckband

With RS of work facing, join yarn at right front edge. Knit the 8 sts of right front (these are the sts on safety pins), k18 of right sleeve, 16 sts of back, 18 sts of left sleeve, 8 sts of left front—68 sts.

Row 1 (WS): K1, purl to last st, k1.

Row 2 (RS): (eyelets for ribbon) K1, *yo, k2tog; rep from * to last st, k1.

Purl 1 row. Knit 1 row.

**Row 5: K1f&b, purl to last 2 sts, p1f&b, k1—70 sts.

Row 6: Knit.

Rep rows 5 and 6 once more, then row 5 once—74 sts.

Row 10 (RS): K1, *yo, k2tog; rep from * to last st, k1.

Row 11: K2tog, purl to last 2 sts, k2tog—72 sts.

Row 12: Knit.

Rep rows 11 and 12 once more, then row 11 once—68 sts. BO all sts**.

Hem for Right Front

With RS of work facing, join yarn in 13th row from CO edge. Pick up and knit 62 sts along right front edge, ending at 4th row of neckband. Work from ** to ** as given for neckband.

Hem for Left Front

Beg at 4th row of neckband, work hem for left front to correspond with right front.

Jacket Finishing

Sew sleeve seams using mattress st or backstitch (see Glossary), then sew sleeves into armholes. Sew shaped corners of hems tog for form miters. Fold hems under at eyelet row and sew in position using whipstitch (see Glossary). Weave in loose tails to WS. Press seams and hems lightly. Thread ribbon through eyelets at neck.

BONNET

Beg with brim, CO 78 sts.
Work 6 rows in St st, ending with purl (WS) row completed.
Row 7 (RS): K1, *yo, k2tog; rep from * to last st, k1.
Beg with purl row, work 7 rows in St st, completing the hem.
Work 16 rows of border patt once. Work 6 rows St st, then rep row 1 of border patt. The brim is turned over on this last eyelet row.
Work 10 rows in k1, p1 rib.
With WS of work facing, k5, *k1f&b, k5; rep from * to last st, k1—90 sts
Row 1: K3, purl to last 3 sts, k3.
Row 2: Knit.
Rep these 2 rows until work measures 8–1/2″ from CO edge, ending with purl (WS) row completed.

Crown shaping:

Row 1: *K8, k2tog; rep from * to end of row—81 sts.
Row 2 and all even-numbered rows: Knit.

Row 3: *K7, k2tog; rep from * to end of row—72 sts.
Row 5: *K6, k2tog; rep from * to end of row—63 sts.
Row 7: *K5, k2tog; rep from * to end of row—54 sts.
Cont dec in this manner, working one st fewer between dec every other row until 9 sts rem. Cut yarn leaving 4″ tail. Thread tail on tapestry needle and draw through rem 9 sts. Pull gently on tail to close sts and top of hat. Weave in tail on WS to secure.

Bonnet Finishing

Fold hem under at first eyelet row and sew in place using whipstitch. Sew up back seam for 3″, working from base of crown, leaving lower section of hat open. Press lightly. Make ribbon rosettes and sew to bonnet as shown.

The baby bonnet and jacket pattern was originally published in this *Beehive for Bairns* pattern book, one of many collections of layette sets available in the 1940s.

Men's Two-Tone Cardigan, published by Bear Brand, 1940

The original cardigan was made using a blend of angora and wool, with two strands worked together as one for the fronts, and a single strand of slightly heavier-weight wool in a second color for the back, sleeves, and front bands. Angora/wool blend is somewhat expensive, especially in a project where the yarn is doubled. We're suggesting a more updated look, using the same yarn, or the same weight yarn in two colors, to avoid doubling one of the yarns. If you prefer, make the whole garment one color, simply adding the amounts of yarns A and B together to obtain the total amount needed in a single color.

STITCH PATTERN
Broad rib pattern:
Row 1 (RS): *P2, k5; rep from * to last 2 sts, p2.
Row 2 (WS): K2, *p5, k2; rep from * to end of row.
Rep rows 1 & 2 for patt.

SPECIAL ABBREVIATIONS
K1f&b (bar inc)—knit into the front loop and then into
the back loop.
K1tbl (through back loop)—knit st through the back loop
(forms twisted st).

BACK
With color A and smaller needles, CO 125 (139, 145) sts.
Row 1 (RS): *K1, p1; rep from * to last st, k1.
Row 2 (WS): *P1, k1; rep from * to last st, p1.
Rep last 2 rows until rib measures 2–1/2" from CO, inc
17 (17, 18) sts evenly spaced across last row of rib—142
(156, 163) sts.
Change to larger needles and broad rib patt beg with
row 1. Work even in patt until back measures 15 (16,
16)" or desired length from CO, ending with WS row
completed.

Underarm shaping:
BO 6 (8, 9) sts at beg of next 2 rows—130 (140, 145)
sts. Maintaining patt, dec 1 st each side every other row
7 (9, 9) times—116 (122, 127) sts.
Work even in patt until back measures 24–1/2 (26,
26–1/2)" or desired length from CO, ending with WS
row completed.

Shoulder shaping:
BO 10 (11, 11) sts beg of next 2 (6, 2) rows—96 (56,
105) sts.
BO 11 (0, 12) sts beg of next 4 (0, 4) rows—52 (56,
57) sts.
BO rem sts for back neck.

LEFT FRONT (AS WORN)
Note: Both fronts are worked in St st. They hang straight
and have a hem at the lower edge, no lower rib.
With color B and larger needles, CO 70 (77, 80) sts.
Work in St st for 9 rows.
Next row (WS): Knit all sts. This row is the turning ridge
for hem at lower edge.
Beg with RS knit row, cont in St st until front measures 6
(6, 6–1/2)" from turning ridge of hem, ending with RS
row completed.

Slanted pocket:
Purl the first 48 (52, 54) sts, sl rem 22 (25, 26) sts on
to strand of waste yarn to hold; *turn work, BO the first
3 sts, knit to end of needle (front edge), turn work, purl
1 row; rep from * 9 (10, 10) times more. Sl the rem 18
(19, 21) sts on needle to separate strand of yarn. Cut
working yarn leaving 4" tail.
CO 30 (33, 33) sts for lower edge of pocket lining, work
in St st for 5 (5, 5–1/2)", ending with WS row
completed. Beg at underarm edge, sl the 22 (25, 26) sts
onto same needle as the 30 (33, 33) pocket sts—52
(58, 59) sts. Work even in St st for 19 (21, 21) rows,
ending with RS row completed, drop yarn.
Turn work. Beg at front edge, sl the 18 (19, 21) front sts
from yarn holder to free needle, pick up yarn and to the
same needle holding front sts, purl the 52 (58, 59) sts
across row to underarm edge—70 (77, 80) sts.
Work even in St st until front measures 15 (16, 16)"
from turning ridge of hem, ending with WS row
completed.

Underarm shaping:
Row 1 (RS): BO 6 (8, 9) sts, knit across row—64 (69,
71) sts.
Row 2 (WS): Purl.
Dec 1 st at armhole edge (RS rows) every other row 6
(8, 8) times—58 (61, 63) sts.

At the same time, when front measures 15–1/2 (16, 16)" from turning ridge of hem, ending with RS row completed, beg neck shaping.

Neck shaping:
Row 1 (WS): P1, p2tog, purl to end.
Row 2 (RS): Knit (remember to cont underarm shaping as necessary).
Rep these 2 rows 12 (13, 11) times more—45 (47, 51) sts. Then dec 1 st at neck edge every 4th row 13 (14, 16) times—32 (33, 35) sts. Work even in St st until front measures 24–1/2 (26, 26–1/2)" from turning ridge of hem, ending with WS side row completed.

Shoulder shaping:
Row 1 (RS): BO 10 (11, 11) sts, knit to end.
Rows 2 and 4 (WS): Purl.
Rows 3 and 5: BO 11 (11, 12) sts, knit to end.
Row 6: BO pwise.

RIGHT FRONT (AS WORN)
Work same as left front, reversing shaping by working underarm shaping beg with WS row, and neckline decs on RS rows. Work shoulder shaping beg of WS rows. Reverse pocket shaping.

SLEEVES
With color A and smaller needles, CO 59 (67, 69) sts.

Cuff:
Work in k1, p1 rib patt same as back until cuff measures 3–1/2" from CO, inc 6 (5, 10) sts evenly spaced across last row of rib—65 (72, 79) sts.

Sleeve shaping:
Change to larger needles and broad rib patt. Working new sts into broad rib patt when possible, inc 1 st each side (make incs 1 st in from edges) every 4th row 27 (19, 22) times—119 (110, 123) sts, then every 6th row 7 (14, 13) times—133 (138, 149) sts.
Work even in broad rib patt until sleeve measures 19–1/2 (20–1/2, 21)" from CO, ending with WS row completed.

Cap shaping:
BO 6 (8, 9) sts beg of next 2 rows—121 (122, 131) sts.
Dec 1 st each side every other row 6 (8, 8) times—109 (106, 115) sts.
Dec 1 st each side every row 17 (13, 12) times—75 (80, 91) sts
Dec 1 st each side every other row 17 (19, 21) times—41 (42, 49) sts.
BO 5 (5, 6) sts at beg of next 4 rows—21 (22, 25) sts.
BO rem sts.
Work second sleeve the same.

Assemble Body
Sew front and back tog at underarms using mattress st (see Glossary). Join shoulders using backstitch (see Glossary).

Cardigan Band
With color A and smaller needles, CO 8 sts.
Row 1: K1f&b in each st—16 sts
Row 2: K1tbl, *wyif sl next st pwise, take yarn to back k1; rep from * ending row with sl st.
Rep row 2 for 1".

Buttonholes:
Work first 4 sts same as row 2, k1, sl 1, pass the knitted st over sl st (BO), *k1, BO 1, sl 1, BO 1; rep from * twice, k1, BO 1; sl 1, k1, sl 1. There should now be 4 sts before and 4 sts after the buttonhole. On next row, CO 4 sts over the 4 bound-off sts to complete buttonhole, and in next row k1f&b in each of the 4 CO sts—16 sts. Make 4 (5, 5) more buttonholes evenly spaced to beg of neck shaping. Work even until band is long enough to go around front edges and neck; baste band to sweater before cutting yarn and sewing band to cardigan to make sure it's neither too short nor too long. When fit is correct, BO as foll: K2tog, k2tog, *pass the first st over the second (BO), k2tog; rep from * to last st, fasten off.

Pocket Bands (make 2)
With color B, CO 6 sts.
Row 1: K1f&b in each st—12 sts.
Row 2: Work same as front band patt.
Rep row 2 for 1/2"; work in patt over the first 6 sts only for about 5 (5–1/4, 5–1/4)" keeping rem 6 sts at back of needle. Cut yarn leaving 4" tail. Join yarn at first 6 sts kept at back of needle and work these sts for about 5 (5–1/4, 5–1/4)" or the same length as previous 6 sts, then work again over all 12 sts for 1/2". BO all sts same as front band. Make second pocket band the same.

FINISHING
Sew sleeve seams using mattress st. Pin sleeves into armholes, easing to fit. On WS work, sew sleeves into place with backstitch. Turn hem on fronts to WS at turning ridge and baste in place. Baste side edges on inner pocket piece to WS of fronts, with lower edge of pocket meeting upper edge of hem; sew hems and side seams of pocket with whipstitch (see Glossary), taking care that sts do not pucker the work or show through on the RS. Baste lower edge of pocket band to edge of pocket opening and both edges of upper half of band to front, just above opening, so entire band forms an outline for pocket opening, as shown in photo. Sew lower edge of upper part of band and the entire outer edge of band to front. Sew buttons on front band about 2 sts in from seam, aligning them with buttonholes. Lightly block to smooth seams and pockets.

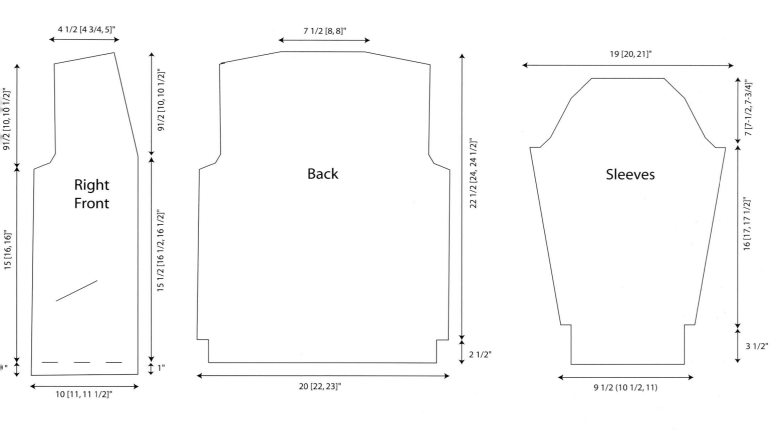

Right Front

4 1/2 [4 3/4, 5]"

9 1/2 [10, 10 1/2]"

9 1/2 [10, 10 1/2]"

15 [16, 16]"

15 1/2 [16 1/2, 16 1/2]"

1"

10 [11, 11 1/2]"

Back

7 1/2 [8, 8]"

22 1/2 [24, 24 1/2]"

2 1/2"

20 [22, 23]"

Sleeves

19 [20, 21]"

7 [7-1/2, 7-3/4]"

16 [17, 17 1/2]"

3 1/2"

9 1/2 (10 1/2, 11)

Stocking Cap and Glove Set, published by Beehive, 1945

Hats and gloves were popular items to knit in the 1940s. Many yarns and color choices weren't always readily available during World War II, and the shortage continued in Europe for several years thereafter. Smaller items could easily be made with yarn obtained from outgrown sweaters, or a few mix-and-match skeins from a knitter's stash (they had some stash, surely!) when new yarns or colors were hard to find. Why not look through your stash to find something suitable for this fun project?

CAP SIZES	SMALL	MEDIUM	LARGE
Head circumference	18"	19"	20"
Length of Cap	36"	38"	40"

MATERIALS

Yarn—CYCA #1 Super Fine, 100% wool, wool blend, alpaca, angora, or other warm yarn: About 265 yds [242 m] each in Light Green (color A), Cyclamen Red (color B), and Dark Green (color C). This yarn amount will make one cap and one pair of gloves for any of the 3 sizes.

Several 12" strands of smooth cotton waste yarn to use as holders for finger sts

Size 3 [3.25 mm] 16" [40 cm] circular needle; set of 4 double pointed needles (dpn)

OPTIONAL: Set of 4 size 3 [3.25 mm] dp glove needles, about 4" [10 cm] long, same size as gauge needles.

Tapestry needle

Stitch marker

4 coilless pins

Safety pin

3 x 6" piece of cardboard, for tassel making

GAUGE

30 sts and 40 rows = 4" on size 3 [3.25 mm] needles in St st. *Adjust needle size as necessary to obtain correct gauge.*

NOTE
When joining new colors and dropping old colors, leave 4" [10 cm] tails to weave in later.

CAP
Starting at cuff, with color C and circ needle, CO 195 (204, 210) sts. Join in rnd, being careful not to twist sts. Place marker to denote beg of rnd.

Rnds 1–6: *P2, k1; rep from * to end of rnd. Cut color C.

Rnd 7: Join color B. *k1, p1; rep from * to end of rnd (inc 1 st for size Small to 196 sts).

Rnd 8: Knit to end of rnd. Cut color B.

Rnd 9: Join color A, *k1, p1; rep from * to end of rnd.

Rnds 10–14: *P2, k1; rep from * to end of rnd. Cut color A.

Rnd 15: Rep rnd 7 (size Small already has 196 sts, not necessary to make another inc).

Rnd 16: Rep rnd 8.

Rnd 17: Join color C, *k1, p1; rep from * to end of rnd (dec 1 st for size Small to 195 sts).

Rnd 18: *P2tog, k1; rep from * to end of rnd—130 (136, 140) sts.

Rnds 19–22: *P1, k1; rep from * to end of rnd. Cut color C.

Rnd 23: Rep rnd 7 (do not inc st).

Rnd 24: Rep rnd 8.

Rnd 25: Join color A, *k1, p1; rep from * to end of rnd.

Rnds 26–30: *P1, k1; rep from * to end of rnd. Cut color A.

Rnd 31: Rep rnd 7 (do not inc st).

Rnd 32: Rep rnd 8.

Rnd 33: Join color C, *k1, p1; rep from * to end of rnd.

Rnd 34: *K30 (32, 68) sts, k2tog; rep from * to end of rnd (size Small ends with k2 tog, k2 sts)—126 (132, 138) sts.

Rnds 35–38: Knit to end of rnd. Cut color C.

Rnd 39: Join color B, *k1, p1; rep from * to end.

Rnd 40: Knit to end of rnd. Cut yarn B.

Rnd 41: Join color A, *k1, p1; rep from * to end.

Rnds 42–46: Knit to end of rnd. Cut yarn A.

Rnd 47: Rep rnd 39.

Rnd 48: Rep rnd 40.

Rnd 49: Join color C, *k1, p1; rep from * to end of rnd.

Rnd 50: *K19 (20, 21) sts, k2tog; rep from * to end of rnd—120 (126, 132) sts.

The stripe for the body of the cap is est on the last 16 rnds (rnds 3 –50). Working in this stripe patt, dec 6 sts in the foll 16th rnd as foll:

*k18 (19, 20) sts, k2tog; rep from * to end of rnd—114 (120, 126) sts.

Cont in this manner, dec 6 sts evenly every 16th rnd until 12 (12, 18) sts rem. Work even in patt until piece measures 36 (38, 40)" from CO edge. Remove m.

Cut yarn leaving 6" tail. Thread tail on tapestry needle and draw through rem sts. Pull tail gently to draw sts tog and close hat. Weave in loose ends on WS and secure.

FINISHING
Tassel: Cut piece of cardboard to 3 x 6". Hold a strand of each color tog as one. Wind yarn around the 6" length about 25 times (75 strands total). Cut yarn. Insert a 12" strand of each color under the wound strands at one of the narrow (3") ends. Adjust 12" strands so that an even amount hangs on each side of the cardboard, then tie these strands tog in a secure knot. Remove cardboard. Cut another set of 12" strands and wind around the tassel about 1" down from the tied end, tuck yarn tails under the wraps to secure. Cut opposite ends and trim. Sew to end of cap.

Cuff: Turn back one half of ribbed cuff, as shown in photo.

GLOVES
To determine your glove size, measure the circumference of your dominant hand (the hand you use when writing) around the knuckles (see Figure 1, Measuring for Gloves, below). To customize your gloves, measure your finger lengths, including fingernails, and adjust instructions as needed.

Sizes	SMALL	MEDIUM	LARGE
Measurement around palm:	5"	6"	7"

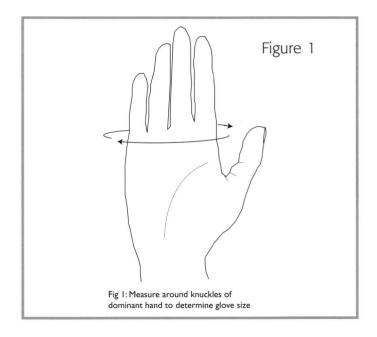

Figure 1

Fig 1: Measure around knuckles of dominant hand to determine glove size

Right Glove
Starting at cuff with color C and dpn, CO 57 (69, 81) sts. Divide sts evenly onto 3 needles. Join sts into rnd, taking care not to twist sts. Pm to denote beg of rnd.

Rnds 1–18: Work patt same as for cap—38 (46, 54) sts.

Rnds 19–33: Work same as for cap. Place coilless pin in last st of rnd 33 when finished.

Work even in stripe patt same as cap body (rnds 35–50) until glove measures 2 (2-1/4, 2-1/2)" from rnd 33 (the rnd marked with coilless pin).

Next rnd: Work in patt over the next 2 sts, transfer next 7 (8, 9) sts to safety pin (to be worked later for thumb); CO 7 (8, 9) sts using backward loop CO (see Glossary) to replace those sts held on safety pin, then work to end of rnd.

Work even in patt until piece measures 1 (1-1/2, 1-3/4)" from CO thumb sts, or until glove, when tried on, reaches to base of index finger. Place safety pins between fingers to mark off finger sts as foll (**Note:** When a finger has an odd number of sts, place the extra st on the back of glove sts.):

Index finger:
Mark off 11 (13, 15) sts for index finger by counting 5 (6, 7) from palm sts and 6 (7, 8) from the back of hand sts.

Middle finger:
Mark off 10 (12, 14) sts, counting 5 (6, 7) sts from palm and same from back of hand.

Ring finger:
Mark off 8 (10, 12) sts, counting 4 (5, 6) sts from palm and same from back of hand.

Little finger:
Mark off 9 (11, 13) sts, counting 4 (5, 6) sts from palm and 5 (6, 7) sts from back.

Cont in patt, work across index finger sts, sl rem sts onto a thread to hold for later.

Optional: Change to 4" [10 cm] dp glove needles to work fingers.

Fingers
Index finger:
Divide the 11 (13, 15) index finger sts among 3 or 4 needles, CO 2 sts between palm and back of hand and work in rnds on these 13 (15, 17) sts until finger reaches 1/4" from fingertip, including fingernail, or measures 2-1/4 (2-1/2, 2-3/4)".
Next rnd: [K2tog] 6 (7, 8) times, k1—7 (8, 9) sts.
Next rnd: K1, [k2tog] 3 times—4 sts. Cut yarn leaving 6" tail and thread on tapestry needle. Insert needle through rem sts and pull yarn gently to draw rem sts tog and close top of finger. Weave tail to WS and through several sts to secure end. *Finish off all fingers and thumb in same manner.*

Middle finger:
Transfer middle finger sts to 2 needles. Attach yarn to last st on back of hand for this finger. Pick up and knit 2 sts over the 2 CO sts of index finger, work across palm sts, CO 2 sts—14 (16, 18) sts. Divide these sts on 3 or 4 needles and work in rnds until finger measures 2-1/2 (2-3/4, 3)" or desired length.
Next rnd: [K2tog] 7 (8, 9) times—7 (8, 9) sts.
Next rnd: [K2tog] 3 (4, 4) times, k1 (0, 1) sts—4 (4, 5) sts.
Finish off finger.

Ring finger:
Transfer ring finger sts to 2 needles. Attach yarn to last st on back of hand for this finger. Pick up and knit 2 sts over the 2 CO sts of middle finger, work across palm sts, CO 2 sts—12 (14, 16) sts. Divide these sts on 3 or 4 needles and work in rnds until finger measures same as index finger or desired length.
Next rnd: [K2tog] 6 (7, 8) times—6 (7, 8) sts.
Next rnd: [K2tog] 3 (3, 4) times, k0 (1, 0)—3 (4, 4) sts.
Finish off finger.

Little finger:
Transfer little finger sts to 2 needles. Attach yarn to last st on back of hand for this finger. Pick up and knit 2 sts over the 2 CO sts of ring finger—11 (13, 15) sts. Divide these sts on 3 or 4 needles and work in rnds until finger measures 1-3/4 (2, 2-1/4)" or desired length.
Next rnd: [K2tog] 5 (6, 7) times, k1—6 (7, 8) sts.
Next rnd: [K2tog] 3 (3, 4) times, k0 (k1, k0)—3 (4, 4) sts.
Finish off finger.

Thumb:
Transfer the 7 (8, 9) thumb sts to 2 needles. Attach yarn and pick up and knit 7 (8, 9) sts over the 7 (8, 9) CO sts—14 (16, 18) sts. Divide these sts on 3 or 4 needles and work in rnds until thumb measures 2 (2-1/4, 2-1/2)" or desired length.
Next rnd: [K2tog] 7 (8, 9) times—7 (8, 9) sts.
Next rnd: [K2tog] 3 (4, 4) times, k1 (0, 1) sts—4 (4, 5) sts.
Finish off thumb. Weave in yarn tails to WS.

Left Glove
Work same as right glove. When glove measures 1 (1-1/2, 1-3/4)" or reaches the base of the index finger, try on glove, turning work until thumb opening is in place for left hand. Finish as for right glove.

Men's Heavy Gloves, published by Beehive, 1945

These gloves are worked circularly from cast on to finger tips. The yarn is DK-weight, a little heavier than the women's project gloves shown in this chapter. The original needles were old English size 11 [3 mm]; we don't have an exact U.S. size conversion, so try size 2 or 3, or whatever size will provide the gauge. The needle size and gauge are meant to be smaller than normally used for this yarn weight in order to provide strength and warmth. Most men appreciate a gift of warm gloves as much as they enjoy a pair of hand-knit socks.

For the Family

(A) *Childrens Gloves*—See page 12.

(B) *Ladys Gloves*—See page 13.

(C) *Mens Gloves*—See page 12.

(D) *Mens Heavy Gloves*—See page 16.

(E) *Ladys Gloves*—See page 13.

(F) *Childrens Gloves*—See page 16.

SIZES

Men's glove size: 7-3/4 through 8-1/4 (M)

Size 8-1/2 through 9 (L). Using larger needle, foll instructions as written for size M.

Note: To determine glove size, measure the circumference of the wearer's dominant hand (the hand used when writing) around the knuckles (see Figure 1, Measuring for Glove Size, opposite). To customize gloves, measure wearer's finger lengths, including fingernails, and adjust instructions if needed.

MATERIALS

Yarn—CYCA #3 Light, 100% wool, wool blend, alpaca, or other warm yarn: About 360 yds

Size 2 or 3 [2.75 or 3.25 mm] knitting needles; set of 4 or 5 double pointed needles (dpn); for larger size gloves use Size 3 or 4 [3.25 or 3.5 mm] dpn

Optional: set of 4" dp glove needles for fingers and thumb in same size needle as used to obtain gauge.

Tapestry needle

2 strands of smooth cotton waste yarn about 10" in length, to use as stitch holders for finger and thumb sts

Stitch marker

GAUGE

26 sts and 36 rows = 4" on size 2 or 3 [2.5 or 3.25 mm] needles in patt st. *Adjust needle size as necessary to obtain correct gauge.*

STITCH PATTERN

Rnds 1 and 2: *K2, p2; rep from * to end of rnd.
Rnds 3 and 4: *P2, k2; rep from * to end of rnd.
These 4 rnds complete 1 patt for hand of glove.
Fingers and thumb are worked in St st (knit each rnd).

RIGHT GLOVE

CO 48 sts. Divide sts evenly on 3 dpn (16-16-16). Join rnd, being careful not to twist sts, and place marker to indicate beg of rnd. Work in K2, p2 rib for 3–1/2" or desired length.
Next 4 rnds: Work 1 complete st patt.

Thumb gusset:
Rnd 1: P1, [k1f&b, k1] twice, p3, *k2, p2; rep from * to end of rnd—50 sts.
Rnd 2: P1, k6, p3, *k2, p2; rep from * to end of rnd.
Rnd 3: P1, k6, p1, k2, *p2, k2; rep from * to end of rnd.
**Rnd 4: P1, inc 1 st in next st, knit to the 2 sts before next purl st, inc 1 st in next st, k1, p1, work in patt to end of rnd—52 sts.
Rnds 5 and 6: P1, knit to next purl st, p1, work in patt to end of rnd**.
Rep instructions from ** to ** until there are 16 sts between the 2 purled sts.
Next 3 rnds: P1, k16, p1, work in patt to end of rnd.
Next rnd: P1, CO 4 sts, sl next 16 sts onto waste yarn holder and leave for thumb. Work in patt to end of rnd. Work 3 complete patts (12 rnds), then work rnds 1 and 2 of 4th patt. Remove m.

Fingers

First Finger:
Knit first 4 sts, sl all but last 10 sts onto waste yarn holder, CO 2 sts, knit last 10 sts—16 sts. Divide these 16 sts on 3 needles and join in rnd.
Knit in rnds for 3" or desired length.
Next rnd: [k2tog] 8 times.

Finish off finger:
Cut yarn, leaving 3" tail and thread on tapestry needle; thread needle and yarn through rem sts, pulling yarn gently to close top of finger. Weave tail to WS and secure. *Finish off all fingers and thumb the same.*

Second Finger:
Knit next 6 sts of rnd (front of glove) from yarn holder, CO 2 sts, knit last 6 sts of rnd from yarn holder, pick up and knit 3 sts at base of first finger (the CO sts of first finger)—17 sts. Divide these 17 sts on 3 dpn and join in rnd.
Knit in rnds for 3–1/2" or desired length.
Next rnd: [K2tog] 8 times, k1.
Finish off finger.

Third Finger:
Knit next 6 sts of rnd from yarn holder, CO 2 sts, knit last

6 sts of rnd from yarn holder, pick up and knit 2 sts at base of second finger—16 sts. Divide these 16 sts on 3 dpn and join in rnd.
Knit in rnds for 3" or desired length.
Next rnd: [K2tog] 8 times.
Finish off finger.

Fourth Finger:
Knit rem sts from waste yarn holder, pick up and knit 4 sts at base of third finger—14 sts. Divide these 14 sts on 3 dpn and join in rnd.
Knit in rnds for 2–1/2" or desired length.
Next rnd: [K2tog] 7 times.
Finish off finger.

Thumb:
Knit the 16 thumb sts from waste yarn holder, pick up and knit 4 sts at base of thumb—20 sts.
Divide these 20 sts on 3 needles and join in rnd.
Next 2 rnds: Knit, dec twice over the 4 sts that were picked up at base of thumb—16 sts after completing second of these 2 rnds.
Knit in rnds for 2–1/2" or desired length.
Next rnd: [K2tog] 8 times.
Finish off thumb.

LEFT GLOVE

Work the same as right glove until fingers are reached.

Fingers

First Finger: Knit first 14 sts, sl rem sts onto a waste yarn holder, CO 2 sts—16 sts. Divide these 16 sts on 3 dpn and join in rnd.
Finish finger and work rem of glove for the same as right glove, beg at back of glove to work sts for rem fingers.

FINISHING

Weave in yarn tails to WS. Wash and block gloves to size. Allow to dry before wearing.

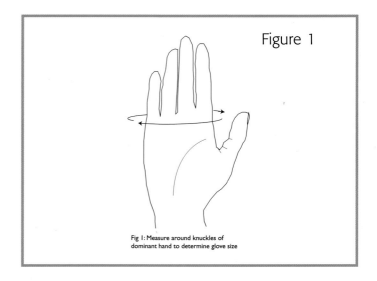

Figure 1

Fig 1: Measure around knuckles of dominant hand to determine glove size

Lady's Pullover, published by Monarch, 1946

This smartly styled pullover combines a wide rib pattern on the body with faux cables added in the upper yoke and sleeve cap. The high neckline opens in back and closes with a small button and crochet loop. Half double crochet completes the crew neck, and single crochet is used to finish around the lower edges and sleeves, although you could use reverse single crochet (crab stitch) instead of single crochet. The original project was offered in one size only, but we've created two extra sizes. The fit is meant to be snug, with very little ease. If you need a tad more breathing room and the next size is too large, try using larger needles, keeping in mind to check the row gauge—otherwise, the neckline, armhole, and sleeve shaping might need adjustments. Or, add a selvedge stitch at each side edge for seaming, remembering not to include these stitches in the overall pattern instructions as you work.

SIZE
Chest: 34 (36, 38)"

FINISHED MEASUREMENTS
Chest circumference: 35 (38–1/2, 41–1/2)"
Length: 23–3/4 (24–3/4, 26–1/4)"
Sleeve length to underarm: 4"

MATERIALS
Yarn—CYCA #1 Super Fine, any yarn that knits to gauge: About 1050 (1175, 1350) yds
Size 2 [2.75 mm]; size 3 [3.25 mm] knitting needles

Size 4 [3.5 mm] crochet hook
Tapestry needle
2 stitch holders
Long sewing pins with large heads
1 button, about 1/2" diameter
Sewing needle and thread to match yarn
Optional: Shoulder pads

GAUGE
30 sts and 40 rows = 4" [10 cm] in patt st on size 2 [2.75 mm] needles. *Adjust needle size as necessary to obtain correct gauge.*

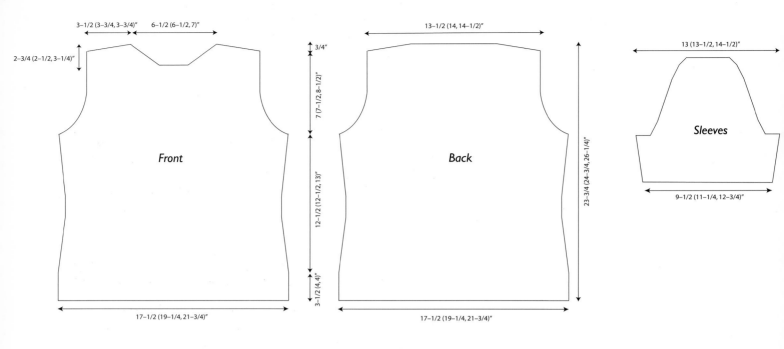

BACK

With larger needles, CO 132 (144, 156) sts.
Row 1 (RS): K3, *p6, k6; rep from * to last 9 sts, p6, k3.
Row 2 (WS): P3, *k6, p6; rep from * to last 9 sts, k6, p3.
Rep last 2 rows until rib patt measures 3–1/2 (4, 4–1/2)" from CO, ending with WS row completed.
1st dec row (RS): K3, *p2, p2tog, p2, k6; rep from * across est patt to last 9 sts, p2, p2tog, p2, k3—121 (132, 143) sts.
Next row (WS): P3, *k5, p6; rep from * across row to last 8 sts, k5, p3.
Next row (RS): K3, *p5, k6; rep from * across row to last 8 sts, p5, k3.
Rep last 2 rows until work measures 6 (6–1/2, 7)" from CO, ending with WS row completed.
2nd dec row (RS): K3, *p2, p2tog, p1, k6; rep from * across row to last 8 sts, p2, p2tog, p1, k3—110 (120, 130) sts.
Next row: P3, *k4, p6; rep from * to last 7 sts, k4, p3.
Next row: K3, *p4, k6; rep from * to last 7 sts, p4, k3.
Rep last 2 rows 4 times more (10 rows total).
Change to smaller needles, work even in est patt until work measures 9 (9–1/2, 10)" from CO. Change to larger needles, work even in est patt for 1", ending with RS row completed.
1st Inc row (WS): P3, *k1, k1f&b in next st, k2, p6; rep from * to last 7 sts, k1, k1f&b, k2, p3—121 (132, 143) sts.
Next row (RS): K3, *p5, k6; rep from * to last 8 sts, p5, k3.
Next row (WS): P3, *k5, p6; rep from * to last 8 sts, k5, p3.

Rep last 2 rows until back measures 11–1/2 (12, 12–1/2)" from CO, ending with RS row completed.
2nd Inc row (WS): P3, *k2, k1f&b in next st, k2, p6; rep from * to last 8 sts, k1, k1f&b, k2, p3—132 (144, 156) sts.
Next row (RS): K3, *p6, k6; rep from * to last 9 sts, p6, k3.
Next row (WS): P3, *k6, p6; rep from * to last 9 sts, k6, p3.
Work even in est patt until back measures 16 (16–1/2, 17)" from CO, ending with WS row completed.

Underarm shaping:

BO 8 (10, 10) sts at beg of next 2 rows, working in est patt across rem sts to end—116 (124, 136) sts.
Dec 1 st each side every other row 7 (9, 13) times—102 (106, 110) sts. *At the same time,* after completing 20 (18, 24) rows from first BO, ending with WS row completed, begin faux cables.

Begin faux cables:
Size 34" only

Row 21 (RS): P6, *insert right-hand needle between 6th and 7th sts on left-hand needle, wind yarn around needle as if to knit and draw up a loop, sl loop to left-hand needle and knit as an extra st, k6, sl extra st over last 6 sts, p6, k6, p6; rep from * to end of row.
Rows 22–26: Work in est rib patt.
Row 27: Work same as row 21 for this size.
Rows 28–40: Work in est rib patt.
Row 41: P6, *k6, p6, insert right-hand needle between

6th and 7th sts on left-hand needle, wind yarn around needle as if to knit and draw up a loop, sl loop to left-hand needle and knit as an extra st, k6, sl extra st over last 6 sts, p6; rep from * to end of row.
Rows 42–46: Work in est rib patt.
Row 47: Work same as row 41 for this size.

Size 36" only
Row 19 (RS): P3, *insert right-hand needle between 6th and 7th sts on left-hand needle, wind yarn around needle as if to knit and draw up a loop, sl loop to left-hand needle and knit as an extra st, k6, sl extra st over last 6 sts, p6, k6, p6; rep from * across row to last 9 sts, *insert right-hand needle between 6th and 7th sts on left-hand needle, wind yarn around needle as if to knit and draw up a loop, sl loop to left-hand needle and knit as an extra st, k6, sl extra st over last 6 sts, p3.
Rows 20–24: Work in est rib patt.
Row 25: P2, then rep row 19 from * to last 2 sts, p2.
Rows 26–38: Work in est rib patt.
Row 39: P2, k6, p6, *insert right-hand needle between 6th and 7th sts on left-hand needle, wind yarn around needle as if to knit and draw up a loop, sl loop to left-hand needle and knit as an extra st, k6, sl extra st over last 6 sts, p6, k6, p6; rep from * across row, working last rep as *insert right-hand needle between 6th and 7th sts on left-hand needle, wind yarn around needle as if to knit and draw up a loop, sl loop to left-hand needle and knit as an extra st, k6, sl extra st over last 6 sts, p6, k6, p2
Rows 40–44: Work in est rib patt.
Row 45: P2, k6, p6, *insert right-hand needle between 6th and 7th sts on left-hand needle, wind yarn around needle as if to knit and draw up a loop, sl loop to left-hand needle and knit as an extra st, k6, sl extra ststitch over last 6 sts, p6, k6, p6; rep from * across row, working last rep as *insert right-hand needle between 6th and 7th sts on left-hand needle, wind yarn around needle as if to knit and draw up a loop, sl loop to left-hand needle and knit as an extra st, k6, sl extra st over last 6 sts, p6, k6, p2.

Size 38" only
Row 25 (RS): K6, p6, *insert right-hand needle between 6th and 7th sts on left-hand needle, wind yarn around needle as if to knit and draw up a loop, sl loop to left-hand needle and knit as an extra st, k6, sl extra st over last 6 sts, p6, k6, p6; rep from * to last 6 sts, k6.
Rows 26–30: Work in est rib patt and cont shaping dec.
Row 31: K4, p6, then rep row 25 from * to last 4 sts, k4.
Rows 32–44: Work in est rib patt.
Row 45: K4, p6, k6, p6, *insert right-hand needle between 6th and 7th sts on left-hand needle, wind yarn around needle as if to knit and draw up a loop, sl loop to left-hand needle and knit as an extra st, k6, sl extra st over last 6 sts, p6, k6, p6; rep from * across row to last 16 sts, *insert right-hand needle between 6th and 7th sts on left-hand needle, wind yarn around needle as if to

knit and draw up a loop, sl loop to left-hand needle and knit as an extra st, k6, sl extra st over last 6 sts, p6, k4.
Rows 46–50: Work in est rib patt.
Row 51: Rep row 45.

All sizes
Work even in est rib patt until armhole measures 5–1/2 (6, 6–1/2)", ending with WS row completed.

Back neck opening:
Next row (RS): Work in patt across first half of row——51 (51, 55) sts, drop yarn, join another ball of yarn and work across second half of row—51 (51, 55) sts. Working both sides at the same time, cont in est patt until armhole measures 7 (7–1/2, 8–1/2)" from BO.

Shoulder shaping:
Maintaining back neck opening and working both sides of opening at the same time, each with its own ball of yarn (both sides of neck opening count as 1 row), at armhole edges BO 8 (9, 9) sts beg of next 2 (4, 2) rows, work in patt to end of row—86 (70, 92) sts.
BO 9 (10, 10) sts beg of next 4 (2, 4) rows, work in patt to end of row—50 (50, 52) sts.
BO rem sts for back neck.

FRONT
Work same as back, including all shaping, until front measures 21 (22, 23)" from CO, ending with WS row completed.

Neckline shaping:
Row 1 (RS): Work 35 (37, 38) sts in est patt, drop yarn and join another ball, BO 32 (32, 34) sts, work in est patt to end of row—35 (37, 38) sts each side of neck. Working both sides of neck at same time, each with its own ball of yarn, dec 1 st at each neck edge every other row 9 times—26 (28, 29) sts each side of neck. *At the same time,* when armhole measures 7 (7–1/2, 8–1/2)" from first armhole BO, ending with WS row completed, beg shoulder shaping.

Shoulder shaping:
Next row (RS): BO 8 (9, 9) sts, work even in patt to end.
Next row (WS): Work even in patt.
Next row: BO 9 (9, 10) sts, work even in patt to end.
Next row: Work even in patt.
Next row: BO rem 9 (10, 10) sts.

SLEEVES (make 2)
With smaller needles, CO 72 (84, 96) sts.
Row 1 (RS): K3, *p6, k6; rep from * to last 9 sts, p6, k3.
Row 2 (WS): P3, *k6, p6; rep from * to last 9 sts, k6, p3.
Rep last 2 rows 6 times more.

Size 34" only
Sleeve shaping:
Change to larger needles and counting the first row as row 1, work as foll:

Inc 1 st each side every other row 13 times, working new sts into est patt—98 sts.
Row 27 (RS): K4, *p6, k6; rep from * to last 10 sts, p6, k4.
Row 28 (WS): P4, *k6, p6: rep from * to last 10 sts, k6, p4.

Cap shaping:
BO 8 sts beg of next 2 rows—82 sts. Dec 1 st each side every other row 22 times—38 sts. *At the same time*, after completing 20 rows from first BO row, beg faux cables.

Faux cables:
Row 21 (RS): P5, *insert right-hand needle between 6th and 7th sts on left-hand needle, wind yarn around needle as if to knit and draw up a loop, sl loop to left-hand needle and knit as an extra st, k6, sl extra st over last 6 sts, p6, k6, p6; rep from * to last 5 sts, p5.
Rows 22–26: Work in est rib patt and cont shaping dec.
Row 27 (RS): P2, *insert right-hand needle between 6th and 7th sts on left-hand needle, wind yarn around needle as if to knit and draw up a loop, sl loop to left-hand needle and knit as an extra st, k6, sl extra st over last 6 sts, p6, k6, p6; rep from * to last 2 sts, p2.
Rows 28–40: Work in est rib patt and cont shaping dec.
Row 41 (RS): K1, p6, *insert right-hand needle between 6th and 7th sts on left-hand needle, wind yarn around needle as if to knit and draw up a loop, sl loop to left-hand needle and knit as an extra st, k6, sl extra st over last 6 sts, p6, k6, p6; rep from * to last 7 sts, p6, k1.
Rows 42–46: Work in est rib patt and cont shaping dec.
Row 47 (RS): P4, *insert right-hand needle between 6th and 7th sts on left-hand needle, wind yarn around needle as if to knit and draw up a loop, sl loop to left-hand needle and knit as an extra st, k6, sl extra st over last 6 sts, p6, k6, p6; rep from * to last 4 sts, p4. BO 4 sts at beg of next 6 rows.
BO rem 14 sts.

Size 36"only
Sleeve shaping:
Change to larger needles and counting the first row as row 1, work as foll:

Inc 1 st each side every other row 4 times, then every 4th row 5 times, working new sts into est patt—102 sts.

Note: the last inc row (WS) is worked as p1, inc 1, p4 *k6, p6; rep from * to last 11 sts, k6, p4, inc 1, p1.

Cap shaping:
BO 9 sts beg of next 2 rows—84 sts. Dec 1 st each side every other row 9 times—66 sts. Dec 1 st each side every 4th row 3 times—60 sts. Dec 1 st each side every other row 9 times—42 sts. *At the same time*, after completing 18 rows from first BO row, beg faux cables.

Faux cables:
Row 19 (RS): K6, p6, *insert right-hand needle between 6th and 7th sts on left-hand needle, wind yarn around needle as if to knit and draw up a loop, sl loop to left-hand needle and knit as an extra st, k6, sl extra st over last 6 sts, p6, k6, p6; rep from * once more to last 6 sts, end row k6.
Rows 20–24: Work in est rib patt and cont shaping dec.
Row 25 (RS): K5, p6, *insert right-hand needle between 6th and 7th sts on left-hand needle, wind yarn around needle as if to knit and draw up a loop, sl loop to left-hand needle and knit as an extra st, k6, sl extra st over last 6 sts, p6, k6, p6; rep from * once more to last 5 sts, k5.
Rows 26–38: Work in est rib patt and cont shaping dec.
Row 39 (RS): P5, k6, p6, *insert right-hand needle between 6th and 7th sts on left-hand needle, wind yarn around needle as if to knit and draw up a loop, sl loop to left-hand needle and knit as an extra st, k6, sl extra st over last 6 sts, p6, k6, p6; rep from * working last rep as *insert right-hand needle between 6th and 7th sts on left-hand needle, wind yarn around needle as if to knit and draw up a loop, sl loop to left-hand needle and knit as an extra st, k6, sl extra st over last 6 sts, p5.
Rows 40–44: Work in est rib patt and cont shaping dec.
Row 45 (RS): P2, k6, p6, *insert right-hand needle between 6th and 7th sts on left-hand needle, wind yarn around needle as if to knit and draw up a loop, sl loop to left-hand needle and knit as an extra st, k6, p6, k6, p6; rep from * working last rep as *insert right-hand needle between 6th and 7th sts on left-hand needle, wind yarn around needle as if to knit and draw up a loop, sl loop to left-hand needle and knit as an extra st, k6, sl extra st over last 6 sts, p2.
Rows 46–50: Work in est rib patt and cont shaping dec.
BO 4 sts beg of next 2 rows—34 sts. BO 5 sts beg of next 4 rows. BO rem14 sts.

Size 38" only
Sleeve shaping:
Change to larger needles and counting the first row as row 1, work as foll:

Inc 1 st each side every 4th row 4 times, then every 6th row 2 times, working new sts into est patt —108 sts.

Note: the last inc row (WS) is worked as P1, inc 1, p1, *k6, p6; rep from * across row to last 8 sts, k6, p1, inc 1, p1.

Cap shaping:

BO 10 sts beg of next 2 rows—88 sts.

Dec 1 st each side every 4th row 4 times—80 sts.

Dec 1 st each side every other row 19 times—42 sts.

At the same time, after completing 24 rows from first BO row, beg faux cables.

Faux cables:

Row 25 (RS): K3, p6, *insert right-hand needle between 6th and 7th sts on left-hand needle, wind yarn around needle as if to knit and draw up a loop, sl loop to left-hand needle and knit as an extra st, k6, sl extra st over last 6 sts, p6, k6, p6; rep from * to last 9 sts end last rep as p6, k3.

Rows 26–30: Work in est patt and cont cap shaping dec.

Row 31 (RS): P6, *insert right-hand needle between 6th and 7th sts on left-hand needle, wind yarn around needle as if to knit and draw up a loop, sl loop to left-hand needle and knit as an extra st, k6, sl extra st over last 6 sts, p6, k6, p6; rep from * to last 6 sts end last rep as p6.

Rows 32–44: Work in est patt and cont cap shaping dec.

Row 45 (RS): K5, p6, *insert right-hand needle between 6th and 7th sts on left-hand needle, wind yarn around needle as if to knit and draw up a loop, sl loop to left-hand needle and knit as an extra st, k6, sl extra st over last 6 sts, p6, k6, p6; rep from * ending last rep as p6, k5.

Row 46–50: Work in est patt and cont cap shaping dec.

Row 51 (RS): K2, p6, *insert right-hand needle between 6th and 7th sts on left-hand needle, wind yarn around needle as if to knit and draw up a loop, sl loop to left-hand needle and knit as an extra st, k6, sl extra st over last 6 sts, p6, k6, p6; rep from * end last rep as p6, k4.

Rows 52–56: Work in est patt and cont cap shaping dec. BO 4 sts beg of next 4 rows—26 sts. BO 3 sts beg of next 4 rows. BO rem 14 sts.

The Lady's Pullover with the faux cable was published in *Monarch Handknit Hits for Ladies Men & Boys* in 1946.

FINISHING

With RS together, sew shoulder seams tog using backstitch (see Glossary). Sew body and underarm sleeve seams with mattress st (see Glossary). Pin sleeve into armhole opening, matching underarm body and sleeve seams. Sew sleeve to body using backstitch. Remove pins. Work second sleeve the same.

Neckband

Note: See Glossary for crochet terms.

With crochet hook and RS facing, beg at left back neck, work 1 sc st in each 25 (25, 26) left back BO sts, then 23 (24, 24) sc along left neck sts, sc across 32 (32, 34) BO front neck sts, sc 23 (24, 24) along right neck sts, and across 25 (25, 26) BO sts along right back neck—128 (130, 134) sts. Turn work.

Row 2 (decs): Ch 2, 1 hdc in each hdc across right back neck, work 2 hdc decs evenly spaced in each of the foll sections, right side of neck, front neck, and left side of neck, 1 hdc in each hdc across left back neck—122 (124, 128) hdc. Turn work.

Row 3: Ch 2, working in front loop only, 1 hdc in each sc around neckline to last st of left back neck. Turn work.

Row 4 (decs): Rep row 2 except, work 1 hdc dec in each section, instead of 2 dec—119 (121, 125) hdc.

Row 5: Ch 1, work 2 sc in first hdc, 1 sc in each hdc around neckline to last hdc before back neck opening, work 2 sc in last hdc, then ch 3 to make button loop, join ch 3 with sl st to the 2nd sc (check to make sure ch 3 will sl over your selected button, adding more chs if needed), work 2 sc every 3 rows along both edges of back neck opening, sl st to first sc on left back neck and finish off. With sewing thread and needle, sew button on left side of neck to align with ch 3 loop.

Edging

Work 1 row sc around lower edge of sweater, also around cuffs (these rows could be worked as reverse sc (crab st—see Glossary) if you prefer. Weave in all loose ends to WS. Block sweater to measurements.

Men's Turtleneck Sweater, published by Monarch, 1946

A big complaint from men is that the sweaters we make for them are too hot to wear indoors, either at the office or home, and many are so bulky they rarely fit comfortably when worn beneath a jacket. If you want to knit something he'll wear more than once, here it is! This finely knit turtleneck will fit nicely under a suit or sport jacket. Just remember that the turtleneck collar fits closely, so make sure you select a soft fiber. Don't judge the yarn by how it feels in your hands or pressed against your face. Ask the intended wearer to wrap a skein around his neck, or a few yards around his wrist, for a few hours, to make sure the yarn is comfortable. We've up-sized this design to fit current sizes and added two more sizes. We also modified the collar a tad to a circular, seamless turtle. The original turtleneck collar was made in two pieces, then seamed on each side of the neck.

SIZE
Chest: 38 (42, 46)"

FINISHED MEASUREMENTS
Chest: 40 (44, 48)"
Length: 25 (27, 29)"
Sleeve length to underarm: 19–1/2 (20–1/2, 21)"
Armhole depth: 9 (10, 11)"

MATERIALS
Yarn—CYCA #2 Fine, 100% merino wool or soft wool
    blend: About 1750 (2000, 2275) yds
Size 2 [2.75 mm] knitting needles; 2 double pointed
    needles (dpn); 16" circular needle
Size 5 [3.75 mm] knitting needles;
    16" circular needle
Tapestry needle
3 stitch holders
Stitch marker
Long sewing pins with large heads

GAUGE
24 sts and 32 rows = 4" [10 cm] in St st on size 5
    [3.75 mm] needles. *Adjust needle size as as
    necessary to obtain correct gauge.*

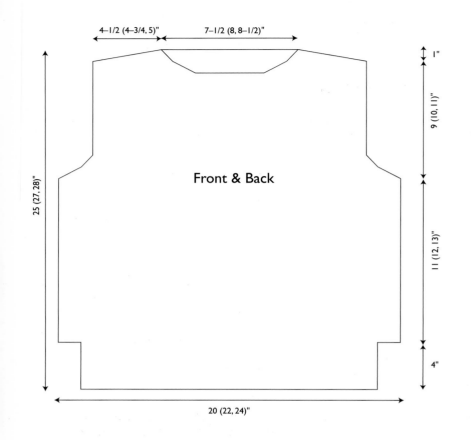

Front & Back

4-1/2 (4-3/4, 5)"   7-1/2 (8, 8-1/2)"

25 (27, 28)"

1"

9 (10, 11)"

11 (12, 13)"

4"

20 (22, 24)"

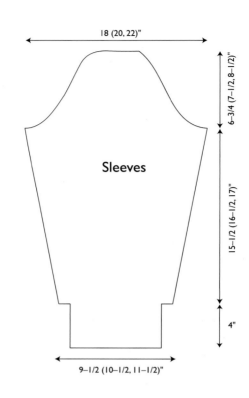

Sleeves

18 (20, 22)"

6-3/4 (7-1/2, 8-1/2)"

15-1/2 (16-1/2, 17)"

4"

9-1/2 (10-1/2, 11-1/2)"

BACK
With smaller needles, CO 118 (130, 142) sts.
Row 1 (RS): *K2, p2; rep from * to last st, k2.
Row 2 (WS): *P2, k2; rep from * to last st, p2.
Rep last 2 rows until rib measures 4" from CO, inc 2 sts evenly spaced across last row of rib—120 (132, 144) sts.
Change to larger needle and work even in St st until back measures 15 (16, 17)" or desired length from CO.

Underarm shaping:
BO 5 (7, 8) sts at beg of next 2 rows, working in St st across rem sts to end—110 (118, 128) sts.
Dec 1 st each side every other row 5 (6, 8) times—100 (106, 112) sts.
Work even in St st until back measures 24 (26, 28)" from CO, ending with RS row completed.

Garter stitch shoulder insert:
Row 1 (WS): K27 (29, 30) sts, p46 (48, 52) sts, k27 (29, 30) sts.
Row 2: (RS) Knit all sts.
Rep last 2 rows once more.

Shoulder shaping (short rows):
Cont working shoulders in garter st and neck sts in St st.
Short row 1 (WS): K27 (29, 30) sts, p46 (48, 52) sts, k18 (20, 20), wrap and turn (w&t) as foll: bring yarn to front, sl next st pwise to right needle, take yarn to back, sl wrapped st back to left needle, turn work leaving the unworked sts on needle.
Short row 2 (RS): Knit to last 9 (9, 10) sts, w&t next st.
Short rows 3 and 4: Work in est patt to last 18 (20, 20) sts, w&t next st.
Short rows 5 and 6: Work across 100 (106, 112) sts in est patts. BO 46 (48, 52) back neck sts. Place shoulder sts on holders.

Note: Don't pick up wraps; in garter st, they'll be less noticeable if left in place.

FRONT
Work same as back until both underarm shaping rows are finished—100 (106, 112) sts. Work even in St st until front measures 22 (23-1/4, 25-1/4)" from CO edge, ending with WS row completed.

Neckline shaping:

K38 (41, 42) sts, sl next 24 (24, 28) sts to holder, join another ball of yarn, K38 (41, 42) sts to end of row—38 (41, 42) shoulder sts on each side of center neck sts. Working both sides tog at the same time, dec 1 st at each neck edge every other row 11 (12, 12) times—27 (29, 30) shoulder sts each side of neck. *At the same time,* change to garter st when front measures 24 (26, 28)" from CO, ending with RS row completed.

Garter stitch shoulder insert:

Rows 1–4: Change to garter st and knit all sts, cont neckline shaping as necessary.

SHOULDER SHAPING (SHORT ROWS):
Left side of neck (as worn):

Short row 1 (WS): Work to last 9 sts before armhole edge, w&t next st.
Short rows 2 and 4 (RS): Knit to neck.
Short row 3: Work to last 18 sts before armhole edge, w&t next st.
Rows 5 and 6: K27 (29, 30) sts. Place sts on holder after row 6 is completed.

Right side of neck (as worn):

Short rows 1 and 3 (WS): Knit to neck.
Short row 2 (RS): Work to last 9 sts before armhole edge, w&t next st.
Short row 4: Work to last 18 sts before armhole edge, w&t next st.
Row 5: Knit to neck.
Row 6: K27 (29, 30) sts. Place sts on dpn.

Join shoulders:

*Sl right back shoulder sts from holder to dpn. Align right back and right front shoulder sts tog with WS facing. Join yarn. With larger needles, work three-needle BO (see Glossary) to close both sets of right shoulder sts tog. Cut yarn leaving 4" tail. Rep from * for left front and left back shoulders. Weave in loose ends to WS.

TURTLENECK COLLAR

With RS facing and smaller circular needle, pick up and knit 46 (48, 52) sts across back neck, 17 (20, 20) sts from right neck edge, 24 (24, 28) sts from front neck, 17 (20, 20) sts left neck edge—104 (112, 120) sts. Place marker to denote beg of rnd. Work in k2, p2 rib until collar measures 3", change to larger circular needle and cont in rib for another 3". BO all sts in patt.

SLEEVES

With smaller needles, CO 58 (62, 70) sts. Work in k2, p2 rib until cuff measures 4" from CO edge, inc 0 (2, 0) sts evenly across last row of rib, ending with WS row completed—58 (64, 70) sts. Change to larger needles and St st.

Begin sleeve shaping:

Inc 1 st each side of row every 4th (4th, 2nd) row 21 (26, 2) times—100 (114, 74) sts, then every 6 (6, 4)th row 4 (2, 29) times—108 (120, 132) sts. Work even in St st until sleeve measures 19–1/2 (20–1/2, 21)" from CO.

Cap shaping:

BO 5 (7, 8) sts each side of next 2 rows—98 (106, 116) sts.
Dec 1 st each side every other row 5 (6, 8) times—88 (94, 100) sts.
Dec 1 st each side every row 16 (13, 15) times—56 (68, 70) sts.
Dec 1 st every other row 11 (14, 14) times—34 (40, 42) sts.
BO 4 (5, 5) sts at beg of next 4 rows—18 (20, 22) sts.
BO rem sts.
Work second sleeve the same.

FINISHING

With RS facing, join body side seams with mattress st (see Glossary), working 1 st in from each side edge to maintain k2, p2 rib patt. Work underarm sleeve seams the same. *With RS tog, pin sleeve into armhole opening, matching underarm body and sleeve seams and easing sleeve cap into armhole. Sew sleeve to body using backstitch (see Glossary). Remove pins. Rep from * for second sleeve. Weave in loose ends to WS of work. Block to size.

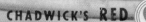

J. & P. COATS · CLARK'S O.N.T.   Sweaters BOOK No. 291   10¢

Everyone wears SWEATERS

CHADWICK'S RED HEART YARNS

1950s

As Americans returned from the war and settled down to start families in the late 1940s and early 1950s, patterns for "family group" knits became all the rage, with patterns for mother-daughter outfits, father-son sweaters, sister-brother jackets, and his-and-her matching cardigans appearing everywhere. For modern knitters who suffer from the dreaded Second Sock Syndrome, the idea of knitting two of the same sweater may be daunting. Thankfully, the 1950s offered plenty of individual projects, too, including dolman-sleeve boleros, turtleneck sweaters, turtleneck hooded sweaters, and shoulderettes—or shrugs, as they are commonly called today. The overall fit of the 1950s sweater was fairly close, and body shaping was limited to ribbing.

A variety of designs in every stitch pattern imaginable were available to the knitter in the 1950s. Patterns for garments featuring argyles (with charts!), multicolor stranded knitting (often with charts), cables, and openwork were offered in a plethora of styles and yarns. Multiple sizes were commonly included in each pattern, and substitute yarns were often suggested.

Knitting patterns for grade school children were plentiful during the decade, because the early members of the baby-boom generation were in school and already claiming their share of the market. Styles ranged from simple raglan cardigans to short-sleeved middy sweaters, often with a nautical theme. Sweaters and shell vests in all-over color patterns or with color bands on solid backgrounds were also popular for children.

Women's Hooded Pullover, published by Fleisher Bear Brand, 1957

A great winter sweater worked in Fisherman's Rib pattern. Easy fit raglan sleeves with a hood/cowl collar are worked in two separate pieces (front and back), then seamed together on each side. The top opening is then pulled around the face to form a hood, or rolled down when worn to form a collar.

SIZE
34 (38, 42)"

FINISHED MEASUREMENTS
Width at chest: 17 (19, 21)"
Length: 23–1/2 (26, 27)"
Sleeve length to underarm: 17 (18–1/2, 18–1/2)"

MATERIALS
Yarn—CYCA #2 Fine, wool or wool blend—choose yarns that have natural elasticity: About 1600 (1800, 2000) yds.
Size 8 [5 mm] knitting needles
Note: **The patt st uses larger needles than normally required for this yarn size.**
Tapestry needle
Open-ring stitch markers
Stitch holders

GAUGE
14 sts and 40 rows = 4" [10 cm] in Fisherman's Rib patt. *Adjust needle size as necessary to obtain correct gauge.*

SPECIAL ABBREVIATION

K1b—Insert right needle tip into center of the st directly below the st on left needle, k1 dropping st from left needle as you complete the st. This is **not** a lifted inc (inc 1 by knitting in the row below, then knit st on left needle), so be sure you drop the old st from the left needle as you complete the knit st.

FRONT

CO 60 (66, 74) sts. Work in p1, k1 rib for 6 rows.

Establish Fisherman's Rib pattern:
Next row: *P1, k1b; rep from * across row.
Rep this row until front measures 14–1/2 (16–1/2, 16–1/2)" from CO. Place marker in center of last row to denote RS of work.

Raglan Shaping:
First dec row: P3tog, work in est patt to end of row—58 (64, 72) sts.

Second dec row: P3tog, work in patt to last st, k1—56 (62, 70) sts.
Next row: Work in patt to last st, k1. Work even in patt for 5 rows.
Rep last 8 rows 9 (10, 11) times more—20 (22, 26) sts. Work even in patt until front measures about 9 (9–1/2, 10–1/2)" from st m.

Neck ribbing:
Work in P1, k1 rib for 10 rows.

Front Collar

Work even in Fisherman's Rib for 12 (13, 13)". BO loosely in patt.

BACK

CO 60 (66, 74) sts. Work same as front until neck rib is completed—20 (22, 26) sts. Do not BO. Place these sts on holder.

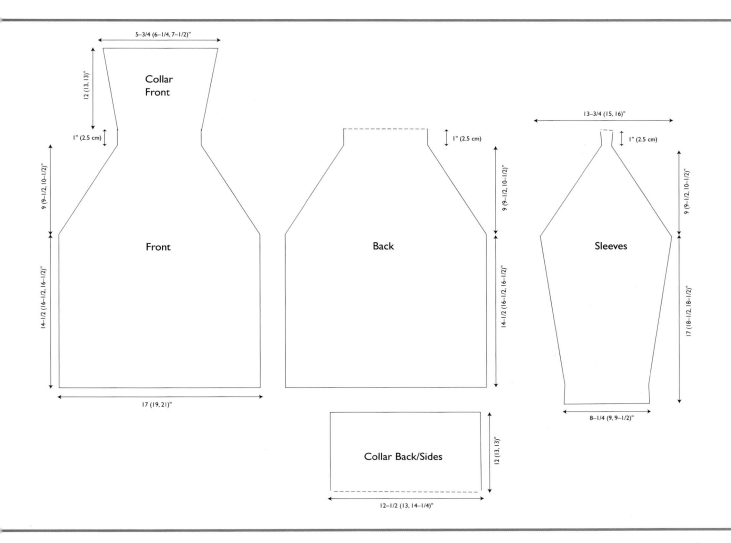

SLEEVES

CO 36 (40, 44) sts. Work in p1, k1 rib for 3 (3–1/2, 3–1/2)".
Work even in Fisherman's Rib until sleeve measures 6–1/2 (7, 7)" from CO.

Sleeve shaping:

Note: Work incs into est patt when there are sufficient incs to do so.
First inc row: Inc 1 in first st, work across row in est patt to last st, inc 1 in last st—38 (42, 46) sts.
Second inc row: Inc 1 in first st, work across row in est patt to last st, inc 1 in last st—40 (44, 48) sts.
Rep the 2 inc rows every 3–1/2" twice more—48 (50, 56) sts. Work even in est patt until sleeve measures 17 (18–1/2, 18–1/2)" from CO. Place marker in center of last row to denote RS of work.
Work second sleeve the same.

Raglan shaping and neck ribbing:

Work the same as front until same number of rows are completed from m—8 sts.

Work in p1, k1 rib for 9 rows.
Work 1 more row of rib, inc 1 st in each of first and last 2 sts—12 sts. Place 12 sts on holder. Work second sleeve same. Do not place these sts on holder.

Join row:

Work in Fisherman's Rib across 12 sts of 2nd sleeve, then work 20 (22, 26) back neck sts from holder, then work across 12 sts from first sleeve—44 (46, 50) sts. Do not BO.

Collar (and hood):

Work even in Fisherman's Rib for 12 (13, 13)" above rib. BO loosely in patt.

FINISHING

Remove all st ms. Sew side seams of body with mattress st (see Glossary). Sew sleeve seams. Sew in sleeves, matching rows of raglan shaping. Sew side edges of collar tog. Weave in loose ends to WS. Steam lightly, blocking to size.

This project features an all-season cardigan for men and women. The classic styling offers set-in sleeves and front bands, which are worked simultaneously with each front. The instructions begin with the women's sizes, and the men's sizes appear on the following pages.

Note: When working decreases for armhole and neck shaping, place an open-ring marker into the first st of the first *full* pattern repeat, then begin the row working the beg partial repeat sts as knit or purl, whichever is needed to maintain the patt of previous rows. When you reach the stitch marker, continue in the main stitch pattern working full repeats to the end of the last full repeat, place another marker in the last st of the last full repeat, then work remaining odd sts in either knit or purl. Move the stitch markers as necessary so they always mark the first and last full pattern repeats.

BACK
CO 114 (122, 130).
Row 1: *K2, p2; rep from * to last 2 sts, k2.
Row 2: *P2, k2; rep from * to last 2 sts, p2.

Rep last 2 rows until ribbing measures 2–1/2 (3, 3)" from CO, ending with WS row completed.

Begin pattern
Row 1 (RS): Knit, inc 12 (13, 14) sts evenly across row—126 (135, 144) sts.
Row 2 (WS): Purl.
Row 3: *K3, p6; rep from * to end of row,
Row 4: *P3, k6; rep from * to last end of row.
Row 5: Knit.
Rep rows 2–5 for pattern. Work even in patt until back measures 15 (16, 16)" or desired length from CO.

Armhole shaping
BO 10 (11, 13) sts beg of next 2 rows—106 (113, 118) sts.
Dec 1 st each side every other row 9 (11, 12) times—88 (91, 94) sts.

WOMEN

SIZE
38 (40, 42)"

FINISHED MEASUREMENTS
Width at chest: 21 (22–1/2, 24)"
Length: 24–3/4 (25–3/4, 26–1/4)"
Sleeve length to underarm: 17–1/2 (18–1/2, 18–1/2)"

MATERIALS
Yarn—CYCA #3 Light, wool or wool blend
Women: About 1600 (1700, 1850) yds;
Men: About 1720 (1920, 2100) yds
Size 5 [3.75 mm] knitting needles
7 buttons, about 3/4" diameter
1–1/2 yds grosgrain ribbon
Sewing thread and needle
Tapestry needle
2 stitch holders
2 open-ring stitch markers

GAUGE
24 sts and 32 rows = 4" [10 cm] in st patt. *Adjust needle size as necessary to obtain correct gauge.*

Work even in patt until back measures 24 (25, 25–1/2)" or desired length from CO, ending with WS row completed.

Shape Shoulders
BO 7 (8, 8) sts beg of next 2 (6, 6) rows—74 (43, 46) sts.
BO 8 (0, 0) sts beg of next 4 (0, 0) rows—42 (43, 46) sts.
BO rem 42 (43, 46) sts.

LEFT FRONT (AS WORN)
CO 57 (61, 65) sts
Row 1 (RS): *K2, p2; rep from * to last 9 sts, k9 (front band).
Row 2 (WS): P9 (front band), *k2, p2; rep from * to end of row.
Row 3: *K2, p2; rep from * to last 9 sts, k3, p3, k3 (front band).
Row 4: P3, k3, p3 (front band), *k2, p2; rep from * to end of row.
Rep last 4 rows until rib measures 2–1/2 (3, 3)" from CO, ending with WS row completed.

Begin pattern
Row 1 (RS): Knit, increasing 6 (5, 7) sts evenly across row (do not make increases in last 9 sts)—63 (66, 72) sts.
Row 2 (WS): Purl.
Row 3: P0 (3, 0), *k3, p6; rep from * to last 9 sts, k3, p3, k3.
Row 4: P3, k3, p3, *k6, p3; rep from * to last 0 (3, 0) sts, k0 (3, 0)
Row 5: Knit.
Rep rows 2–5 for patt until front measures 15 (16, 16)" or desired length from CO, ending with WS row completed.

Armhole shaping
Row 1 (RS): BO 10 (11, 13) sts, work in established patt to end of row—53 (56, 59) sts.
Row 2 (WS): Work even in patt.
Row 3: Dec 1 st beg of row, work in patt to end of row—52 (55, 58) sts.
Rep rows 2 and 3 another 8 (10, 11) times—44 (45, 47) sts. Cont in patt st until front measures 22–3/4 (23–3/4, 24–1/4)" from CO, ending with RS row completed.

Begin neck shaping
Row 1 (WS): Beg at neck edge, work 14 (15, 16) sts in patt, slip these sts onto a stitch holder, work in patt to end of row—30 (30, 31) sts.
Row 2 (RS): Work in patt to end of row.
Row 3 (WS): At neck edge, dec 1 st, work in patt to end of row—29 (29, 30) sts.
Rep rows 2 and 3 another 6 (5, 6) times—23 (24, 24) sts. *At the same time*, when front measures 24 (25, 25–1/2)" ending with WS row completed, begin shoulder shaping, cont armhole shaping as necessary.

Shoulder shaping
Row 1 (RS): BO 7 (8, 8) sts, work in patt to end of row—16 sts rem.
Rows 2 and 4 (WS): Work even in patt.
Row 3: BO 8 (8, 8) sts, work in patt to end of row—8 sts.
Row 5: BO rem 8 sts.
Carefully mark 6 button placements along front band with yarn and thread, beg 3/4" up from lower edge and 4 sts in from front edge. The seventh button will be attached to the neckband later. Use these button markers to help you align the buttonholes when working the Right Front (for women).

RIGHT FRONT (AS WORN)
CO 57 (61, 65) sts.
Note: Work 6 buttonholes in the 9-st front band, aligning the buttonhole positions with the button markers on left front band. Beg buttonholes at front edge on RS rows as follows: Work 3 sts, BO 3 sts, work as instructed to end of row. On next row, work as instructed to BO sts, CO 3 sts over the BO sts using backward loop CO (see Glossary), then work final 3 sts as instructed.
Row 1 (RS): K9 (front band), *p2, k2; rep from * to end of row.
Row 2 (WS): *P2, k2; rep from * to last 9 sts, p9 (front band).
Row 3: K3, p3, k3 (front band), *p2, k2; rep from * to end of row.
Row 4: K2, p2; rep from * to last 9 sts, p3, k3, p3 (front band).
Rep last 4 rows until rib measures 2–1/2 (3, 3)" from CO, ending with WS row.
Begin pattern
Row 1 (RS): Knit, increasing 6 (5, 7) sts evenly across row (do not make increases in first 9 sts)—63 (66, 72) sts.
Row 2 (WS): Purl.
Row 3: K3, p3, k3, *p6, k3; rep from * to last 0 (3, 0) sts, p0 (3, 0) sts.
Row 4: K0 (3, 0), *p3, k6; rep from * to last 9 sts, p3, k3, p3.
Row 5: Knit.
Rep rows 2–5 for patt until front measures 15 (16, 16)" or desired length from CO, ending with RS row completed.

Armhole shaping
Row 1 (WS): BO 10 (11, 13) sts, work in established patt to end of row—53 (56, 59) sts.
Row 2 (RS): Work even in patt.
Row 3 (WS): Decrease 1 st beg of row, work in patt to end of row—52 (55, 58) sts.
Rep rows 2 and 3 another 8 (10, 11) times—44 (45, 47) sts. Cont in patt st until piece measures 22–3/4 (23–3/4, 24–1/4)" from CO, ending with WS row completed.

Begin neck shaping
Row 1 (RS): Beg at neck edge, work 14 (15, 16) sts in est patts, slip these sts onto a stitch holder, continue in

patt to end or row—30 (30, 31) sts.
Row 2 (WS): Work in patt to end of row.
Row 3 (RS): At neck edge, decrease 1 st, work in patt to end of row—29 (29, 30) sts.
Rep rows 2 and 3 another 6 (5, 6) times—23 (24, 24) sts. *At the same time*, when front measures 24 (25, 25–1/2)" ending with RS row completed, begin shoulder shaping, cont armhole shaping as necessary.

Shoulder shaping
Row 1 (WS): BO 7 (8, 8) sts, work in patt to end of row—16 sts rem.
Rows 2 and 4 (RS): Work even in patt.
Row 3: BO 8 sts, work in patt to end of row—8 sts rem.
Row 5: BO 8 sts.

SLEEVES
CO 50 (50, 54) sts. Work in k2, p2 rib same as back for 2–1/2 (3, 3)".
Row 1 (RS): Knit, inc 7 (7, 6) sts evenly across row—57 (57, 60) sts.
Basic sleeve pattern set up:
Row 2 (WS): Purl.
Row 3: P0 (0, 3), *k3, p6; rep from * to last 3 sts, k3.
Row 4: P0 (0, 3), *k3, p6; rep from * to last 3 sts, k3.
Row 5: Knit (beg inc as indicated in sleeve shaping).

Sleeve shaping
Rep rows 2–5 for pattern, working increases into patt when there are sufficient sts to do so. Beg with row 5 above, inc 1 st each side every fourth row 19 (17, 23) times—95 (91, 106) sts, then every 6th row 6 (8, 4) times—107 (107, 114) sts. Work even in patt until sleeve measures 17–1/2 (18–1/2, 18–1/2)".

Begin cap shaping
BO 10 (11, 13) sts beg of next 2 rows—87 (85, 88) sts.
Dec 1 st each side every other row 9 (11, 12) times—69 (63, 64) sts.
Dec 1 st each side every row 6 (4, 1) time(s)—57 (55, 62) sts.
Dec 1 st each side every other row 12 (11, 13) times—33 (33, 36) sts.
BO 4 sts at beg of next 4 rows—17 (17, 20) sts.
BO rem 17 (17, 20) sts. Make second sleeve same.

FINISHING
With RS facing, thread tapestry needle and sew side seams together using mattress st, working 1 st in from each side edge to maintain rib patt. Sew sleeve seams together the same. With WS facing, sew shoulder seams together using backstitch. Turn work to RS.

Neck band
Note: Size 40 will require 1 st fewer across back neck sts than was originally BO in order to accommodate neck band patterns. Follow instructions as given below.

With RS facing k14 (15, 16) sts from right front stitch holder, pick up and k11 sts along right side of neck, 42 (42, 46) back neck sts, 11 sts along left side of neck, then k14 (15, 16) sts from left front stitch holder—92 (94, 100) sts.
Row 1: Work in est patt across first 9 sts, p2 (1, 2) *k2, p2; rep from * to last 13 (12, 13) sts, work last rep as k2, p2 (1, 2), work in patt across last 9 sts to end of row.
Working first and last 9 sts in front band patt, work rem sts in rib patt as established, until neckband measures about 1/2" from pick up row, make a buttonhole at the right front edge and aligned with the buttonholes in the front band. Continue neckband for another 1/2". BO loosely in ribbing. Weave in ends to WS. Block cardigan to measurements. On WS, sew grosgrain ribbon to front bands with sewing needle and thread, cutting in buttonholes in the ribbon to align with those in front band. Work buttonhole stitch around buttonholes to secure edges. Sew on buttons.

MEN'S CARDIGAN
(see Materials and Gauge, page 88)

SIZE
38 (40, 42)"

FINISHED MEASUREMENTS
Width at chest: 21 (22–1/2, 24)"
Length: 26–3/4 (27–3/4, 28–3/4)
Sleeve length to underarm: 19–1/2 (21, 21–1/2)"

Note: When working decreases for armhole and neck shaping, place an open-ring marker into the first st of the first *full* pattern repeat, then begin the row working the beg partial repeat sts as knit or purl, whichever is needed to maintain the patt of previous rows. When you reach the stitch marker, continue in the main stitch pattern working full repeats to the end of the last full repeat, place another marker in the last st of the last full repeat, then work remaining odd sts in either knit or purl. Move the stitch markers as necessary so they always mark the first and last full pattern repeats.

BACK
CO 114 (122, 130) sts.
Row 1: *K2, p2; rep from * to last 2 sts, k2.
Row 2: *P2, k2; rep from * to last 2 sts, p2.
Rep last 2 rows until rib measures 3 (3–1/2, 3–1/2)" from CO, ending with WS row completed.

Begin pattern
Work same as women's back until piece measures 16–1/2 (17–1/2, 18)" or desired length from CO—126 (135, 144) sts.

Armhole shaping

BO 7 (8, 10) sts beg of next 2 rows—112 (119, 124) sts.
Decrease 1 st each side every other row 6 (8, 9) times—100 (103, 106) sts.
Work even in patt until back measures 26 (27, 28)" or desired length from CO, ending with WS row completed.

Shape Shoulders

BO 9 sts beg of next 6 (4, 2) rows—46 (67, 88) sts.
BO 0 (10, 10) sts beg of next 0 (2, 4) rows—46 (47, 48) sts.
BO rem 46 (47, 48) sts.

RIGHT FRONT (AS WORN)

Note: Do not make buttonholes on this front.
CO 57 (61, 65) sts. Work same as women's right front, omitting buttonholes, until rib measures 3 (3–1/2, 3–1/2)" from CO edge.

Begin pattern

Continue to follow the instructions for women's right front until piece measures 16–1/2 (17–1/2, 18)" or desired length from CO, ending with RS row completed—63 (67, 72) sts.

Armhole shaping

Row 1 (WS): BO 7 (8, 10) sts, work in established patt to end of row—56 (59, 62) sts.
Row 2 (RS): Work even in patt.
Row 3: Decrease 1 st beg of row, work in patt to end of row—55 (58, 61) sts.
Rep rows 2 and 3 another 5 (7, 9) times—50 (51, 52) sts. Cont in patt until piece measures 23–3/4 (24–3/4, 25–1/4)" from CO edge, ending with WS row completed.

Begin neck shaping

Row 1 (RS): At neck edge, work 12 sts in patt, slip these sts onto a stitch holder, continue in patt to end of row—38 (39, 40) sts.
Row 2 (WS): Work in patt to end of row.
Row 3: At neck edge, dec 1 st, work in patt to end of row—37 (38, 39) sts.
Rep rows 2 and 3 another 10 times—27 (28, 29) sts.
At the same time, when front measures 26 (27, 28)" ending with RS row completed, begin shoulder shaping, continuing armhole shaping as necessary.

Shoulder shaping

Row 1 (WS): BO 9 sts, work in patt to end of row—18 (19, 20) sts.
Rows 2 and 4 (RS): Work even in patt.
Row 3: BO 9 (9, 10) sts, work in patt to end of row—9 (10, 10) sts.
Row 5: BO rem 9 (10, 10) sts.
Carefully mark 6 button placements along front band with yarn and thread, beginning 3/4" up from lower edge and 4 sts in from front edge. The 7th button will

be attached to the neckband later. Use these button markers to help you align the buttonholes when working the Left Front (for men).

LEFT FRONT (AS WORN)

Note: Work 6 buttonholes in the 9-st front band, aligning the buttonhole positions with the button markers on right front band. Work buttonholes at front edge on RS rows as follows: Work across row to last 9 sts in buttonhole row, k3, BO 3 sts, k3 sts (this number includes the st already on right needle from the final BO st). On next row, work first 3 sts in patt, CO 3 sts over the BO sts using backward loop CO (see Glossary), k3, then work to end of row in main patt.
CO 57 (61, 65) sts. Work same as women's left front until rib measures 3 (3–1/2, 3–1/2)" from CO edge.

Begin pattern

Continue to follow the instructions for women's right front until piece measures 16–1/2 (17–1/2, 18)" or desired length from CO, ending with WS row completed—63 (67, 72) sts.

Armhole shaping

Row 1 (RS): BO 7 (8, 10) sts, work in established patt to end of row—56 (59, 62) sts.
Row 2 (WS): Work even in patt.
Row 3: Decrease 1 st beg of row, work in patt to end of row—55 (58, 61) sts.
Rep rows 2 and 3 another 5 (7, 9) times—50 (51, 52) sts. Continue in patt until piece measures 23–3/4 (24–3/4, 25–1/4)" from CO edge, ending with RS row completed.

Begin neck shaping

Row 1 (WS): At neck edge, work 12 sts in est patts, slip these sts onto a stitch holder, continue in patt to end of row—38 (39, 40) sts.
Row 2 (RS): Work in patt to end of row.
Row 3: At neck edge, decrease 1 st, work in patt to end of row—37 (38, 39) sts.
Rep rows 2 and 3 another 10 times—27 (28, 29) sts.
At the same time, when front measures 26 (27, 28)" ending with WS row completed, begin shoulder shaping, continuing armhole shaping as necessary.

Shoulder shaping

Row 1 (RS): BO 9 sts, work in patt to end of row—18 (19, 20) sts.
Rows 2 and 4 (WS): Work even in patt.
Row 3: BO 9 (9, 10) sts, work in patt to end of row—9 (10, 10) sts.
Row 5: BO rem 9 (10, 10) sts.

SLEEVES

Cast on 50 (54, 58) sts. Work in k2, p2 ribbing same as back for 3 (3–1/2, 3–1/2)".

Row 1 (RS): Knit, increasing 8 (6, 6) sts evenly across row—58 (60, 64) sts.

Pattern set up, size 38 and 40 only
Row 2 (WS): Purl.
Row 3: P2 (3), *k3, p6; rep from * to last 2 (3) st(s), k2 (3).
Row 4: P2 (3), *k6, p3; rep from * to last 2 (3) sts, k2 (3).
Row 5: Knit.

Size 42 only
Row 2 (WS) Purl.
Row 3 (RS): K1, *p6, k3; rep from * to end of row.
Row 4: *P3, k6; rep from * to last st, p1.
Row 5: Knit (beg inc as indicated in sleeve shaping).
Cont all sizes

Sleeve shaping
Rep rows 2–5 for pattern, working increases into patt when there are sufficient sts to do so. Beg with row 5 above, inc 1 st each side every 4th row 22 (15, 16) times—102 (90, 96) sts, then every 6th row 6 (12, 12) times—114 (114, 120) sts. Work even in patt until sleeve measures 19–1/2 (21, 21–1/2)" from CO edge.

Cap shaping
BO 7 (6, 8) sts each side—100 (102, 104) sts.
Dec 1 st each side every other row 6 (7, 8) times—88 sts.
Dec 1 st each side every row 13 (11, 11) times—62 (66, 66) sts.

Dec 1 st every other row 13 (14, 13) times—36 (38, 40) sts.
BO 4 sts at the beg of next 4 rows—20 (22, 24) sts.
BO rem 20 (22, 24) sts.

FINISHING
Follow seaming instructions for women's finishing.

Neckband
Size 40 will require 1 st fewer across back neck sts than was originally BO in order to accommodate neck band pattern. Follow instructions as given below:
With RS facing k12 sts from right front stitch holder, pick up and k17 (17, 20) sts along right side of neck, 46 (46, 48) back neck sts, 17 (17, 20) sts along left side of neck, then k12 sts from left front stitch holder—104 (104, 112) sts.
Row 1: Work in patt across first 9 sts, p2, *k2, p2; rep from * to last 9 sts, k9.
Working first and last 9 sts in front band patt, work rem sts in rib patt as established, until neckband measures about 1/2" from pick up row, make a buttonhole at the left front edge and aligned with the buttonholes in the front band. Continue neckband for another 1/2". BO loosely in ribbing. Weave in ends to WS. Block cardigan to measurements. On WS, sew grosgrain ribbon to front bands with sewing needle and thread, cutting in buttonholes in the ribbon to align with those in front band. Work buttonhole stitch around buttonholes to secure edges. Sew on buttons.

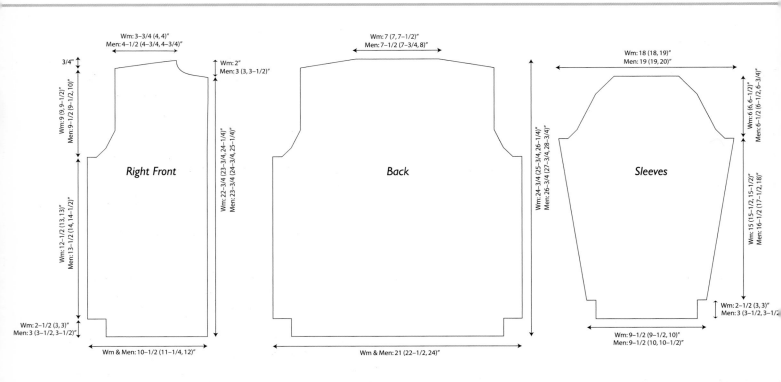

Embroidered Mittens, published by Coats & Clark, 1957

Everyone can use a pair of warm mitts. Although these are decorated with flowers, if you omit the flowers, sequins, and beads you can use the same pattern for both sexes. The original mitts used a commercial motif of petal shapes, which were then attached to the mitts, adorned with beaded centers, then embroidered with lazy daisy leaves. We suggest making the petals with lazy daisy embroidery stitches before adding the beaded centers and lazy daisy stitch leaves (Figure 1: Lazy Daisy flower).

RIGHT MITTEN

Starting at cuff with larger needles, CO 48 (52, 56) sts. Divide sts on 3 needles and join into rnd, being careful not to twist sts. Change to smaller needles and work in k2, p2 rib for 2-1/2 (2-1/2, 3)" or desired length from CO.

Change to larger needles and work in St st (knit each rnd) for 5 (6, 7) rnds.

Thumb gore:

Rnd 1 (inc): Place marker on needle, p and k in first st, k1f&b (see Glossary) in next st, pm on needle and knit to end of rnd—50 (54, 58) sts.

Rnds 2 and 3: Knit.

Rnd 4 (inc): Inc 1 st after the first m and 1 st before second m, knit to end of rnd—52 (56, 60) sts.

Rep last 3 rnds until there are 16 (16, 18) sts between ms.

Next 3 rnds: Knit even.

Next rnd: Sl 16 (16, 18) sts of thumb gore onto st holder or safety pin. CO 2 sts for inner side of thumb. Join 48 (52, 56) rem sts and work in rnds of St st until mitt measures 5-1/2 (5-3/4, 6)" from last rnd of rib or until mitt, when tried on, reaches tip of little finger.

Mitten top shaping:

Rnd 1: *Ssk, k20 (22, 24), k2tog, pm on needle; rep from * once more—44 (48, 52) sts.

Rnd 2: Knit, sl ms in place.

Rnd 3: *Ssk, knit to within 2 sts before next m, k2tog; rep from * once more—40 (44, 48) sts.

Rep rnds 2 and 3 another 4 (4, 5) times more, or until 24 (28, 28) sts rem. Remove ms.

Close top:

Cut yarn leaving 18" tail. Place 12 (14, 14) palm sts on one needle and 12 (14, 14) back of hand sts on second needle.

With WS tog and RS facing, hold needles parallel to each other. Thread tapestry needle and close sts tog with Kitchener st (see Glossary). With tapestry needle, weave in ends to WS and secure.

Thumb

Sl 16 (16, 18) thumb sts onto 3 needles, pick up 2 sts over the 2 CO sts—18 (18, 20) sts. Knit in rnds until thumb measures about 2-1/2" or reaches 1/4" from top of thumb nail.

Thumb tip shaping:

Rnd 1: *K2tog, k1; rep from * around (end largest size with k2tog)—12 (12, 13) sts.

Rnd 2: Knit.

Rnd 3: *K2tog; rep from * around (end largest size with k1)—6 (6, 7) sts.

Cut yarn leaving 8" tail. Thread tapestry needle and weave through rem sts twice. Pull tail gently to close thumb top. Weave yarn to WS and secure. Weave in loose ends.

LEFT MITTEN

Work the same as right mitten to within first rnd of thumb gore. Work thumb gore as foll:

Rnd 1: Knit around all sts to within last 2 sts, pm on needle, p and k into next st, k1f&b into next st, pm on needle. Position of thumb gore for left mitten has now been est; complete left mitten the same as right mitten.

FINISHING

Press mittens under damp cloth to smooth sts before embroidery. With 6 strands white embroidery thread and needle, embroider 7 flowers on back of each mitt using lazy daisy st (Figure 2: Embroidery Placement). With needle and sewing thread, add sequin topped with bead to the center of each flower. With 6 strands green embroidery thread and needle, accent each flower with 2 leaves in lazy daisy st. Weave all ends to WS and secure.

SIZES
WOMEN'S SMALL (MEDIUM, LARGE)
Circumference: 6 (6–1/2, 7)"

Note: To determine your mitten size, measure the circumference of your dominant hand (the hand you use when writing) around the knuckles (see Figure 1: Measuring for Gloves, page 71). To customize mitts, add more stitches to make wider mitts. (8 stitches add an extra inch in circumference at the suggested gauge.) If adding stitches, remember to factor them in when placing thumb gore, or working decreases to shape the mitt top. To make longer mitts, measure your finger lengths, including fingernails, then work any length adjustment prior to shaping tip as needed. Minor size adjustments can be made by simply using a slightly thicker yarn (or 2 strands of super fine yarn held together) and larger needles. Mitts, like gloves and socks, are often warmer and stronger when made on small needles at a fine gauge.

MATERIALS
Yarn—CYCA #1 Super Fine, 100% wool, wool blend, alpaca, angora, or other warm yarn: About 300 yds.
Size 1 [2.5 mm] knitting needles; set of 4 double pointed needles (dpn)
Size 2 [2.75 mm] knitting needles; set of 4 dpn
Tapestry needle
Embroidery needle
Embroidery floss: 1 skein each of white and green
14 assorted cup sequins
14 small beads
Stitch marker
Stitch holder or safety pin

GAUGE
32 sts and 48 rnds = 4" on size 2 [2.75 mm] needles in St st. *Adjust needle size as necessary to obtain correct gauge.*

Figure 1: Lazy Daisy flower with sequin and beaded center

Figure 2: Embroidery placement

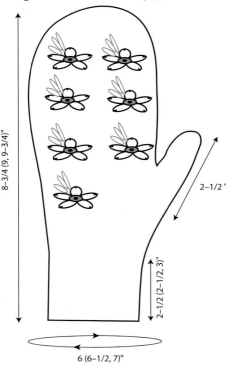

8-3/4 (9, 9-3/4)"

2-1/2 "

2-1/2 (2-1/2, 3)"

6 (6–1/2, 7)"

94

Versatile Shoulderette,
published by Minerva, 1951

It's hard to believe this Versatile Shoulderette is a project from the 1950s. A quick browse through many current knitting publications would yield many similar projects. In addition to the overall style, the Jiffy Garter Stitch knitting pattern uses small needles to work one row and much larger needles to work the next row. Many long-time knitters may remember this technique and its variations as "condo-knitting," a popular method from the 1980s worked in garter or stockinette stitch. The lesson learned here: Never throw away those old knits or knitting patterns . . . what goes around, always comes back around.

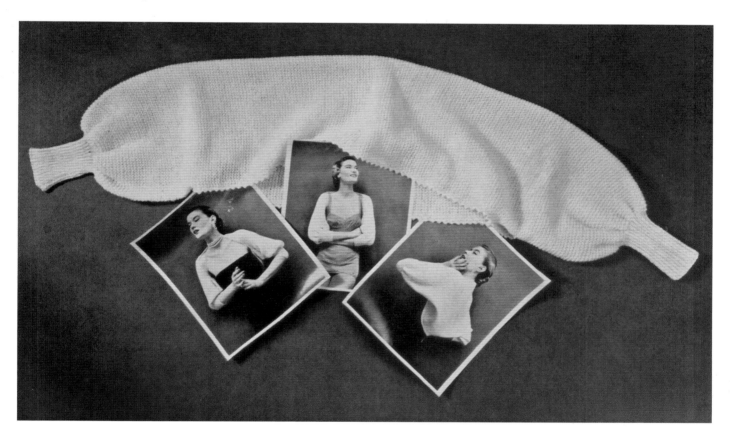

SIZE
One size fits many

FINISHED MEASUREMENTS
Width, mid-arm to mid-arm: 50"
Length, top to bottom: 20"

MATERIALS
Yarn—CYCA #1 Super Fine, any yarn that knits to gauge: About 1100 yds.

Size 3 [3.25 mm]; size 10 [5 mm] knitting needles
Size C/2 [2.75 mm] crochet hook
Tapestry needle

GAUGE
20 sts = 4" [10 cm] in Jiffy Garter St patt on sizes 3 and 10 needles [2.75 and 5 mm] needles.
Adjust needle size as necessary to obtain correct gauge.

Note: The project is worked side-to-side across the body, beginning with one mid-arm cuff and ending at the second mid-arm cuff. In order to maintain the same appearance at the beginning and ending edges, we suggest you begin with a provisional CO. After the garment is finished, remove the waste yarn from the provisional CO, place the live sts on needles, join yarn, and then BO. This will match the BO on the other arm. Or, work the permanent crochet chain CO (see Glossary), which matches the standard BO.

FIRST CUFF

With smaller needles, CO 51 sts. Work in k1, p1 rib for 5", ending RS rows with k1 and WS rows p1.
Next row: Change to larger needles, k1, *k1f&b; rep from * to last st, k1—100 sts.
** Next row: Change to smaller needles, knit.
Next row: Change to larger needles, knit**.
Rep last 2 rows from ** to ** until work measures about 45" or desired length from CO edge.
Note: To change width, work until piece measures 5" shorter than you want it, then add final cuff.
Next row: K1, ***K2tog; rep from *** to last st, k1—51 sts.

SECOND CUFF

Working with smaller needles only, work in k1, p1 rib for 5", ending RS rows with k1 and WS rows with p1. BO all sts.

FINISHING

Cut yarn leaving about 20" tail to sew cuff and sleeve. Thread tapestry needle with long tail, with RS facing join cuff tog using mattress st (see Glossary), inserting needle into center of first and last sts in order to maintain k1, p1 patt. After completing 5" cuff seam, cont seam, changing to invisible weaving for garter st (see Glossary) for 7" after the rib section is finished. Total seam length should be about 12" from CO edge. Cut yarn leaving 4" tail to weave in later. Seam other cuff and sleeve the same.

Edging

Join yarn at one end of opening. With crochet hook, work 1 row of sc all around opening. Adjust sts if necessary to achieve multiple of 3.
Next rnd: *Ch 3, 1 sc in first ch, skip 1 sc, 1 sc in next st; rep from * to end of rnd. Cut yarn leaving 4" tail and fasten off. Weave in all ends to WS of work.

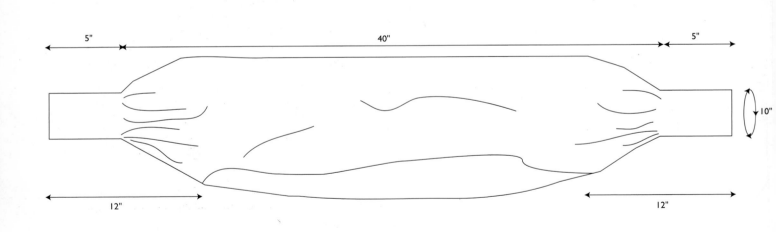

Boy's and Girl's Cardigan, published by Minerva, 1951

Comfortably snug, these front-zipper cardigans are just the thing for school or playground. With raglan sleeves, collar, and patch pockets (just the right size to carry a frog or some flowers), the cardigan is simple enough to make this a "project-to-carry along," yet the pattern is interesting enough to keep the knitter from daydreaming.

SIZES
4 (6, 8) years

FINISHED MEASUREMENTS
Width at chest: 13 (13–3/4, 14–1/2)"
Length: 15–1/4 (15–1/2, 17–1/2)"
Sleeve length to underarm: 10–1/2 (12, 12–1/2), plus 2" turn-back at cuff.

MATERIALS
Yarn—CYCA #2 Fine, most yarn types—a superwash wool will be practical, warm, and comfy: About 800 (875, 900) yds.

Size 2 [2.75 mm] knitting needles; 16" circular needle for collar
Size 3 [3.75 mm] knitting needles; 16" circular needle for collar
Size C/2 [2.75 mm] crochet hook
1 separating zipper, about 13 (12–3/4, 14–1/2)" long
Sewing thread and needle
Tapestry needle

GAUGE
32 sts and 40 rows = 4" [10 cm] in st patt. *Adjust needle size as necessary to obtain correct gauge.*

BACK

CO 104 (110, 116) sts.
Row 1 (RS): *K1, p1; rep from * to end.
Row 2 (WS): *P1, k1; rep from * to end.
Work rows 1 and 2 for a total of 6 rows. Now reverse patt as foll:
Row 7 (RS): Rep row 2.
Row 8 (WS): Rep row 1.
Work rows 7 and 8 for 6 rows.
Rep these 12 rows for patt until work measures 9 (9, 10–1/2)" from CO, ending with WS row completed.

Begin raglan shaping:

BO 8 sts beg of next 2 rows—88 (94, 100) sts.
Dec 1 st each side every other row 25 (26, 30) times—38 (42, 40) sts.
Dec 1 st each side every 4th row 3 (3, 2) times—32 (36, 36) sts.
BO rem 32 (36, 36) sts.

LEFT FRONT (AS WORN)

CO 52 (54, 66) sts.
Work in 12-row rib patt same as back until front measures 9 (9, 10–1/2)", ending with WS row completed. Work raglan shaping same as back until front measures about 13 (12–3/4, 14–1/2)" from CO edge.

Neck shaping:

Row 1 (WS): Beg at neck edge, BO 8 (9, 9) sts, work in patt to end of row.
Row 2 (RS): Work in patt to end of row.
Row 3 (WS): At neck edge, dec 1 st, work in patt to end of row.
Rep rows 2 and 3 another 7 (7, 8) times. Work even at neckline and cont raglan shaping same as back; when front measures same as back, BO.

RIGHT FRONT (AS WORN)

CO 52 (54, 66) sts. Work the same as left front until work measures 9 (9, 10–1/2)", ending with RS row completed. Work raglan shaping same as left front until front measures about 13 (12–3/4, 14–1/2)" from CO edge, ending with WS row completed.

Neck shaping:

Row 1 (RS): Beg at neck edge, BO 8 (9, 9) sts, work in patt to end of row.
Row 2 (WS): Work in patt to end of row.
Row 3 (RS): At neck edge, dec 1 st, work in patt to end of row.
Rep rows 2 and 3 another 7 (7, 8) times. Work even at neckline, cont raglan shaping same as back; when front measures same as back, BO.

SLEEVES

With smaller needles, CO 58 (60, 64) sts. Work in 12-row rib patt same as back for 2" (turn-back cuff).
Change to larger needles.

Sleeve shaping:

Cont in est patt, inc 1 st on each side every 4th (6th, 6th) row 1 (11, 8) times—60 (82, 80) sts. Then inc 1 st each side every 6th (8th, 8th) row 12 (3, 6) times—84 (88, 92) sts. Work even in patt until sleeve measures 12–1/2 (14, 14–1/2)" from CO edge (this measurement includes 2" turn-back cuff).

Cap shaping:

BO 8 sts beg of next 2 rows—68 (72, 76) sts.
On next RS row, dec 1 st each side—66 (70, 74) sts.
Dec 1 st each side every other row 28 (31, 32) times—10 (8, 10) sts.
Dec 1 st each side every 4th row 1 (0, 1) time—8 sts.
BO rem 8 sts.
Work second sleeve the same.

With RS facing and threaded tapestry needle, sew sleeves into raglan armholes with mattress st (see Glossary), then sew underarm and sleeve seams also with mattress st.

COLLAR

With RS of work facing and smaller circular needles, pick up and knit 37 (42, 43) sts from right front neck, 32 (36, 36) sts from back neck, 37 (42, 43) sts from left front neck—106 (120, 122) sts.
Sl first st in each row to create an even edge, work in 12-row rib patt for 12 rows.
Change to larger circular needles and work even until collar measures about 2–3/4" to 3" from row where larger needles began.
BO loosely in patt.

Pockets (Make 2)

With larger needles, CO 24 (28, 32) sts. Work in 12-row rib patt for 3 (4, 4)", then work 6 rows with smaller needles. BO in patt with larger needles.
Work second pocket the same.

FINISHING

Pin pockets to fronts, positioning them as shown in photo; keep the 6 rows made with smaller needles facing upward for pocket opening. Thread tapestry needle and whipstitch (see Glossary) around 3 edges of each pocket, leaving top edge open. With sewing needles and matching sewing thread, sew separating zipper along center front edges using backstitch (see Glossary).

Zipper Cord

With crochet hook and yarn, make a ch about 10" long, cut yarn and fasten off. Draw cord through tab of slide fastener and tie knot to secure.

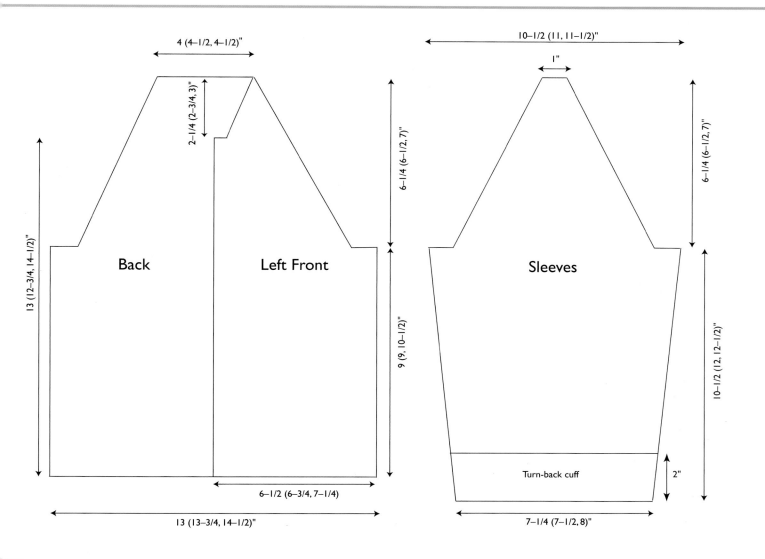

Back

4 (4–1/2, 4–1/2)"

2–1/4 (2–3/4, 3)"

13 (12–3/4, 14–1/2)"

Left Front

6–1/4 (6–1/2, 7)"

9 (9, 10–1/2)"

6–1/2 (6–3/4, 7–1/4)

13 (13–3/4, 14–1/2)"

Sleeves

10–1/2 (11, 11–1/2)"

1"

6–1/4 (6–1/2, 7)"

10–1/2 (12, 12–1/2)"

Turn-back cuff

2"

7–1/4 (7–1/2, 8)"

Men's Pullover,
published by Lux, 1952

This sweater is an updated version of a traditional military-style pullover from the 1940s, with a cozy fold-over collar. The sweater is worked in a slightly unusual rib pattern—k2, p2 rib across the first row, and p1, k1 rib on the second row. All knit stitches are worked through the back loop, and all purl stitches are worked normally.

SIZE
Chest: 36 (38, 40, 42)"

FINISHED MEASUREMENTS
Chest circumference: 38–1/2 (41, 44, 45)"
Length: 26–1/4 (27–1/4, 27–3/4, 28–3/4)"

MATERIALS
Yarn—CYCA #3 Light, 100% wool or blend: About 1750 (1925, 2050, 2200) yds
   Note: **With the twisted rib pattern and large collar, this project may not work well in 100% cotton. Choose a blend or a yarn with plenty of elasticity for better results.**
Size 3 [3.25 mm]; size 5 [3.75 mm] knitting needles
Tapestry needle
2 buttons, about 3/4" in diameter
Stitch holders
Open-ring stitch marker

GAUGE
24 sts and 32 rows = 4" [10 cm] in main rib patt on size 5 [3.75 mm] needles. *Adjust needle size as necessary to obtain correct gauge.*

STITCH GUIDE
Main Pattern
Row 1 (RS): *K2tbl , p2; rep from * to end of row.
Row 2 (WS): *P1, k1tbl; rep from * to end of row.
Rep these 2 rows for main patt.

BACK
With smaller needles, CO 103 (111, 119, 123) sts.
Row 1 (RS): *K1, p1; rep from * to last st, k1.
Row 2 (WS): *P1, k1; rep from * to last st, p1.
Rep last 2 rows until rib measures 3" from CO, inc 13 sts evenly spaced across last row of rib—116 (124,132,136) sts. Change to larger needles and beg main patt as foll:

Row 1 (RS): *K2tbl, p2; rep from * to end of row.
Row 2 (WS): *P1, k1 tbl; rep from * to end of row.
Rep the last 2 rows until back measures 16–1/2 (17, 17–1/2, 18)" or desired length from CO, ending with WS row completed.

Underarm shaping:
BO 7 (8, 9, 9) sts at beg of next 2 rows—102 (108, 114, 118) sts.
Next row: K1, ssk, work in est patt to last 3 sts, k2tog, k1—100 (106, 112, 116) sts.
Next row: Work even in patt.
Rep last 2 rows 5 (6, 6, 6) times more—90 (94, 100, 104) sts.

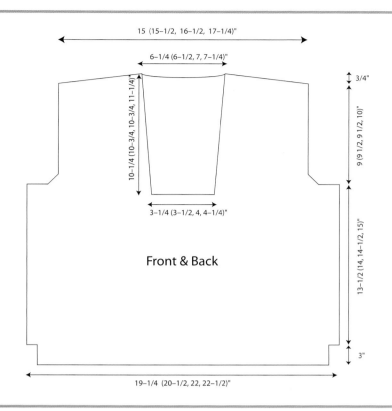

Front & Back

15 (15-1/2, 16-1/2, 17-1/4)"

6-1/4 (6-1/2, 7, 7-1/4)"

10-1/4 (10-3/4, 10-3/4, 11-1/4)"

3-1/4 (3-1/2, 4, 4-1/4)"

3/4"

9 (9-1/2, 9 1/2, 10)"

13-1/2 (14, 14-1/2, 15)"

3"

19-1/4 (20-1/2, 22, 22-1/2)"

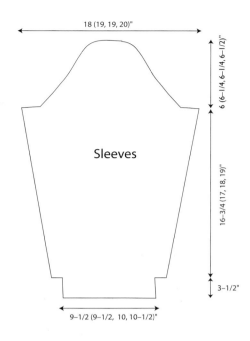

Sleeves

18 (19, 19, 20)"

6 (6-1/4, 6-1/4, 6-1/2)"

16-3/4 (17, 18, 19)"

3-1/2"

9-1/2 (9-1/2, 10, 10-1/2)"

Work even in patt until armhole measures 9 (9–1/2, 9–1/2, 10)" from beg of armhole shaping, ending with WS row completed.

Divide stitches for neck:
With RS facing, work in est patt for 29 (30, 32, 33) sts. Place these sts on st holder for right shoulder. BO 32 (34, 36, 38) sts for back neck. Work in patt across rem sts—29 (30, 32, 33) shoulder sts each side of neck BO.

Left shoulder shaping:
Keeping armhole edge even, dec 1 st at neck edge next 2 rows—27 (28, 30, 31) sts each shoulder.
Next row (armhole edge): BO 8 (8, 9, 9) sts, work across rem sts in patt to last 3 sts, dec 1 st, work 1 st in patt—18 (19, 20, 21) sts.
Next row (neck edge): Work 1 st in patt, dec 1 st, work to end of row—17 (18, 19, 20) sts.
Rep last 2 rows once more—7 (8, 8, 9) sts.
BO rem 7 (8, 8, 9) sts.

Right shoulder shaping:
Attach yarn at neck edge. Work even across row, then foll directions for left shoulder.

FRONT
Work same as back until front measures 16 (16–1/2, 17, 17–1/2)" or 1/2" less than back from CO edge, ending with WS row completed.

Divide stitches for neck:
Work in patt over 48 (51, 54, 55) sts; place sts on holder for left front neck. Cont row by working in patt over next 20 (22, 24, 26) sts, place these sts on holder for neck. Work in patt over 48 (51, 54, 55) sts for right front neck.

RIGHT FRONT NECK
Work even in est patt for 4 rows.
Row 5 (armhole edge): BO 6 (8, 9, 9) sts, work across rem sts to last 3 sts, dec 1, work 1 st in patt (neck edge)—41 (42, 44, 45) sts.
Rows 6, 8, 10, 12: Work even.
Row 7: Work across row to last 3 sts, dec 1, work 1 st in patt—40 (41, 43, 44) sts.
Row 9: Work 1 st, dec 1 st, work in patt to last 3 sts, dec 1, work 1 st in patt—38 (39, 41, 42) sts.
Row 11: Work 1 st, dec 1 st, work even to end of row—37 (38, 40, 41) sts.
Rep rows 9–12 twice more—31 (32, 34, 35) sts.
Next row: Work across row to last 3 sts, dec 1, work 1 st in patt—30 (31, 33, 34) sts.
Next 3 rows: Work even in patt.
Rep last 4 rows 7 times more—23 (24, 26, 27) sts.
Place marker in last neck dec.
Work even in est patt until armhole measures same depth as back, ending with RS row completed at armhole edge.

Shoulder shaping:

Row 1 (WS): BO 8 (8, 9, 9) sts, work even to end of row—15 (16, 17, 18) sts.
Row 2: Work even in patt.
Rep rows 1 and 2 once more—7 (8, 8, 9) sts.
BO rem 7 (8, 8, 9) sts.

LEFT FRONT NECK

Attach yarn at neck edge. Work across row in patt. Foll instructions for right front neck.

WRAP-OVER ROLL COLLAR

Note: All shaping is made on the outer edge—first dec at left shoulder side. Shaped edge is then sewn to neckline when assembling the pieces.

With smaller needles, RS of work facing, and starting at right shoulder side of the row, place the 20 (22, 24, 26) sts from holder on needle. Attach yarn at left shoulder edge.
Row 1 (RS): *K1, p1; rep from * across.
Rep row 1 another 3 times, ending at left shoulder edge.

Begin increases:

Row 1 (RS): K1, m1(see Glossary), work in rib to end of row—21 (23, 25, 27) sts.
Rows 2, 3, and 4: Work even in est rib patt.
Rep last 4 rows twice more—23 (25, 27, 29) sts.
Row 13 (buttonhole row): Rib 1, m1, rib to last 8 sts, BO 4 sts, rib to end—24 (26, 28, 30) sts.
Row 14: Rib 4 sts, CO 4 sts using backward loop CO (see Glossary), rib to end of row.
Rows 15 and 16: Work even.
Rep rows 1–4 another 6 times—30 (32, 34, 36) sts.
Rep rows 13–16 once more (2nd buttonhole)—31 (33, 35, 37) sts.
Rep rows 1–4 once more—32 (34, 36, 38) sts.
Work even in rib until collar fits along left front, around back of neck, and along right front to the st m on right front edge.

Begin decreases:

Row 1 (RS): Rib 1 (dec 1 st by working 2 sts tog), work in rib to end of row—31 (33, 35, 37) sts.
Rows 2, 3, and 4: Work even.
Rep last 4 rows 11 times more—20 (22, 24, 26) sts.
Next 4 rows: Work even in rib. BO all sts.

SLEEVES

With smaller needles, CO 57 (57, 59, 63) sts.
Row 1 (RS): *K1, p1; rep from * to last st, k1.
Row 2 (WS): *P1, k1; rep from * to last st, p1.
Rep rows 1 and 2 until cuff measures 3–1/2", inc 1 st in last WS row—58 (58, 60, 64) sts.
Change to larger needles and work main patt rows 1 and 2.

Sleeve shaping:

Inc 1 st on each side every 4th row 15 (20, 13, 12) times, working new sts into main patt when possible—88 (98, 86, 88) sts.
Inc 1 st each side every 6th row 10 (8, 14, 16) times—108 (114, 114, 120) sts.
Work even in patt until sleeve measures 20–1/4 (20–1/2, 21–1/2, 22–1/2)" from CO.

Cap shaping:

BO 5 (5, 7, 7) sts each side of next row—98 (104, 100, 106) sts.
Dec 1 st each side every other row 5 (5, 6, 6) times—88 (94, 88, 94) sts.
Dec 1 st each side every row—16 (17, 13, 13) times—56 (60, 62, 68) times.
Dec 1 st each side every other row 11 (12, 13, 14) times—34 (36, 36, 40) sts.
BO 4 (4, 4, 5) sts beg of next 4 rows—18 (20, 20, 20) sts.
BO rem 18 (20, 20, 20) sts.
Work second sleeve the same.

FINISHING

With RS tog and threaded tapestry needle, sew shoulders using backstitch (see Glossary). Join body side seams and sleeve seams using mattress st (see Glossary), working 1/2 st in from each side edge of rib to maintain k1, p1 rib patt at lower edges. Set sleeves in armholes, easing sleeve cap where necessary. Sew BO edge of collar under first collar row. Sew buttons on to correspond with buttonholes. Weave in ends to WS and secure.

Dolman Bolero, published by Lux, 1952

This bolero is ideal for teenagers or anyone young at heart. The design is simple enough for anyone with advanced beginner knitting skills to make. The dolman sleeves offer ease of movement, without excess bulk, and a bolero is just the thing for year-round wear. Make one in cotton blend to protect against the chill of air conditioning in the summer, or cool, breezy evenings at the coast or in high country. Or, make one in a warmer yarn like wool, cashmere, or alpaca to keep you cozy in fall and winter.

SIZE
Chest: 30 (32, 34)"

FINISHED MEASUREMENTS
Back chest width: 18–1/2 (20, 21)"
Length: 13–1/4 (14–3/4, 16)"

MATERIALS
Yarn—CYCA #1 Fine, any fiber: About 800 (840, 960) yds
Size 2 [2.75 mm] knitting needles
1 button, about 3/4" diameter
Tapestry needle

GAUGE
28 sts and 36 rows = 4" [10 cm] in St st on size 2 [2.75 mm] needles. *Adjust needle size as necessary to obtain correct gauge.*

RIGHT FRONT (AS WORN)

CO 18 (21, 24) sts. Work in St st (knit 1 row, purl 1 row) as foll:

Rows 1 and 2: Work even in St st.

Row 3 (RS): CO 2 sts at beg of row (center front) using backward loop CO (see Glossary). Knit those 2 sts, then knit across row—20 (23, 26) sts.

Row 4 (WS): Work even.

Rep rows 3 and 4 another 4 times—28 (31, 34) sts.

Row 13: K1, m1, work even to end of row—29 (32, 35) sts

Row 14: Work even.

Rep last 2 rows 4 times more—33 (36, 39) sts. Work should measure about 2-1/4" from CO.

Underarm shaping:

Row 1: K1, m1 at center front edge, knit to last st, m1, k1—35 (38, 41) sts.

Rows 2 and 4: Work even.

Row 3: Rep row 13—36 (39, 42) sts.

Row 5: Rep row 1—38 (41, 44) sts.

Rep rows 2–5 until there are 56 (62, 66) sts on needle, ending at armhole edge.

Sleeve shaping:

Cont to inc 1 st every 4th row at center front, and shape sleeve as foll:

Next row (WS): CO 10 sts (armhole edge), purl those 10 CO sts, then purl to end of row.

Next row (RS): Knit.

Rep last 2 rows until there are 50 new sleeve sts added—108 (114, 118) sts.

Keeping armhole edge even (no more incs), cont to inc 1 st at center-front edge every 4th row as before until there are 115 (120, 124) sts on needle.

Keeping both armhole and center-front edges even, work even in St st until sleeve (at cuff edge) is 4-1/2 (5, 5-1/2)", ending with WS row completed at center front.

Neckline shaping:

Next row (RS): BO 7 (8, 9) sts. Knit to end of row—108 (112, 115) sts.

Next row (WS): Work even.

Next row: Dec 1 st at neck edge, knit to end of row—107 (111, 114) sts.

Rep last 2 rows 2 times more—105 (109, 112) sts.

Shoulder shaping:

Next row (WS): BO 9 sts, purl to end of row (center front)—96 (100, 103) sts.

Next row (RS): Dec 1 st, knit to end of row—95 (99, 102) sts.

Next row (WS): BO 8 sts, purl to end of row—87 (91, 94) sts.

Next row: Dec 1 st, knit to end of row—86 (90, 93) sts.

Rep last 2 rows 4 times more—50 (54, 57) sts.

Next row: BO 10 (11, 12) sts, purl to end of row—40 (43, 45) sts.

Next row: Dec 1 st, knit to end of row—39 (42, 44) sts.

Next row: BO 10 (11, 12) sts, purl to end of row—29 (31, 32) sts.

Next row: Work even.

Next row: BO 10 sts, purl to end—19 (21, 22) sts.

Rep last 2 rows once more—9 (11, 12) sts.

BO rem 9 (11, 12) sts.

LEFT FRONT (AS WORN)

CO 18 (21, 24) sts. Knit 1 row even.

Foll directions for right front, starting with row 1. Shaping is reversed.

BACK

CO 100 (106, 112) sts.

Work 9 (11, 13) rows k1, p1 rib.

Work 2-1/4" in St st, ending with WS row completed. The St st section should measure the same length as fronts to underarm shaping.

Underarm shaping:

Cont in St st, inc 1 st each end of needle on next row, then every other row until 15 (17, 18) inc rows are worked, ending with WS row completed—130 (140, 148) sts.

SLEEVES

Row 1 (RS): CO 10 sts, knit these 10 sts then knit to end of row—140 (150, 158) sts.

Row 2 (WS): CO 10 sts, purl these 10 sts, then purl to end of row—150 (160, 168) sts.

Rep these 2 rows 4 times more—230 (240, 248) sts.

Work even in St st until sleeve (at cuff edge) measures 4-1/2 (5, 5-1/2)", ending with WS row completed.

Shoulder shaping:

BO 9 sts beg each of next 6 rows—176 (186, 194) sts.

BO 8 sts beg each of next 10 rows—96 (106, 114) sts.

BO 10 (11, 12) sts beg each of next 4 rows—56 (62, 66) sts

BO 9 (11, 12) sts beg each of next 2 rows—38 (40, 42) sts.

Place rem 38 (40, 42) sts on holder.

Front Borders

With RS facing, pick up and knit 7 sts for each inch along right-front edge (excluding neckline)—about 130 (138, 146) sts.

Work 9 (11, 13) rows in k1, p1 rib.

BO loosely in rib patt.

Work left front border the same.

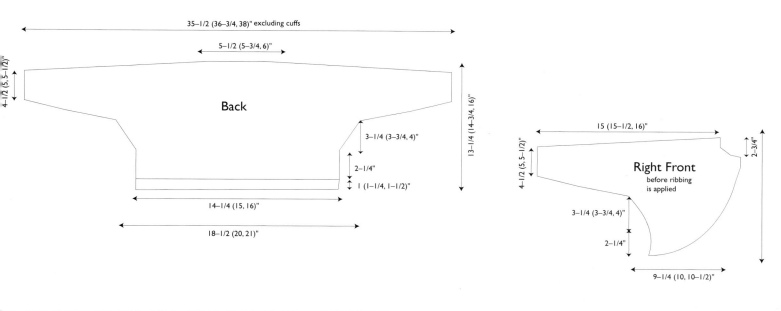

Cuff Borders

Sew shoulder/sleeve top seams tog. Pick up and knit 7 sts for each inch along cuff edge—about 76 (86, 96) sts. Work in k1, p1 rib for 9 (11, 13) rows.
Work second cuff border the same.

Neckband

Beg at right-center front edge. With RS facing, pick up and knit 7 sts for each inch along right-front neck—about 35 (36, 37) sts, then k38 (40, 42) back neck sts from holder, then pick up and k35 (36, 37) sts from left-front neck—108 (112, 116) sts.
Next row (WS): Work in k1, p1 rib to end of row.

Next row (beg buttonhole): Rib 3 sts, BO 4 sts, rib to end of row.
Next row (complete buttonhole): Rib across row to BO sts, CO 4 sts, rib to end.
Work 6 (8, 10) rows more in ribbing.
BO loosely in rib patt.

FINISHING

Weave in all ends to WS. Sew side seams (including sleeve underarms). Add button on left front neck to correspond with buttonhole. Lightly block to measurements.

Ski Fashions
by COLUMBIA·MINERVA

BOOK 758
PRICE $1.00

1960s

The fashions of the 1950s remained in vogue into the early 1960s, but styles changed dramatically by the late 1960s. The mini skirt, white knee boots, wild colors, and crochet tops and dresses made popular in the mid 1960s would later come to define the decade. Wools, blends, and synthetics were commonly used to create handknit garments, and specialty fibers like angora were no longer reserved for adding flair along cuffs or hemlines—they were now used for entire sweaters, especially shells. Mohair sweaters were trendy for women and teens.

Aran sweaters and other styles from around the world were favorite knitting projects in the early part of the decade. Bulky knits were in, and the overall fit of knit sweaters was more relaxed than it had been in the 1950s. Many men's sweaters, in fact, fit so loosely that they were too bulky to be worn under a suit or sport jacket.

While some sweaters from the 1960s still featured raglans and fitted cap sleeves, many projects now included a modified drop shoulder with capless sleeves. Sweater lengths varied from upper hip for shells to mid-hip or lower hip for other sweaters and cardigans. Waistline shaping disappeared by the end of the decade. (No more stockings, no more girdles!)

The "family group" sweaters popular in the 1950s carried over into the 1960s but followed a sports theme. Ski and skating sweaters using identical stitch motifs were available for family members, ranging from children's size 8 to Dad's size 46″. Ski hats and headbands in multicolor motifs were also in style.

Woman's Shell,
published by Bear Brand, 1965

Bear Brand's classic-style shell with fitted rib waist and turtleneck collar is shown here in mohair, but this project would look great in mohair blend or a blend of angora/merino.

BACK
With smaller needles, CO 60 (64, 68) sts.
Row 1 (RS): *K2, p2; rep from * across row.
Row 2 (WS): *P2, k2; rep from * across row.
Rep last 2 rows until rib patt measures 3" from CO, ending with WS row completed.
Change to larger needles and work in St st (knit 1 row, purl 1 row) until work measures 10" above rib, end with RS row completed.

Underarm shaping:
BO 3 sts at beg of next 2 rows—54 (58, 62) sts.
Dec 1 st each side every other row 5 (6, 7) times—44 (46, 48) sts. Work even in St st until armhole measures 8 (8, 8–1/2)" from BO, ending with RS row completed.

Shoulder shaping:
BO 4 sts beg of next 4 rows—28 (30, 32) sts.
BO 3 (4, 5) sts at beg of next row—25 (26, 27) sts.
Next row: BO first 2 (3, 4) sts, loosen loop on right needle and pass ball of yarn through st, binding off 3rd (4th, 5th) st; k1, *inc 1 st in next st, k1; rep from * to last 3 sts, inc 1 st in next st, k2—32 sts. Do not BO 32 back neck sts. Place on holder.

FRONT
With smaller needles, CO 64 (68, 72) sts. Work same as back, including underarm shaping, until work measures 5–1/2 (5–1/2, 6)" from armhole BO, ending with WS row completed—48 (50, 52) sts.

Divide for neck shaping:
Row 1 (RS): K17 (18, 19) sts, place on holder for left side, k1, *inc 1 st in next st, k1; rep from * 5 times more, k1; place these 20 sts on holder for neck, knit to end for right side of neck—17 (18, 19) sts. Working these sts for right side of neck, dec 1 st at neck

SIZE
Chest: 32 (34, 36)"

FINISHED MEASUREMENTS
Chest circumference: 35–1/4 (37–3/4, 40)"
Length: 21–3/4 (21–3/4, 22–1/4)"

MATERIALS
Yarn—CYCA #5 Bulky, any yarn that knits to gauge:
    About 480 (480, 560) yds

Size 6 [4 mm] knitting needles; 16" circular needle for
    turtleneck collar
Size 10–1/2 [6.5 mm] knitting needles
Tapestry needle
Stitch holders

GAUGE
14 sts and 18 rows = 4" [10 cm] in St st on size 10–1/2
    [6.5 mm] needles. *Adjust needle size as necessary
    to obtain correct gauge.*

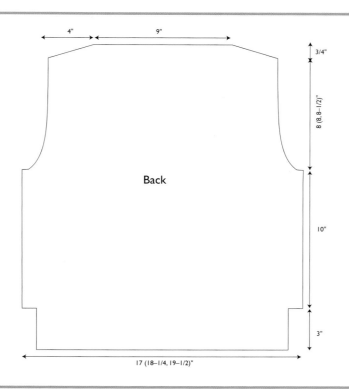

Back

4" 9" 3/4"

8 (8, 8-1/2)"

10"

3"

17 (18-1/4, 19-1/2)"

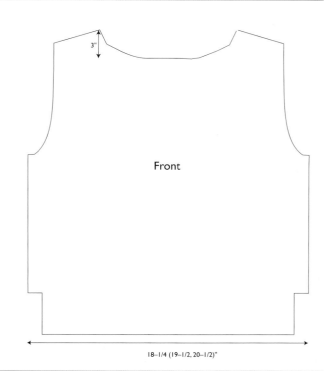

Front

3"

18-1/4 (19-1/2, 20-1/2)"

edge every row 4 times—13 (14, 15) sts, then every other row 2 times—11 (12, 13) sts.

Work even until armhole length is same as back, then shape shoulder the same as back shoulder.

Sl 17 (18, 19) sts of left side from holder, join yarn at neck edge, and finish to correspond to right side. With threaded tapestry needle, join shoulders tog with back-stitch (see Glossary).

Turtleneck ribbed collar:

With smaller circular needle and WS facing, join yarn, pick up and k18 sts on left side of neck, k20 sts of front neck from holder, pick up and k18 sts on right side of neck, k32 sts from back neck holder—88 sts.

Work in rnds of k2, p2 on these 88 sts until turtleneck measures 5–1/2".

BO loosely in rib patt.

ARMHOLE RIBBING

Make left armhole:

With smaller needles and RS facing, beg at underarm edge of left front armhole, pick up k3 sts in 3 BO sts, 74 (78, 82) sts along armhole edge, 3 sts in 3 BO sts of back armhole—80 (84, 88) sts. Work in k2, p2 rib for 3/4". BO in rib patt. Work rib along right armhole edge to correspond, beg with right back armhole.

FINISHING

With RS facing, sew underarm seams with mattress st (see Glossary). Weave in loose ends to WS. Steam seams lightly.

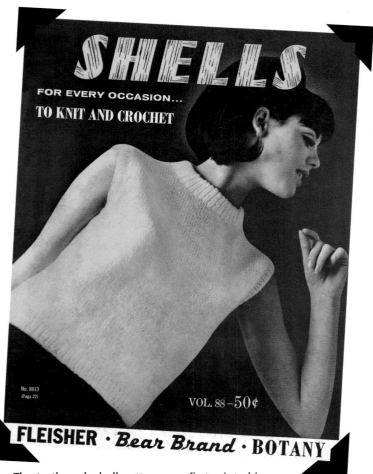

The turtleneck shell pattern was first printed in *Shells for Every Occasion . . . to Knit and Crochet* in 1965.

Girl's Lucky Lady Cardigan, published by Galt, 1966

Here's a quick-to-knit cardigan worked in bulky-weight yarn on large needles that we offer in five sizes. An interesting cable runs lengthwise on each front to break up the stockinette stitch, and the knit-in garter stitch front bands ensure that this project is a quickie to make. The sleeves are set-in and full-length (although they look a little shorter than full-length on this model).

NOTE

When seaming sides together, plan to work mattress st into the centers of each edge st. Using a whole stitch at each edge will reduce the finished circumference by almost 2" because of the large gauge (2–1/2 sts = 1"). If you wish to maintain more width after seaming, add 2 extra sts when casting on for the back and sleeves, and 1 extra st at side edge of both fronts. Work these stitches in patt but don't include them in the stitch count. These stitches will then be used to seam the pieces together.

BACK

With smaller needles, CO 33 (35, 37, 39, 41) sts.
Row 1 (RS): *K1, p1; rep from * to last st, k1.
Row 2 (WS): *P1, k1; rep from * to last st, p1.
Rep rows 1 and 2 until rib measures 3" from CO edge, inc 1 st in last row—34 (36, 38, 40, 42) sts.
Change to larger needles, work in St st until piece measures 10–1/2 (11, 12, 13, 14)" from CO edge.

Armhole shaping:

BO 2 sts beg of next 2 rows—30 (32, 34, 36, 38) sts.
Dec 1 st each side every other row 3 times—24 (26, 28, 30, 32) sts.
Work even in St st until armholes measure 5 (5–1/2, 6, 6–1/2, 7)" from BO.

Shoulder shaping:

BO 5 sts beg of next 2 rows—14 (16, 18, 20, 22) sts.
BO 4 (4, 5, 5, 6) sts beg of next 2 rows—6 (8, 8, 10, 10) sts.
BO rem 6 (8, 8, 10, 10) sts.

LEFT FRONT (AS WORN)

Note: There will be a few more sts rem at front shoulders after shaping than back shoulders because of cable sts.
With smaller needles, CO 22 (22, 24, 26, 28) sts.
Row 1 (RS): K1, *p1, k1; rep from * to last 3 sts, k3 (front border).
Row 2 (WS): K3 (front border), p1, *k1, p1; rep from * to end of row.
Rep rows 1 and 2 until rib measures 3" from CO edge, ending with WS row completed.
Change to larger needles and work in St st, setting up cable patt.

Cable pattern:

Row 1 (RS): K6 (6, 7, 8, 9) sts, p1, k8, p1, knit to last 3 sts, k3 (front border).
Rows 2 and 4 (WS): K3 (border), p3 (3, 4, 5, 6), k1, p8, k1, purl to end of row.
Row 3 (cable): K6 (6, 7, 8, 9) sts, p1, place next 2 sts

SIZES
4 (6, 8, 10, 12) years

FINISHED MEASUREMENTS
Width at chest: 13–1/2 (14–1/2, 15–1/4, 16, 16–3/4)"
Length: 16 (17, 18–1/2, 19–1/2, 21)"
Sleeve length to underarm: 11 (12, 13, 14, 15)"

MATERIALS
Yarn—CYCA #5 Bulky, all yarn types: About 365 (430, 510, 600, 680) yds

Size 9 [5.5 mm]; size 13 [9 mm] knitting needles
Cable needle
6 buttons, about 3/4" diameter
Sewing thread and needle
Tapestry needle

GAUGE
10 sts and 20 rows = 4" [10 cm] in St st patt. *Adjust needle size as necessary to obtain correct gauge.*

on cable needle and hold in back, k2 from needle, k2 from cable needle, place next 2 sts on cable needle and hold in front, k2 from needle, k2 from cable needle, p1, knit to end.

Rep last 4 rows for patt until front measures same as back to underarm, ending with WS row completed.

Armhole shaping:
Row 1 (RS): BO 2 sts at armhole edge, work in est patt to end of row—20 (20, 22, 24, 26) sts.
Row 2 (WS): Work even.
Dec 1 st at armhole edge every RS row 3 (2, 3, 3, 3) times—17 (18, 19, 21, 23) sts.
Work even until armhole measures 2" less than back armholes to shoulders, ending with RS row completed.

Neck shaping:
Row 1 (WS): K3 (border sts), work across in est patt—14 (15, 16, 18, 20) sts.
Cont on rem sts, dec 1 st at neck edge every row 3 (3, 4, 5, 6) times—11 (12, 12, 13, 14) sts.
Work even (if necessary) until armhole measures same as back armholes to shoulders, ending with WS row completed.

Shoulder shaping:
Row 1 (RS): BO 5 sts, work in est patt across row—6 (7, 7, 8, 9) sts.
Row 2 (WS) Work even in patt..
Row 3: BO rem 6 (7, 7, 8, 9) sts.
Mark front border for buttons, pm at center of lower rib and 4 ms evenly spaced along front band. The 5th button will be sewn on neckband when completed.

Key

☐ Knit on RS; purl on WS

⊡ Purl on RS; knit on WS

☐ Pattern repeat frame

⨯ 2/2 RC; place 2 sts on cable needle and hold in back; k2, k2 from cable needle.

⨯ 2/2 LC; place 2 sts on cable needle and hold in front; k2, k2 from cable needle.

Row 3

Row 1

RIGHT FRONT (AS WORN)

Note: There will be a few more sts rem at front shoulders after shaping than back shoulders because of cable sts.

CO and work the same as left front, reversing all shaping as foll: Starting front border at beginning of first row, BO for armhole and shoulder on WS rows, beginning neck shaping on RS row. Work buttonholes in right front border to correspond with ms on left front border as foll: Beg at front edge, k2, BO 1, work in patt to end of row. Next row: Work in patt to last 2 sts, CO 1 st over the BO st, k2.

Neckband

Sew shoulder seams tog with backstitch (see Glossary), gently easing extra fullness (because of cables) of front shoulder sts to back shoulder sts. Pick up and knit 41 (41, 43, 45, 47) sts around entire neck edge. Keeping the 3 border sts each side worked in garter st, work even in k1, p1 rib for 4 rows, working a buttonhole as before in 2nd row of right front border. BO loosely in rib.

SLEEVES

With smaller needles, CO 16 (18, 20, 22, 24) sts. Work in k1, p1 rib for 2–1/2".

Sleeve shaping:
Change to larger needles and work in St st, inc 1 st each side every 4th row 4 times—24 (26, 28, 30, 32) sts. Work even until sleeve measures 11 (12, 13, 14, 15)" or desired length from CO edge to underarm, ending with WS row completed.

Cap shaping:
BO 2 sts beg of next 2 rows—20 (22, 24, 26, 28) sts. Beg with next RS row, dec 1 st each side every other row 3 (4, 5, 6, 7) times; work even on WS rows—14 sts. BO 1 st each side every row 3 (3, 2, 1, 1) time(s)—8 (8, 10, 12, 12) sts rem.
BO all sts.
Make second sleeve the same.

FINISHING

With threaded tapestry needle, sew underarm and sleeve seams with mattress st (see Glossary). Sew in sleeves to armholes. With sewing needle and thread, attach buttons to left front, aligning with buttonholes. Do not block cables.

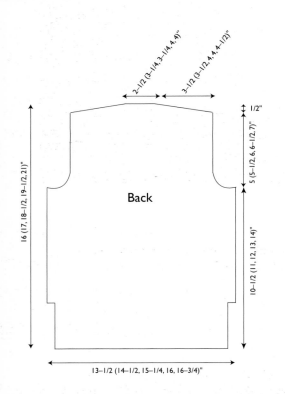

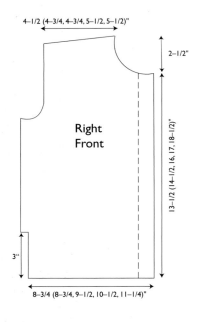

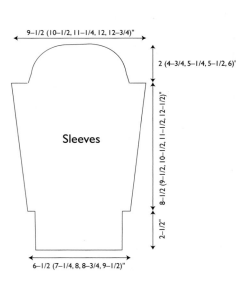

Men's Striped Sweater, published by Spinnerin, 1961

This design is reminiscent of the suave European ski sweaters of the 1960s. Not the Nordic multicolor motifs, but sleeker, closer-fitting models, with simple stripes along the shoulders and arms. A wonderful classic made in lighter-weight yarn and offered in six sizes.

BACK

With smaller needles and MC, CO 109 (115, 121, 127, 133, 139) sts.
Row 1 (RS): K1, *p1, k1; rep from * to end.
Row 2 (WS): P1, *k1, p1; rep from * to end.
Rep last 2 rows until rib measures 2–1/2" from CO, ending with WS row completed.

Cont with MC, change to larger needle and work in patt, inc 1 st each side every 32 rows 3 times, working incs into patt when possible—115 (121, 127, 133, 139, 145) sts. Work even in patt until back measures 18–1/2" from CO edge.

Underarm shaping:
BO 2 sts at beg of next 8 (10, 12, 14, 16, 18) rows—99 (101, 103, 105, 107, 109) sts.
Work even in patt until armholes measure 7 (7, 8, 8–1/2, 9, 9–1/2)", ending with WS row completed.

Shoulder and neck shaping:
BO 3 sts at beg of next 10 rows—69 (71, 73, 75, 77, 79) sts.
Next row (RS): BO 3 sts for right shoulder, work until 25

SIZE
Chest: 36 (38, 40, 42, 44, 46)"

FINISHED MEASUREMENTS
Chest: 39 (41, 43, 45, 47, 49)"
Length: 26–1/2 (26–1/2, 27–1/2, 28, 28–1/2, 29)"
Sleeve length to underarm: 18"

MATERIALS
Yarn—CYCA #2 Fine, 100% wool or blend: About 2000 (2175, 2375, 2375, 2590, 2590) yds main color (MC); 195 yds each of colors A and B

Size 5 [3.75 mm] knitting needles; 16" circular needle
Size 6 [4 mm] knitting needles
Tapestry needle
3 stitch holders
Stitch marker
4 yarn bobbins

GAUGE
24 sts and 32 rows = 4" [10 cm] in patt st on size 6 [4 mm] needles. *Adjust needle size as necessary to obtain correct gauge.*

(26, 26, 27, 28, 29) sts on right needle, place center 13 (13, 15, 15, 15, 17) sts on st holder for back neck, join another ball of MC, work last 28 (29, 29, 30, 31, 32) sts in patt.

Work both sides of neck at the same time, each with its own ball of yarn.

Next row (WS): BO 3 sts for left shoulder, work to end. Cont to BO 3 sts at shoulder edges every other row 3 times more. *At the same time*, BO 5 sts from neck edges twice, then BO 4 (5, 5, 5, 5, 5) sts at neck edges once, then BO rem 2 (2, 2, 3, 4, 4) sts from shoulder edges—29 (29, 29, 30, 30, 31) sts are BO from each shoulder.

FRONT

Note: Front is slightly larger than back.

With MC and smaller needles, CO 115 (121, 127, 133, 139, 145) sts. Work the same as back to armholes—121 (127, 133, 139, 145, 151) sts.

The Men's Striped Sweater was first published in the *Spinnerin Gentlemen Prefer* pattern book in 1961.

Underarm shaping:
BO 2 sts at beg of next 10 (12, 14, 16, 18, 20) rows—101 (103, 105, 107, 109, 111) sts.
Work even in patt until front measures same as back from CO.

Shoulder and neck shaping:
BO 3 sts at beg of next 4 rows—89 (91, 93, 95, 97, 99) sts.
Next row (RS): BO 3 sts for right shoulder, work across row until there are 34 (35, 35, 36, 37, 37) sts on right needle, place center 15 (15, 17, 17, 17, 19) sts on holder for neck front, join another ball of MC, work last 37 (38, 38, 39, 40, 40) sts in patt.
Work both sides of neck at the same time, each with its own ball of yarn.
Next row (WS): BO 3 sts for left shoulder, work to end. Cont to BO 3 sts at shoulder edges every other row 6 times more. *At the same time*, BO 3 sts from neck edges every other row 4 times, then BO rem 2 (3, 3, 3, 3, 3) sts once from each shoulder. BO rem 2 (2, 2, 3, 4, 4) sts from armhole edges.

SLEEVES
Note: Wind 2 bobbins with MC and 1 bobbin each with colors A and B. When changing colors, pass yarn to be used under yarn previously used to avoid holes in work at color change.

Left Sleeve
With MC and smaller needles, CO 43 (43, 47, 51, 51, 51) sts. Work k1, p1 rib same as back until rib measures 3", inc 10 sts evenly spaced across last row—53 (53, 57, 61, 61, 61) sts. Cut yarn.

Sleeve shaping:
Next row: Change to larger needles, join MC bobbin (back edge of sleeve), work patt row 1 for 26 (26, 28, 30, 30, 30) sts, join color A bobbin, continue patt for 4 sts, join color B bobbin, cont patt for 2 sts, join 2nd MC bobbin, continue in patt across last 21 (21, 23, 25, 25, 25) sts.
Working colors as est, continue in patt, inc 1 st each edge every 6th row 16 times—85 (85, 89, 93, 93, 93) sts, then inc 1 st each edge every 4th row 8 times—101 (101, 105, 109, 109, 109,) sts.
Work even until sleeve measures 16–1/2" above rib or desired length to underarm, ending with WS row completed.

Cap shaping:
Next row (RS): BO 2 sts at beg of row, work in patt to last 5 sts, k2, sl 1, k2tog, psso (double dec). Cont to BO 2 sts from back edge every other row 21 (21, 22, 23, 23, 23) times more. *At the same time*, dec 2 sts at front edge every other row 18 (18, 19, 20, 20, 20) times—19 sts.

Saddle shoulder:
Work even on 19 sts for 4–3/4 (4–3/4, 4–3/4 5, 5–1/4, 5–1/4)". BO 3 sts from front edge every other row 6 times. Fasten off last st.

Right Sleeve
With MC and smaller needles, CO 43 (43, 47, 51, 51, 51) sts. Work rib same as left sleeve.
Next row: Join MC bobbin, work in patt for 21 (21, 23, 25, 25, 25) sts, join color B bobbin work 2 sts, join color A bobbin work 4 sts, join 2nd MC bobbin work 26 (26, 28, 30, 30, 30) sts.
Complete right sleeve the same as left sleeve, reversing shaping.

FINISHING
Block pieces to measurements. With RS facing, join body side seams with mattress st (see Glossary), work underarm sleeve seams the same. Using backstitch (see Glossary) sew front edges of sleeve caps to front armholes, back edges to back armholes, easing in any extra length in caps. Using whipstitch (see Glossary) sew edges of saddle shoulders to back and front shoulders, easing in any extra length in saddles. Weave in loose ends to WS.

Neckband
With circular needle, MC, and RS facing, pick up and knit 118 (118, 120, 120, 122, 122) sts around neck edge, including sts on holders. Join sts in rnd and work k1, p1 rib for 2". BO in rib. Fold neck and sleeve rib in half to WS and sew in place with whipstitch.

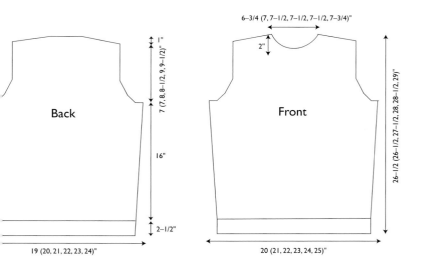

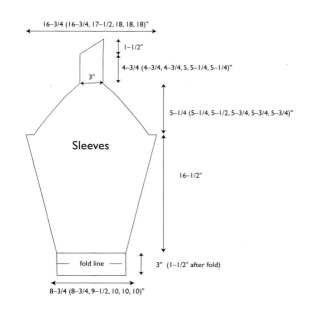

115

Boy's Cowboy Pullover, published by Newlands, 1962

Does your favorite young man love cowboys? Then this pullover is sure to be his sweater of choice. You can knit the cowboy motif as you work the front by following the full-size chart, using the intarsia method of working in color; or you can wait until the pullover is finished and apply the cowboy using duplicate stitch. The V-neck and set-in sleeves are comfortable to wear and make it easy for any young'un to dress himself.

BACK
With smaller needles and MC, CO 75 (81) sts.
Row 1: *K1, p1; rep from * to last st, k1.
Row 2: *P1, k1; rep from * to last st, p1.
Rep rows 1 and 2 for 1–1/2 (2)", inc 9 (10) sts evenly spaced across last row—84 (91) sts.
Change to larger needles and work in St st until back measures 8 (9)" from CO.

Underarm shaping:
BO 7 (6) sts at beg of next 2 rows—70 (79) sts.
Dec 1 st each side every other row 7 (6) times—56 (67) sts.
Work even in patt until armhole measures 4–1/4 (5)" from armhole BO.

Shoulder shaping:
BO 4 sts beg of next 2 rows—48 (59) sts.
BO 4 (5) sts at beg of next 4 rows—32 (39) sts.
BO rem 32 (39) sts for back neck.

FRONT
Note: To prevent a hole when changing colors, bring color to be used under last color used. Wind colors on individual yarn bobbins or count the number of sts in each color and allow about 1/2" of yarn for each st. Cut long strands and let the strands dangle, pulling them into position when the chart indicates using that color. Work same as back until 4th row of St st after rib is finished, ending with WS row completed. Begin cowboy chart.

Cowboy chart:
Cont in St st and foll cowboy chart, working rows 1–56, beg with RS row.
When chart is completed, work even until armhole shaping and work same as back. *At the same time,* when front measures 8–1/2 (9–1/2)" from CO edge, ending with RS row completed, begin neck shaping.

Neck shaping:
Work to center st, place center st on holder (use safety pin or coilless pin), attach another ball of yarn, and complete row.
Next row (RS): Using a separate ball of yarn for each

side of neck, dec 1 st at each neck edge every row 12 times, then every row 4 (7) times—12 (14) sts.
Work even in St st until front measures 12–1/4 (14)" from CO, ending with WS row completed.

Shoulder shaping:
Work both shoulders at same time, using separate ball for each side.
Row 1 (RS): BO 4 sts at armhole edge, drop yarn, pick up second yarn, work to end of other shoulder—8 (10) sts on first shoulder.
Row 2 (WS): Rep row 1—8 (10) sts on both shoulders.
Row 3: Rep row 1—4 sts on first shoulder.
Row 4: BO 5 sts at armhole edge, work across both shoulders—5 sts on second shoulder.
Rep rows 3 and 4 once more. Fasten off last st.

SLEEVES
With smaller needles and MC, CO 39 (45) sts.
Work in k1, p1 rib same as back for 2", inc 5 sts evenly spaced across last row—44 (50) sts.

Sleeve shaping:
Change to larger needles. Working in St st, inc 1 st each side every 8th row 5 (10) times—54 (70) sts.
Inc 1 st each side every 10th (0) row 2 (0) times—58 (70) sts. Work even until sleeve measures 9 (11)" or desired length from CO.

Cap shaping:
BO 7 sts beg of next 2 rows—44 (58) sts.
Dec 1 st each side every other row 11 (14) times—22 (30) sts.

Size 21" only:
Dec 1 st every 3rd row 2 times—18 sts.
Size 23" only:
Dec 1 st each side every row 5 times—(20) sts.
Both sizes:
BO 2 sts beg of next 4 rows—10 (12) sts.
Work second sleeve the same.

Block all pieces and allow to dry completely. Sew shoulder seams tog with backstitch (see Glossary). Sew sleeves in place with backstitch. Sew underarm and sleeve seams with mattress st (see Glossary), inserting needle through middle of each edge st to maintain rib patt.

Neck Ribbing
With smaller circular needle, MC, and RS facing, pick up and knit 32 (39) sts from back neck, 26 (32) sts from left neck edge. Place marker in center, m1, place marker, pick up 26 (32) sts from right neck edge, place marker (use another color marker) at end of rnd—85 (104) sts.
Rnd 1: Work in k1, p1 rib to within 2 sts of first center m, ssk, sl m, k1 (this is the center st), sl m, k2tog, work in k1, p1 rib to end of rnd.

Rnd 2: Work in est rib patt to within 2 sts of center m, ssk, sl m, k1, sl m, k2tog, work in est rib patt to end of rnd. Rep rnd 2 for about 1" from pick up rnd. Remove ms. BO in loosely in rib.

FINISHING
Weave in loose ends to WS to secure. Using a damp press cloth, lightly press seams to flatten, lightly press intarsia work to smooth out sts.

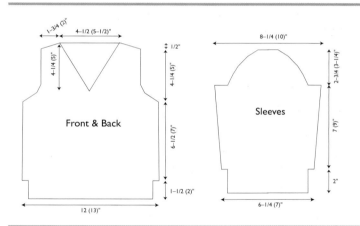

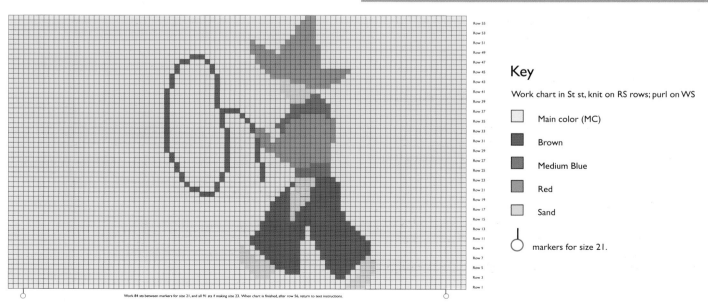

Key

Work chart in St st, knit on RS rows; purl on WS

☐ Main color (MC)

☐ Brown

☐ Medium Blue

☐ Red

☐ Sand

○ markers for size 21.

Work 84 sts between markers for size 21, and all 91 sts if making size 23. When chart is finished, after row 56, return to text instructions.

Men's Cardigan with Solid or Striped Sleeves, published by Newlands, 1962

Here is another good, basic cardigan for the men in your life, featuring set-in sleeves worked either in the main color or the main color with a band of five stripes added to one sleeve. It also features pockets, and front bands worked along with the two fronts. This sweater is offered in six sizes, from 36 to 46".

SIZE
Chest: 36 (38, 40, 42, 44, 46)"

FINISHED MEASUREMENTS
Chest circumference: 38 (40, 42, 44, 46, 48)", with front band buttoned
Length: 25–1/2 (25–3/4, 26, 26–1/4, 26–1/2, 26–3/4)"
Sleeve length from underarm to cuff: 19–3/4 (20, 20–1/4, 20–1/2, 20–3/4, 21)"

MATERIALS
Yarn—CYCA #3 Light, 100% wool or blend; about 1500 (1750, 1750, 2000, 2000, 2250) yds main color (MC); 125 yds contrast color (CC) for sleeve with stripes

Size 3 [2.75 mm]; size 4 [3.5 mm] knitting needles:
  1 spare needle, size 4 [3.5 mm]
6 buttons, about 3/4" diameter
Sewing thread and needle to attach buttons
Tapestry needle
2 stitch holders
Long sewing pins with large, colored heads
Coilless pins

GAUGE
24 sts and 32 rows = 4" [10 cm] in St st on size 4 [3.5 mm] needles. *Adjust needle size as necessary to obtain correct gauge.*

BACK
With smaller needles, CO 111 (117, 123, 129, 135, 141) sts.
Work in St st (purl 1 row, knit 1 row) for 12 rows for hem facing, ending with knit (RS) row completed.
Turning ridge row (WS): With larger needles, K1tbl in each st to end of row. This row produces a purl ridge on the RS of fabric.
Next row (RS): Knit.
Work even in St st until back measures 16" from turning ridge row, ending with WS row completed.

Underarm shaping:
BO 6 sts at beg of next 2 rows—99 (105, 111, 117, 123, 129) sts.
Dec 1 st each side every other row 6 times—87 (93, 99, 105, 111, 117) sts.
Work even in St st until armhole measures 8–3/4 (9, 9–1/4, 9–1/2, 9–3/4, 10)" from armhole BO.

Shoulder shaping:
BO 7 (9, 11, 13, 15, 17) sts beg of next 2 rows—73 (75, 77, 79, 81, 83) sts.
BO 10 sts beg of next 4 rows—33 (35, 37, 39, 41, 43) sts.
BO rem 33 (35, 37, 39, 41, 43) sts for back neck.

Pocket Linings (Make 2)
With larger needles, CO 27 (28, 29, 30, 31, 32) sts.
Work in St st for 5–1/4", ending with WS row completed.
Sl sts on holder. Cut yarn leaving 4" tail.

RIGHT FRONT (AS WORN)
Note: The front bands are worked simultaneously with the fronts. When the right front is completed, mark the front band for button placement using the coilless pins or small safety pins, then use these ms as your guide for buttonhole placement when you work the left front.

With smaller needles, CO 53 (56, 59, 62, 65, 68) sts.
Work in St st for 12 rows same as back, ending with RS row completed. Change to larger needles and work turning ridge row same as back. With a 33" strand of yarn, CO 20 sts for front border and facing onto a spare larger needle and knit these sts onto the same needle holding sts of right front. Knit 1 row across all 73 (76, 79, 82, 85, 88) sts. Work even in St st until front measures 6–3/4" above turning ridge row, ending with RS row completed.

Pocket Opening
(WS): P13 (14, 15, 16, 17, 18) sts, work turning ridge on next 27 (28, 29, 30, 31, 32) sts and sl these sts on holder for pocket, p33 (34, 35, 36, 37, 38) sts.
Next row (RS): K33 (34, 35, 36, 37, 38) sts, k27 (28, 29, 30, 31, 32) sts of pocket *lining* from holder, k13 (14, 15, 16, 17, 18) sts—73 (76, 79, 82, 85, 88) sts.
Work even until front measures same as back to beg of armhole BO, ending with RS row completed.

Underarm and neck shaping:
Row 1 (WS): BO 6 sts beg of next row for underarm, purl to end—67 (70, 73, 76, 79, 82) sts.
Work 2 rows even.
Row 4 (RS) decs: K19 for border and facing, ssk, knit to last 2 sts of row end, k2tog—65 (68, 71, 74, 77, 80) sts.
Rep dec at armhole edge every other row 5 times, and dec at inner edge of border every 4th row 13 (14, 15, 16, 17, 18) times—47 (49, 51, 53, 55, 57) sts. Work even until front armhole measures same as back armhole to beg of shoulder shaping.

Shoulder shaping:
Shape shoulders same as for back. Work even on rem 20 sts for 2–1/4 (2–1/2, 2–1/2, 2–3/4, 3, 3)" for back neck border. Sl these sts on holder. Cut yarn leaving 24" tail for weaving.

Pocket Hem

With smaller needles, sl 27 (28, 29, 30, 31, 32) pocket sts from holder onto needle. With RS facing, join yarn at right edge, knit 1 row, purl 1 row for 9 rows. BO all sts.

Mark for buttons:

Working upward along front band and about 2 sts in from center front edge, place button ms (coilless pins), inserting first m about 6 rows from lower edge and last m at beg of neck shaping. Place rem 4 button ms evenly spaced between these two ms.

LEFT FRONT (AS WORN)

With smaller needles, CO 53 (56, 59, 62, 65, 68) sts. Work in St st for 12 rows. CO 20 sts at end of last knit row for front border and facing. With larger needles, work ridge row across all sts.
Knit 1 row, purl 1 row for 5 rows, ending with **knit** (RS) row completed at front edge.

Buttonholes:

Note: 2 buttonholes are made in the same row, one in the facing and the other in the band. First buttonhole row (WS): P2, BO 5 sts, purl until 6 sts from BO, BO 5 sts, purl to end of row.
Next row completes buttonholes (RS): Knit across row CO 5 sts over each buttonhole.
Cont in St st until same number of rows as right front to pocket opening, rep buttonholes when necessary to match button ms on right front.

Pocket opening:

(WS): P33 (34, 35, 36, 37, 38) sts, work ridge row on next 27 (29, 29, 30, 31, 32) sts and sl these sts on holder for pocket, p13 (14, 15, 16, 17, 18) sts.
Next row (RS): K13 (14, 15, 16, 17, 18) sts, k27 (28, 29, 30, 31, 32) sts of pocket lining from holder, k33 (34, 35, 36, 37, 38) sts. Work even until same length as right front to underarm, cont to work buttonholes to match button ms on right front, completing 6th buttonholes at front edge on RS row before armhole and neck shaping begins. Purl 1 row.

Underarm and neck shaping:

Row 1 (RS): BO 6 sts beg of next row for underarm, knit to end—67 (70, 73, 76, 79, 82) sts.
Purl 1 row.
Row 3 (RS) decs: K2tog, knit to within 21 sts of end or row, ssk, k19 for border and facing—65 (68, 71, 74, 77, 80) sts.
Finish left front and all shaping to correspond with right front.

SLEEVES

With smaller needles, CO 50 (50, 54, 58, 62, 62) sts.

Cuff:

Row 1 (RS): *K2, p2; rep from * to last 2 sts, k2.
Row 2 (WS): *P2, k2; rep from * to last 2 sts, p2.
Rep rows 1 and 2 until cuff measures 4" from CO. Knit 1 row, inc 10 (13, 12, 11, 10, 13) sts evenly spaced across row—60 (63, 66, 69, 72, 75) sts.

Sleeve shaping:

With larger needles and working in St st, inc 1 st each side every inch (about 8 rows per inch) 15 times—90 (93, 96, 99, 102, 105) sts.
Work even in St st until sleeve measures 15–3/4 (16, 16–1/4, 16–1/2, 16–3/4, 17)" above rib, ending with RS row completed.

Cap shaping:

BO 6 sts beg of next 2 rows—78 (81, 84, 87, 90, 93) sts.
Dec 1 st each side every other row 3 (4, 5, 6, 7, 8) times—72 (73, 74, 75, 76, 77) sts.
BO 2 sts at beg of next 20 rows—32 (33, 34, 35, 36, 37) sts.
BO 3 sts at beg of next 2 rows—26 (27, 28, 29, 30, 31) sts.
BO rem 26 (27, 28, 29, 30, 31) sts.

For Sleeve with Stripes

Work same as plain sleeve, until piece measures 12" above inc row, ending with RS row completed.

Make stripes:

Cont inc as for plain sleeve. At the same time work [4 rows in CC, 6 rows MC] twice, then 4 rows CC. Work even with MC until sleeve is same length as plain sleeve to underarm. Finish same as plain sleeve.

FINISHING

Block all pieces and allow to dry completely. Fold pocket hem along turning ridge and with threaded tapestry needle, whipstitch (see Glossary) to WS. Sew pocket linings to WS of fronts. Turn back front facing for 10 sts and hem to WS with whipstitch. Sew buttonholes tog, working through both thicknesses of band and facing. Kitchener st (see Glossary) both ends of neck border tog. With threaded tapestry needle, sew seams tog with mattress st (see Glossary). Whipstitch inner edge of neck border to back neck edge, and hem other edge over this seam. Turn back hem at lower edge along ridge and whipstitch to WS. Sew in sleeves to armhole on WS using backstitch (see Glossary). Steam all seams.

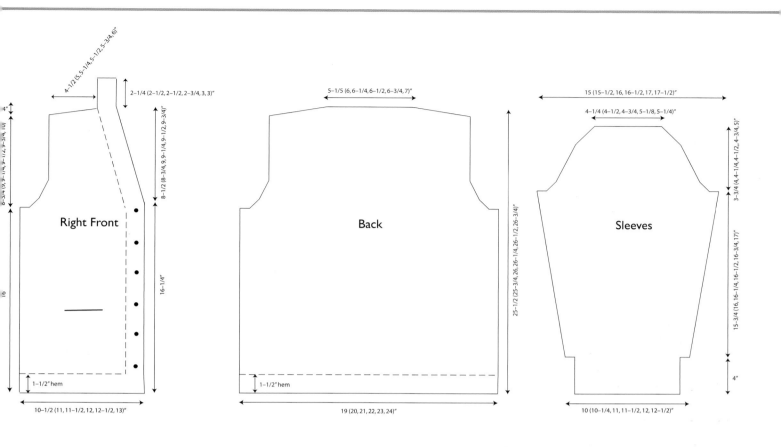

Right Front

4-1/2 (5, 5-1/4, 5-1/2, 5-3/4, 6)"

2-1/4 (2-1/2, 2-1/2, 2-3/4, 3, 3)"

8-1/2 (8-3/4, 9, 9-1/4, 9-1/2, 9-3/4)"

6-3/4 (9, 9-1/4, 9-1/2, 9-3/4, 10)"

4"

16

16-1/4"

1-1/2" hem

10-1/2 (11, 11-1/2, 12, 12-1/2, 13)"

Back

5-1/5 (6, 6-1/4, 6-1/2, 6-3/4, 7)"

25-1/2 (25-3/4, 26, 26-1/4, 26-1/2, 26-3/4)"

1-1/2" hem

19 (20, 21, 22, 23, 24)"

Sleeves

15 (15-1/2, 16, 16-1/2, 17, 17-1/2)"

4-1/4 (4-1/2, 4-3/4, 5-1/8, 5-1/4)"

3-3/4 (4, 4-1/4, 4-1/2, 4-3/4, 5)"

15-3/4 (16, 16-1/4, 16-1/2, 16-3/4, 17)"

4"

10 (10-1/4, 11, 11-1/2, 12, 12-1/2)"

Men's Jacket,
published by Columbia Minerva, 1960s

This good-looking jacket is knit in worsted-weight yarn and sized for men or teens. It's an easy pattern that knits up quickly on large needles. The zippered front, slanted pockets, set-in sleeves, and contrast color trim add style and interest.

PATTERN STITCH (MULTIPLE OF 3 STS)
Row 1 (WS): Purl.
Row 2 (RS): K1, *wyib, sl 1 pwise tbl , k2; rep from * across to last 2 sts, sl 1, k1.
Rep rows 1 and 2 for patt.

BACK
With smaller needles and MC, CO 96 (102, 108, 114) sts.
Change to larger needles and work in patt until back measures 15–1/2" from CO.

Shape underarm:
BO 5 sts at beg of next 2 rows—86 (92, 98, 104) sts.
Dec 1 st each side every other row 4 (4, 5, 5) times—78 (84, 88, 94) sts.
Work even in patt until armhole measures 9 (9–1/2, 10, 10–1/2)" from armhole BO.

Shoulder shaping:
BO 9 (9, 10, 11) sts beg of next 4 rows—42 (48, 48, 50) sts.
BO 7 (10, 9, 10) sts at beg of next 2 rows—28 (28, 30, 30) sts.
BO rem 28 (28, 30, 30) sts for back neck.

Pocket Linings (make 2)
With larger needles and MC, CO 21 sts. Work in patt for 2–1/2", ending with WS row completed for right pocket and RS row for left pocket. Sl sts on holder. Cut yarn leaving 4" tail.

RIGHT FRONT (AS WORN)
With smaller needles and MC, CO 39 (42, 45, 48) sts. Change to larger needles and work in patt until front measures 3" from CO edge, ending with RS row completed.

Pocket:
Next row (WS): Purl 15 and sl these sts to holder, purl to end of row—24 (27, 30, 33) sts.
Next 3 rows: Work even on rem sts.
Next row (WS): P2tog, purl to end of row—23 (26, 29, 32) sts.
Dec 1 st at same edge every 4th row 8 times more—15 (18, 21, 24) sts.
Next 2 rows: Work even.
Sl the rem 15 (18, 21, 24) sts on holder, *do not break yarn.*
Sl 21 sts of pocket lining for right pocket to larger needles. With another strand of MC work across the 21 pocket lining sts, then across the 15 sts at side edge.

SIZE
Chest: 36 (38, 40, 42)"

FINISHED MEASUREMENTS
Chest circumference: 37-3/4 (40-1/2, 42-1/2, 44-3/4)"
Length : 26 (26-1/2, 27, 27-1/2)", including lower border
Sleeve length from cuff to underarm: 20"

MATERIALS
Yarn—CYCA #4 Medium, 100% wool or blend: About 1400 (1400, 1680, 1680) yds main color (MC); 280 yds contrast color (CC) for trim

Size 4 [3.5 mm]; size 9 [5.5 mm] knitting needles
Size 0 steel crochet hook
Separating zipper for center fronts
Tapestry needle
2 stitch holders
Long sewing pins with large, colored heads

GAUGE
20 sts and 24 rows = 4" [10 cm] in patt st on size 9 [5.5 mm] needles. *Adjust needle size as necessary to obtain correct gauge.*

Men's jacket, right.

Work these 36 sts for 37 rows more until even with pocket opening, ending with WS row completed.
Next row (RS): BO 12 sts, work to end of row—24 sts.
Next row: Purl. Cut yarn leaving 4" tail.
Next row (RS): Sl the 15 (18, 21, 24) sts at front edge to same needle holding 24 sts—39 (42, 45, 48) sts.
Work even on these sts in patt to underarm.

Underarm shaping:
Row 1 (WS): BO 5 sts beg of row for underarm, work in patt to end of row—34 (37, 40, 43) sts.
Row 2 (RS): Work even.
Row 3: Dec 1 st beg of row, work in patt to end of row—33 (36, 39, 42) sts.

Rep Rows 2 and 3 another 3 (3, 4, 4) times—30 (33, 35, 38) sts.
Work even until armhole measures 6–1/2 (7, 7–1/2, 8)" from armhole BO, ending with WS row completed.

Neck shaping:
Row 1 (RS): BO 3 (3, 4, 4) sts at front edge, work in patt to end of row—27 (30, 31, 34) sts.
Row 2 (WS): Work even.
Row 3: Dec 1 st at neck edge, work in patt to end of row—26 (29, 30, 33) sts.
Rep last 2 rows once more—25 (28, 29, 32) sts. Work even in patt until armhole measures same as back, ending with RS row completed.

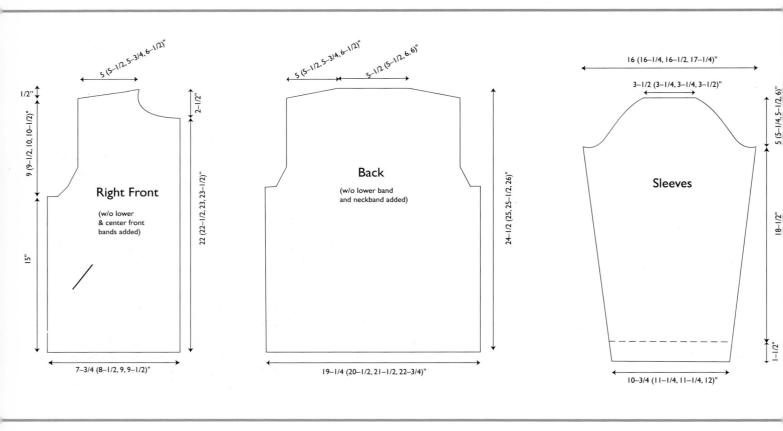

Right Front
(w/o lower & center front bands added)

5 (5-1/2, 5-3/4, 6-1/2)"
1/2"
2-1/2"
9 (9-1/2, 10, 10-1/2)"
22 (22-1/2, 23, 23-1/2)"
15"
7-3/4 (8-1/2, 9, 9-1/2)"

Back
(w/o lower band and neckband added)

5 (5-1/2, 5-3/4, 6-1/2)"
5-1/2 (5-1/2, 6, 6)"
24-1/2 (25, 25-1/2, 26)"
19-1/4 (20-1/2, 21-1/2, 22-3/4)"

Sleeves

16 (16-1/4, 16-1/2, 17-1/4)"
3-1/2 (3-1/4, 3-1/4, 3-1/2)"
5 (5-1/4, 5-1/2, 6)"
18-1/2"
1-1/2"
10-3/4 (11-1/4, 11-1/4, 12)"

Shoulder shaping:
Row 1 (WS): BO 9 (9, 10, 11) sts at armhole edge—16 (19, 19, 21) sts.
Row 2 (RS): Work even in patt.
Rep Rows 1 and 2 once more—7 (10, 9, 10) sts
Row 5 (WS): BO rem 7 (10, 9, 10) sts.

LEFT FRONT (AS WORN)
Work same as right front for 3", ending with RS row completed.

Pocket:
Next row: Purl to last 15 sts, sl these sts on holder.
Finish left front to correspond to right front, working armhole and shoulder shaping on RS rows, and neck shaping on WS rows.

Sleeves
With smaller needles and CC, cast on 54 (56, 56, 60) sts.
Row 1 (RS): Work in k1, p1 rib. Cut CC leaving 4" tail.
Row 2 (WS): Join MC, purl.
Next 10 rows: Work in rib with MC. Cut MC leaving 4" tail.
Next row: Join CC, knit 1 row.
Next 2 rows: Cont with CC, work in rib. Cut CC leaving 4" tail
With larger needles, join MC; purl 1 row, inc 1 st for sizes 40 and 42" only—54 (57, 57, 60) sts.

Sleeve shaping:
Working in patt, inc 1 st each side every 10th row 4 (3, 4, 4) times—62 (63, 63, 68) sts.
Inc 1 st each side every 6th row 9 times—80 (81, 83, 86) sts. Work even until sleeve measures 20" or desired length from CO.

Cap shaping:
BO 5 sts beg of next 2 rows—70 (71, 73, 76) sts.
Dec 1 st each side every other row 2 (3, 4, 5) times—66 (65, 65, 66) sts.
BO 2 sts at beg of next 24 rows—18 (17, 17, 18) sts.
BO rem 18 (17, 17, 18) sts.
Work second sleeve the same.
Block all pieces and allow to dry completely. Sew shoulder seams tog with backstitch (see Glossary). Sew sleeves in place with backstitch. Sew underarm and sleeve seams with mattress st (see Glossary).

Borders
With smaller needle and CC, starting at left front edge on RS of work pick up and knit 175 (187, 199, 211) sts around lower edge.
Row 1 (WS): P1 *k1, p1; rep from * across.
Row 2 (RS): Work in rib, inc 1 st each side—177 (189, 201, 213) sts. Cut CC leaving 4" tail.
Row 3: With MC, purl across row.
Row 4: With MC, rep row 2—179 (191, 203, 215) sts.
Row 5: Work in ribbing.
Rows 6–9: Rep rows 4 and 5 twice.
Row 10: Rep row 4. Cut MC leaving 4" tail.
Row 11: With CC, purl.
Row 12: Rep row 2. BO in rib.

Neck:
With smaller needles and CC, starting at right neck edge on RS, pick up and knit 77 (77, 83, 83) sts.
Row 1 (WS): Knit.
Row 2 (RS): Inc 1 st in first st, k1, *p1, k1; rep from * to last st, inc 1 st in last st—79 (79, 85, 85) sts. Cut CC leaving 4" tail.
Row 3: Starting with row 3, work same as border on lower edge. BO in rib.

Right Front Border
With smaller needles and CC, starting at lower right front on RS pick up and knit 119 (123, 127, 131) sts to neck. Work same as neck border.

Left Front Border
With smaller needles and CC, starting at neck on RS pick up and knit 119 (123, 127, 131) sts. Work same as right front border.

FINISHING
Seam mitered edges of borders. Sew pocket linings in place. Pin zipper in place then sew using backstitch (see Glossary). Remove pins. With CC, on RS crochet 1 row of sl st on pocket edges. Ch 1, turn and work 1 more row of sl sts. If desired, face pocket edge with 1" grosgrain ribbon. Weave in all loose ends to WS. Lightly steam seams.

Women's Irish Panel Sweater, published by Minerva, 1965

Although it is shown here as a ski sweater, this project is suitable for any occasion. Its main pattern is simple, with enough interest to hold the knitter's attention. The easy Irish panel of cables, twists, and popcorn stitches is centered on the front, and also forms the muff pocket.

Women's Irish Panel Sweater, right.

SIZE
32 (34, 36, 38)"

FINISHED MEASUREMENTS
Width at chest: 18 (18–3/4, 19–1/4, 20–1/4)"
Length: 24 (24–1/2, 24–3/4, 25)"
Sleeve length to underarm: 15 (15–1/2, 16, 16)"

MATERIALS
Yarn—CYCA #5 Bulky, any yarn that has some natural
    elasticity: About 1000 (1150, 1300, 1450) yds.

Size 9 [5.5 mm]; size 10–1/2 [6.5 mm] knitting needles
Size G/6 [4 mm] crochet hook
Cable needle
Tapestry needle
Stitch holders

GAUGE
14 sts and 20 rows = 4" [10 cm] in main patt on size
    10–1/2 [6.5 mm] needles. *Adjust needle size as
    necessary to obtain correct gauge.*

BACK

With smaller needles, CO 61 (63, 65, 69) sts.
Row 1 (RS): K1, *p1, k1; rep from * across row.
Row 2: P1, *k1, p1; rep from * across row.
Row 3: Rep row 1.
Row 4: Purl, inc 1 st each side—63 (65, 67, 71) sts.
Change to larger needles. Work main patt as foll:

Main pattern:

Rows 1, 3, and 5 (RS): Knit
Rows 2 and 4: Purl
Row 6 (WS): Knit.
Rep these 6 rows for main patt. Work even until back
measures 15–1/2" from CO edge.

Underarm shaping:

BO 4 sts beg of next 2 rows—55 (57, 59, 63) sts. Dec 1
st each side every other row 4 (4, 4, 5) times—47 (49,
51, 53) sts. Work even until armhole measures about
6–1/2 (6–3/4, 7, 7–1/4)" from first BO row, ending
with RS row completed.

Neck and shoulder shaping:

Next row (WS): P16 (17, 17, 18) sts and sl them to a st
holder, BO center 15 (15, 17, 17) sts for back neck, purl
to end of row—16 (17, 17, 18) sts.
Next row (RS): Work even.
Next row (WS): BO 2 sts at neck edge once—14 (15,
15, 16) sts. Work even until armhole measures 7–1/2
(7–3/4, 8, 8–1/4)", ending with WS row completed.
Next row (RS): BO 5 sts at armhole edge, work even in
patt—9 (10, 10, 11) sts.
Next row (WS): Work even.
Rep last 2 rows 1 (2, 2, 1) time(s) more—4 (0, 0, 6) sts.

Sizes 32 and 38"only

BO 4 (0, 0, 6) sts at beg of next armhole edge. Starting
at neck edge, work other side.

FRONT

Note: The extra sts on front accommodate the difference
in gauges for the front panel.

With smaller needles, CO 63 (67, 69, 73) sts. Work in rib
same as back for 3 rows.
Next row (incs): P 18 (20, 21, 23) sts, inc 1 in next st,
then in every 5th st 5 times more, purl to end of row—
69 (73, 75, 79) sts.

Muff pocket:

Row 1 (RS): Change to larger needles, k18 (20, 21, 23)
sts, sl next 33 sts to holder for Easy Irish panel, CO 27 sts
on right-hand needle, then knit rem 18 (20, 21, 23) sts.
Cont in main patt on the 63 (67, 69, 73) sts for 30 rows
more, ending with row 1 of patt completed.
Next row: P18, (20, 21, 23) sts and sl them to a holder,
BO center 27 sts, purl to end of row, sl rem 18 (20, 21,
23) sts to another holder, do not cut yarn, leave yarn
attached to work for later.
Sl the center 33 sts from holder to smaller needles.

Easy Irish panel:

Row 1 (RS): Join new ball of yarn. With larger needles,
work the 33 center sts as foll: P2, k6, p6, sl next 3 sts to
cable needle and hold in back of work, k2 from left
needle, p1 and k2 from cable needle, p6, k6, p2.
Rows 2, 4, 6, 8, 10, and 12 (WS): Knit the knit sts and
purl the purl sts as they appear.
Row 3: P2, k6, p5, [*right twist:* sl next st to cable needle
and hold in back, knit next 2 sts from left needle, p1
from cable needle], p1, [*left twist:* sl next 2 sts to cable
needle and hold in front, purl next st from left needle, k2
from cable needle], p5, k6, p2.
Row 5: P2, [*twist cable:* sl next 3 sts to cable needle and
hold in back, k3 from left needle, k3 from cable needle],
p4, work right twist same as row 3, p3, work left twist
same as row 3, p4, work cable twist, p2.
Row 7: P2, k6, p3, right twist, p5, left twist, p3, k6, p2.
Row 9: P2, k6, p2, right twist, p7, left twist, p2, k6, p2.
Row 11: P2, k6, p1, right twist, p9, left twist, p1, k6, p2.
Row 13: P2, twist cable, p1, k2, p5, work popcorn as foll:
knit in front, back, front, back, front loops of next st (5
loops from 1 st), p1, turn work, k1, p5, turn work, k5,
then p5, k2, p1, twist cable, p2.

Row 14 (WS): K2, p6, k1, p2, k5, to complete popcorn skip first st on left needle, then with point of right needle pass 2nd, 3rd, 4th, and 5th sts on left needle over first st, then knit this st, k5, p2, k1, p6, k2 to finish row.
Row 15: P2, k6, p1, left twist, p9, right twist, p1, k6, p2.
Rows 16, 18, 20, and 22: Knit the knit sts and purl the purl sts.
Row 17: P2, k6, p2, left twist, p7, right twist, p2, k6, p2.
Row 19: P2, k6, p3, left twist, p5, right twist, p3, k6, p2.
Row 21: P2, twist cable, p4, left twist, p3, right twist, p4, twist cable, p2.
Row 23: P2, k6, p5, left twist, p1, right twist, p5, k6, p2.
Row 24: Knit the knit sts and purl the purl sts. End of patt rep.
After completing 24 rows of Easy Irish panel, work rows 1–8 of same patt, cut yarn.
On RS with attached yarn, knit across 18 (20, 21, 23) sts on holder, cont with Easy Irish panel (row 9) across center 33 sts, then knit across the 18 (20, 21, 23) sts from other holder—69 (73, 75, 79) sts. Cont in both patts as est on these sts until front is the same length as back to underarm.

Underarm shaping:
BO 4 sts at beg of next 2 rows—61 (65, 67, 71) sts. Dec 1 st each side every other row 4 (4, 4, 5) times—53 (57, 59, 61) sts. Work even in patts until armhole measures about 4–3/4 (5, 5–1/4, 5–1/2)" above BO sts, ending with RS row completed.

Neck and shoulder shaping:
Work 20 (21, 21, 22) sts and sl them to a holder, BO center 13 (15, 17, 17) sts for front neck, work in patt to end of row—20 (21, 21, 22) sts.
Next row (RS): Work even.
Next row (WS) BO 2 sts at neck edge, work in patt to end—18 (19, 19, 20) sts.
Rep last 2 rows 2 times more—14 (15, 15, 16) sts. Work even until armholes measure same as back.
On next RS row BO 5 sts at armhole edge—9 (10, 10, 11) sts.
Next row (WS): Work even.
Rep last 2 rows 1 (2, 2, 1) time(s)—4 (0, 0, 6) sts.

Sizes 32 and 38" only
Next row: BO 4 (0, 0, 6) sts at armhole edge. Starting at neck edge, work other side.

SLEEVES
With smaller needles, CO 35 (37, 39, 41) sts. Work in rib same as back for 3 rows. Purl 1 row.
Rows 1–6: Change to larger needles and work in main patt, beg with row 1.
Inc 1 st each side beg with row 7—37 (39, 41, 43) sts, then every 8th row 3 times—43 (45, 47, 49) sts, then every 10th row 3 times—49 (51, 53, 55) sts.
Work even until sleeve measures about 15 (15–1/2, 16, 16)" from CO.

Cap:
BO 4 sts at beg of next 2 rows—41 (43, 45, 47) sts. Dec 1 st every other row 10 (11, 12, 13) times and 21 sts.
BO 3 sts at beg of next 4 rows—9 sts.
BO 9 sts.
Work second sleeve the same.

Collar Back
With smaller needles, CO 57 (57, 59, 59) sts for collar back. Work in rib same as back for 3 rows. Purl 1 row.
Rows 1–3: Change to larger needles and work in main patt.
Dec 1 st each side beg of next row—55 (55, 57, 57) sts.
Rep dec row every 4th row 6 times more—43 (43, 45, 45) sts.
Work 2 more rows, ending with row 6 of main patt completed.
Change to smaller needles and work 4 rows in rib.
BO in rib.

Collar Front
With smaller needles, CO 61 (63, 65, 65) sts for front collar. With 4 (6, 6,) sts more throughout, shape same as back collar—47 (49, 51, 51) sts.

FINISHING
Sew shoulder seams, then sleeves in place with backstitch (see Glossary). Sew underarm and sleeve seams with mattress st (see Glossary). Sew CO and BO edges of pocket in place with whipstitch (see Glossary). Sew side edges of collar front and back tog with mattress st. With WS tog, sew collar neatly in place around neckline, aligning collar seams at shoulders. Fold collar over to RS. On RS, crochet 1 row sc (see Glossary) on sides of pocket. Weave in loose ends to WS.

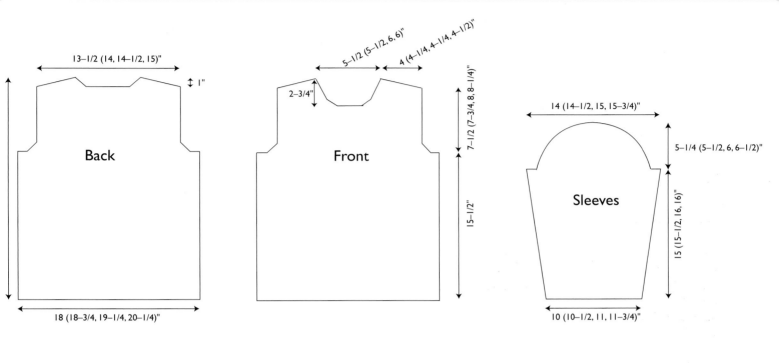

Back

13–1/2 (14, 14–1/2, 15)"

1"

18 (18–3/4, 19–1/4, 20–1/4)"

Front

5–1/2 (5–1/2, 6, 6)"

4 (4–1/4, 4–1/4, 4–1/2)"

2–3/4"

7–1/2 (7–3/4, 8, 8–1/4)"

15–1/2"

Sleeves

14 (14–1/2, 15, 15–3/4)"

5–1/4 (5–1/2, 6, 6–1/2)"

15 (15–1/2, 16, 16)"

10 (10–1/2, 11, 11–3/4)"

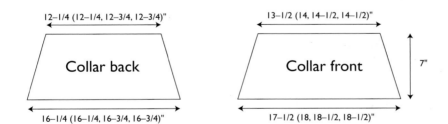

Collar back

12–1/4 (12–1/4, 12–3/4, 12–3/4)"

16–1/4 (16–1/4, 16–3/4, 16–3/4)"

Collar front

13–1/2 (14, 14–1/2, 14–1/2)"

7"

17–1/2 (18, 18–1/2, 18–1/2)"

Women's Mohair Sweater with Hood, published by Fleisher, 1965

This mohair sweater is hip-length and features a reverse stockinette stitch border adorned with popcorns. Easy-fit, bracelet-length raglan sleeves with the same popcorn border and a snug-fitting hood framed with popcorns completes the look. Worked in a blend of mohair and wool on large needles for an oversized fit, this project can be completed in no time at all. Don't like popcorns around the hips? Work the borders in reverse stockinette stitch without them, or in garter stitch.

NOTE
2 strands are held tog and worked as one throughout the sweater.

STITCH GUIDE
Popcorn
(RS) Work popcorn as foll: k1, p1, k1, p1, k1 all in 1 st, turn work, purl these 5 sts, turn work, knit these 5 sts; *with left needle lift the 2nd st on right needle over first st on right needle and drop it; rep from * with 3rd, 4th, 5th sts, until only 1 st rem of the 5 popcorn sts.

BACK
With smaller needles, CO 59 (65) sts.
Facing: [Purl 1 row. Knit 1 row] 2 times, purl 1 row.

Establish border pattern:
Row 1 (RS): Change to larger needles, purl.
Rows 2, 4, 6 (WS): Knit.
Row 3 (popcorns): P5, *work a popcorn (see stitch guide above) in next st, p5; rep from * to end.
Row 5: Purl.
Row 7 (popcorns): P2, *work popcorn in next st, p5; rep from * to last 3 sts, work popcorn in next st, p2.
Row 8: Knit.
Rep rows 1–8 once more to complete border.
Change to St st (knit 1 row on RS, purl 1 row on WS).
Work even until St st portion measures 10" above border and facing or desired length, ending with WS row completed.

Raglan Shaping:
Dec row (RS): K2, ssk, knit to last 4 sts, k2tog, k2—57 (63) sts.
Next row: Purl.
Rep last 2 rows 21 (22) times more, ending with RS row completed—15 (19) sts.

Sizes 30–32" only
Next row (WS): Purl

Sizes 34–36" only
Next row (WS): Purl, dec 4 sts evenly spaced across row—(15) sts.

SIZE
30–32 (34–36)"

FINISHED MEASUREMENTS
Width at chest: 19–1/2 (21–1/2)"
Length: 23–1/2 (26, 27)"
Sleeve length to underarm: 17 (18–1/2, 18–1/2)"

MATERIALS
Yarn—CYCA #5 Bulky, any mohair/wool blend that has some natural elasticity: About 1520 (1719) yds.
Size 9 [5.5 mm]; size 10–1/2 [6.5 mm] knitting needles. Plus spare size 10–1/2 [6.5mm] needle.
Tapestry needle
Stitch holders

GAUGE
12 sts and 18 rows = 4" [10 cm] in St st on size 10–1/2 needles. *Adjust needle size as necessary to obtain correct gauge.*

All sizes
Place rem 15 sts on holder for hood.

FRONT
Work same as back until there are 16 (17) raglan dec rows completed, ending with RS row completed—27 (31) sts.

Divide for neck:
Next row (WS): P12 (14) sts, place these sts on holder for right side of neck; p3, place on holder for neck rib; purl rem 12 (14) sts for left side of neck.
Dec row (RS): Dec raglan as before, knit to within 2 sts of end, k2tog at neck edge; 10 (12) sts.
Next row: Purl.

Rep these last 2 rows 3 (4) times more—4 sts.
Next row: K1, sl 1, k2tog, psso (double dec made)—2 sts.
Next row: P2tog. Fasten off last st.
With WS of work facing, remove 12 (14) sts from holder holding right neck sts and sl onto needle, join yarn at neck edge and work as foll:
Dec Row (RS): Ssk, knit to last 4 sts, k2tog, k2—10 (12) sts.
Next Row (WS): Purl.
Rep these last 2 rows 3 (4) times more—4 sts.
Next row: Sl 1, k2tog, psso (double dec made), k1—2 sts.
Next row: P2tog. Fasten off last st.

SLEEVES
With smaller needles and 2 strands of yarn, CO 23 sts.

Facing: [Purl 1 row. Knit 1 row] 2 times, purl 1 row.

Establish border pattern:
Change to larger needles and work 16 border rows same as back.
Next row (RS): K1f&b (see Glossary), *k1, k1f&b; rep from * to end of row—35 sts.
Next row: Purl.
Cont in St st, inc 1 st each side every 8th (6th) row 4 (6) times—43 (47) sts.
Work even until sleeve measures 9" above the border patt, ending with WS row completed.
Next row (RS): Knit, inc 1 st each side of row—45 (49) sts.
Next row (WS): Purl.
Rep last 2 rows twice more—49 (53) sts.
Work raglan dec rows same as back until 7 (9) sts.
Purl 1 row after last dec row.
Next row (RS): K2 (3), k3tog, k2 (3) sts—5 (7) sts.

Sizes 30–32" only
Next row (WS): Purl.

Sizes 34–36" only
Next row (WS): Purl, dec 2 sts evenly spaced across row—5 sts.

All sizes
Place rem 5 sts on holder.

HOOD
From WS of work, sl 5 sts of first sleeve, 15 sts of back, and 5 sts of 2nd sleeve to smaller needles—25 sts.
Row 1 (RS): With smaller needle and 2 strands of yarn, k1, *p1, k1; rep from * to end.
Row 2 (WS): P1, *k1, p1; rep from * to end.
Rep last 2 rows once more (4 rows total).
Change to larger needle and St st. Work even until hood measures about 9–1/2" above rib, ending with WS row completed.

Border
With spare larger needle and 2 strands of yarn, with RS facing and beg at first row above neck rib pick up and knit 23 sts along right side edge of 9–1/2" of St st just worked, drop separate strands of yarn; with same needle, knit across the 25 sts of back of hood; with 48 sts now on needle and RS facing, pick up and knit 23 sts along left side edge of St st to correspond with other side—71 sts.
Next row (WS): Knit.
Work 16 rows of border patt same as back. Change to smaller needles and [Knit 1 row. Purl 1 row] 3 times (6 rows total). BO kwise. Roll these 6 rows back onto RS of work and using 1 strand of yarn, hem in place with whipstitch (see Glossary).

This great Mohair Sweater with Hood
first appeared in *New Mohair Hand Knits,*
published by Bear Brand and Fleisher Yarns in 1965.

Front Neck Ribbing

With smaller needle, 2 strands of yarn, and RS facing, pick up and knit 8 sts on left neck edge, knit 3 sts from holder, pick up and knit 8 sts on right neck edge—19 sts.
Row 1 (WS): P1, *k1, p1; rep from * to end.
Row 2 (RS): K1, *p1, k1; rep from * to end.
Rep last 2 rows once more.
BO in rib.

FINISHING

Using single strand of yarn, sew raglan seams, joining sleeves to front and back with mattress st (see Glossary). Sew underarm and sleeve seams using same method. Turn back facings to WS and whipstitch in place. Sew lower edges of front hood border to top of front neck rib. Weave in loose ends to WS. Steam lightly, blocking to size.

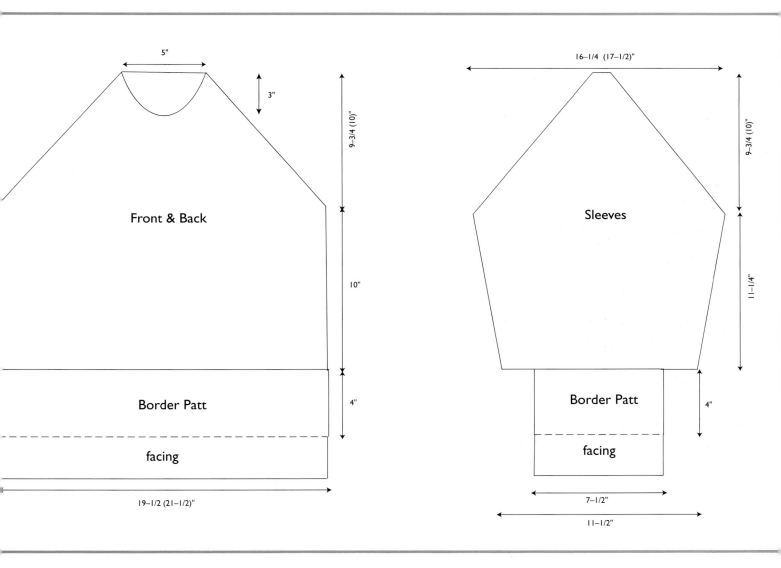

W

Woolcrest

knitting trends

PATTERNS FOR THE FAMILY IN KNITTING & CROCHET

by the F.W. Woolworth Co. Limited

1970s

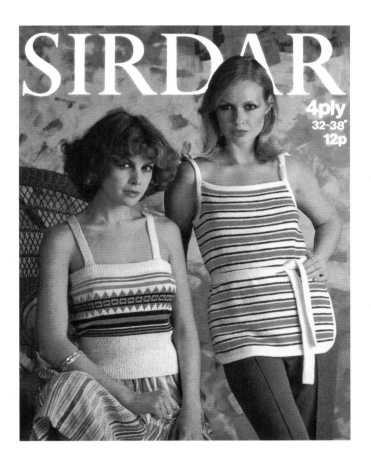

Discos, platform shoes, hip-hugging bell bottoms, shiny fabrics, and ethnic styles are all synonymous with the 1970s. Knitters could choose from such projects as long vests in small geometric patterns worked in stranded knitting; long or short halter tops; knit or crocheted tanks or shells paired with long cardigans; scoop-neck tanks designed to be worn over blouses; or full-length leg warmers decorated with bands of zig-zag, paired with a matching turtleneck sweater in bulky yarn.

The ethnic clothing craze that had gained acceptance in the 1960s flourished in the 1970s, and patterns for multicolored shawls, ponchos, and hooded capes were widely available. Patterns for everything from Tyrolean cardigans and hats embellished with traditional-style embroidery to bikinis, short pants, and maxi-length skirts were popular in the 1970s, along with updated designs for classic V-neck and crew-neck sweaters.

In the 1970s, many thicker (and some bulky) yarns were common. Synthetic yarns were widely available and heavily promoted, although projects made with natural yarns were still available. Very long scarves (think Dr. Who), hats, and mitts worked in either natural fibers or synthetics were staples in many fall and winter issues of craft publications and were regularly teamed with matching sweaters.

Halter Top,
published by Woolcrest, 1975

This great little top is very stylish and easy to knit. With a back that is open and very low and front straps that tie around the neck, this halter is perfect for those warm summer days and evenings.

NOTE
Any length adjustment should be made in the rib before the upper shaping begins.

LEFT FRONT
With smaller needles, CO 108 (114, 122, 128) sts and work in k1, p1 rib for 5–1/2" or desired length. Change to larger needles.
Next row: K34 (37, 37, 40) sts, turn work, CO 40 (40, 48, 48) sts.
Work on these 74 (77, 85, 88) sts first for left front, leaving rem sts on a spare needle or st holder.
Next row: Purl.
Next row: Knit to last 2 sts, k2tog—73 (76, 84, 87) sts.
Next row: Purl.
Rep the last 2 rows until 63 (66, 74, 77) sts rem, ending at side edge.

Raglan armhole shaping:
Next row: BO 2 (3, 5, 6) sts, knit to last 2 sts, k2tog—60 (62, 68, 70) sts.

Next row: Purl.
Next row: K1, ssk, knit to last 2 sts, k2tog—58 (60, 66, 68) sts.
Rep the last 2 rows until 26 (28, 18, 20) sts rem.
Cont armhole dec as before, now dec 1 st at front edge on every foll 4th row until 8 sts rem, ending with **a purl** (WS) row completed.
Keeping front edge straight (no decs), cont armhole dec only until 3 sts rem. Place marker at this point. Work even in St st on these 3 sts until strap measures 12" from marker.
BO all sts.

RIGHT FRONT
Sl 74 (77, 85, 88) sts from holder to larger needle. With RS of work facing and larger needles, rejoin yarn to inner edge of these sts and knit to last 34 (37, 37, 40) sts, mark the last st with a safety pin, knit to end.
Next row: Purl.
Dec 1 st at beg (front edge) of next row, then every

SIZE
32 (34, 36, 38)"

FINISHED MEASUREMENTS
Chest circumference: 34 (36–1/2, 40, 41–3/4)"
Length to shoulder: 16–1/4 (16–3/4, 17–1/4, 17–3/4)"

MATERIALS
Yarn—CYCA #1 Super Fine, silk, cotton blend, sparkly
   synthetic, wool: About 780 (890, 975, 1070) yds

Size 2 [2.75 mm]; size 3 [3.25 mm] knitting needles
Tapestry needle
Stitch holders

GAUGE
27 sts and 36 rows = 4" [10 cm] in St st on size 3
[3.25 mm] needles. *Adjust needle size if necessary
to obtain correct gauge.*

other row, until 62 (65, 73, 76) sts rem, ending with RS row completed.

Raglan armhole shaping:

Next row (WS): BO 2 (3, 5, 6) sts, purl to end—60 (62, 68, 70) sts.

Next row: k2tog, knit to last 3 sts, k2tog, k1—58 (60, 66, 68) sts.

Next row: Purl.

Complete the same as left front.

BACK

Using smaller needles, CO 108 (114, 122, 128) sts and work 5–1/2" or desired length in k1, p1 rib. Change to larger needles and work 3 rows in St st beg with RS row.

Shape back:

Next row (WS): Purl 21 sts, BO center 66 (72, 80, 86) sts, purl to end.

Complete this side first, leaving rem sts on spare needle or st holder.

Dec 1 st at back edge on every row until 2 sts rem. BO. With RS of work facing, rejoin yarn to inner edge of rem sts and complete the same as first side, reversing all shaping.

FINISHING

Block pieces to size. Join side seams with mattress st (see Glossary). Using whipstitch (see Glossary), sew CO sts neatly at lower edge of left front behind right front to m.

Edging

With crochet hook and RS of work facing, rejoin yarn to lower edge of right front and work 2 rows of firm sc (see Glossary), working up along the front, around neck, all around straps, down side of front, down back slope, across back, and all around lower edge of left front. Begin new rows with Ch 1. Fasten off.

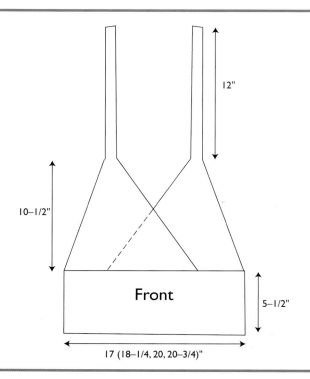

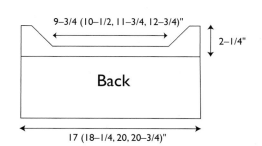

Men's Waistcoat, published by Woolcrest, 1975

This close-fitting waistcoat is suitable for wearing under suit jackets or sport coats. The back is worked all in rib, which helps maintain the tailored fit, and the fronts are worked in a basic slip-stitch pattern. Buttonholes are made when the left front is worked. The front and back of the neck are edged with three rows of single crochet to prevent the edges from rolling.

BACK

With smaller needles, CO 100 (104, 110, 116, 120, 126) sts. Work in k1, p1 rib for 2". Change to larger needles and cont in rib until back measures 12 (12, 13, 13, 14, 14)" or desired length from CO. To determine the correct length, ease out rib until back width measures 18 (19, 20, 21, 22, 23)" and pin in place on blocking board or folded towels before taking length measurement. You may have to remove sts from needle or divide them between 2 needles. Once measured, remove pins and cont work.

Shape underarm:

BO 5 sts at beg of next 2 rows—90 (94, 100, 106, 110, 116) sts.
Dec 1 st each side of next 4 (4, 5, 5, 6, 6) rows—82 (86, 90, 96, 98, 104) sts.
Dec 1 st each side every other row 6 (6, 6, 7, 7, 8) times—70 (74, 78, 82, 84, 88) sts.
Work even in rib patt until armholes measure 8–1/2 (9, 9, 9–1/2, 10, 10)" from BO.

Shoulders and back neck shaping:

BO 5 (5, 5, 6, 6, 6) sts beg of next 3 rows, working rest of row in rib patt—55 (59, 63, 64, 66, 70) sts.
Next row: BO 5 (5, 5, 6, 6, 6) sts, working in patt until there are 11 (12, 13, 12, 12, 13) sts on right-hand needle after BO, then BO next 28 (30, 32, 34, 36, 38) sts, work in patt to end. Complete this side first.
*Row 1: BO 5 (5, 5, 6, 6, 6) sts, work to last 2 sts, k2tog.
Row 2: K2tog, work to end.
BO rem 4 (5, 6, 4, 4, 5) sts*.
With RS facing, rejoin yarn to neck edge of rem sts and work to end. Rep from * to * to complete second shoulder.

RIGHT FRONT (AS WORN)

With smaller needles, CO 3 sts.
Row 1 (RS): K1, yf, sl 1 pwise, yb, k1, turn work, CO 3 sts—6 sts.
Row 2: Purl to end, turn work, CO 2 sts—8 sts
Row 3: *Yf, sl 1 pwise, yb, k1; rep from * to end, turn work CO 2 sts—10 sts.

Row 4: Work as row 2—12 sts.
Row 5: *K1, yf, sl 1 pwise, yb; rep from * to end, turn work CO 2 sts—14 sts.
Rep the last 4 rows until there are 48 (48, 48, 56, 56, 56) sts, ending with row 2 completed.
Next row: *Yf, sl 1, yb, k1; rep from * to end, turn work, CO 8 (12, 14, 10, 12, 16) sts—56 (60, 62, 66, 68, 72) sts.
Next row: Purl to last st, inc in last st—57 (61, 63, 67, 69, 73) sts.
Work even in patt until side edge measures 1/2" less than back to beg of armhole, ending with RS row completed at side edge.

Shape underarm and front neck:

Next row (WS): BO 5 sts, work in patt to last 2 sts, p2tog—51 (55, 57, 61, 63, 67) sts.
Dec 1 st at neck edge every other row. *At the same time,* dec 1 st at armhole edge on next 4 rows, then every other row 6 (8, 8, 10, 10, 12) times—33 (33, 35, 35, 37, 37) sts. Keeping armhole edge straight, dec 1 st at neck edge on every foll 4th row until 21 (21, 21, 23, 23, 23) sts rem. Work even until armhole measures same as back armhole to shoulder, ending at side edge.

Shoulders shaping:

BO 4 (4, 4, 5, 5, 5) sts at beg of next row, then every other row 3 times more—5 (5, 5, 3, 3, 3) sts.
Next row: Work even.
BO rem 5 (5, 5, 3, 3, 3) sts.
Mark positions along front edge for 5 buttons. Pm for first button about 1/2" above the end of point shaping at the lower edge. Pm for last button about 1" below first neck dec. Space rem of ms evenly between these two.

LEFT FRONT (AS WORN)

With smaller needles, CO 3 sts.
Row 1: Purl to end, turn work CO 3 sts—6 sts.
Row 2: *K1, yf, sl 1 pwise, yb; rep from * to end, turn work,

SIZE
Chest: 34 (36, 38, 40, 42, 44)"

FINISHED MEASUREMENTS
Chest circumference (buttoned): 36 (38, 40, 42, 44, 46)"
Length 21–1/4 (21–3/4, 22–3/4, 23–1/4, 24–3/4, 24–3/4)", not including front points

MATERIALS
Yarn—CYCA #3 Light, 100% wool or blend: About 1000 (1000, 1000, 1000, 1250, 1250) yds

Size 3 [3.25 mm]; size 6 [4 mm] knitting needles
Size D/3 [3.25 mm] crochet hook
5 buttons about 3/4" diameter
Stitch holders
Tapestry needle
Sewing needle and matching thread

GAUGE
24 sts and 38 rows = 4" [10 cm] in sl st patt used for fronts on size 6 [4 mm] needles. *Adjust needle size as necessary to obtain correct gauge.*

CO 2 sts—8 sts.
Row 3: Purl to end, turn work, CO 2 sts—10 sts.
Row 4: *Yf, sl 1 pwise, yb, k1; rep from * to end, turn work CO 2 sts—12 sts.
Row 5: Work as row 3.
Rep the last 4 rows until there are 48 (48, 48, 56, 56, 56) sts, ending with row 2 completed.
Next row: Purl to end, turn work CO 8 (12, 14, 10, 12, 16) sts—56 (60, 62, 66, 68, 72) sts.
Next row: *Yf, sl 1, yb, k1; rep from * to last st, inc in last st—57 (61, 63, 67, 69, 73) sts.
Work same as right front, reversing shaping and making buttonholes on WS rows to match button ms on right front. Work buttonholes as foll:

Buttonholes:

Row 1: Work 2 sts, BO next 3 sts, work to end of row.
Row 2: Work to BO sts, CO 3 sts, work last 2 sts in patt.
Rep these 2 rows for each buttonhole made.

FINISHING AND EDGING

Block pieces to size. When completely dry, join shoulder seams with backstitch (see Glossary), easing back shoulders to fit fronts as necessary. With crochet hook, RS facing, and beginning at right-side edge, work 1 row of firm sc (see Glossary) across right front, up front edge, around neck, down left front edge, and across to left-side seam. Work 1 more row sc, working 2 sc into sc at center point and lower-edge corner of each front. Work a 3rd row of sc, working 2 sc into each of the 2 sts at points and corners. Fasten off.

Armhole Edging

With smaller hook, work 3 rows of sc along each armhole edge. Fasten off. Pin back and front-side edges tog, easing as necessary. Join side seams with mattress st (see Glossary). Remove pins, lightly steam seams. With sewing needle and thread, sew on buttons.

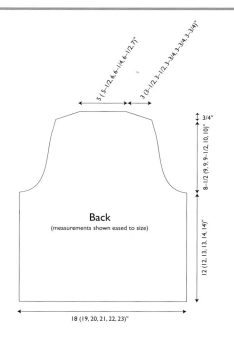

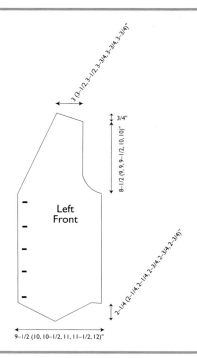

Kid's Footsie Sweater,
published by Woolcrest, 1975

Remember those little embroidered feet that adorned Hang Ten T-shirts and shorts back in the day? Perhaps those tiny footprints were the inspiration for this motif in the 1970s. The basic raglan design is a great sweater for children. If you prefer, omit the feet and insert another motif of your choosing, or make the front plain, without a motif.

BACK
With smaller needles and MC, CO 65 (67, 75, 81) sts.
Row 1: *K1, p1; rep from * to last st, k1.
Row 2: *P1, k1; rep from * to last st, p1.
Rep rows 1 and 2 for 2", inc 7 (9, 11, 10) sts evenly spaced across last row—72 (76, 86, 91) sts.
Change to larger needles and work in St st until back measures 9 (10, 12, 13)" from CO.

Begin raglan shaping:
BO 6 at beg of next 2 rows—60 (64, 74, 79) sts.
Dec 1 st each side every other row 15 (14, 21, 21) times—30 (36, 32, 37) sts.
Dec 1 st each side every 4th row 4 (5, 3, 4) times—22 (26, 26, 29) sts.
BO rem 22 (26, 26, 29) sts.

FRONT
Note: To prevent a hole when changing colors, bring color to be used under last color used. Wind colors on individual yarn bobbins, or count the number of sts in each color section and allow about 1/2" of yarn for each st. Cut long strands and let the strands dangle, pulling them into position when the chart indicates using that color.

Work same as back until last row of rib and inc are *completed*—72 (76, 85, 91) sts.
Change to larger needles and work in St st for 4 (5, 6, 7)" from CO edge, ending with WS row completed.
Next row (RS): K13 (15, 20, 23) sts, place marker, begin row 1 of chart, work 45 sts as shown on chart, changing colors as necessary, place marker, with MC, knit 14 (16, 20, 23) sts to end of row.
Next row (WS): Purl to m, sl m, work 45 sts as shown on chart row 2, sl m; with MC, purl to end of row. Keeping continuity of chart patt correct between ms, work in St st until front measures same as back to armholes, ending with WS row completed.

Begin raglan shaping:
BO 6 at beg of next 2 rows—60 (64, 74, 79) sts.
Dec 1 st each side every other row 15 (14, 21, 21) times, cont chart until completed. Then decrease 1 st each side every 4th row 4 (5, 3, 4) times.

At the same time, when front measures 13 (13–3/4, 16–1/2, 18)" from CO, begin neck shaping.

Neck shaping:
Work to center 10 (14, 13, 15) sts, attach a second ball of MC, drop previous yarn and with new yarn BO center 10 (14, 13, 15) sts, work to end of row. Working both sides of neck at the same time, each with its own ball of yarn, dec 1 st each neck edge every other row 6 (6, 6, 6, 8) times. Finish raglan shaping. BO.

SLEEVES
With smaller needles and MC, CO 35 (37, 41, 43) sts.
Work in k1, p1 rib same as back for 2", inc 5 sts evenly spaced across last row—40 (42, 46, 48) sts.

Sleeve shaping:
Change to larger needle, working in St st, inc 1 st each side every 6th (6th, 6th, 8th) row 8 (2, 3, 8) times—56 (46, 52, 64) sts.

SIZE
Chest: 23 (25, 28, 30)"

FINISHED MEASUREMENTS
Chest width: 13 (13–3/4, 15–1/2, 16–1/2)"
Length: 15-1/4 (16–1/2, 19–1/2, 21)"
Sleeve length to underarm: 10-1/2 (12, 14, 15-1/2)"

MATERIALS
Yarn—CYCA #3 Light, 100% superwash wool or blend:
About 500 (600, 800, 900) yds main color (MC);
about 50 yds in contrast color (CC) for feet motif

Size 3 [3.25 mm] knitting needles; 16" circular needle
Size 6 [4 mm] knitting needles
Tapestry needle
Stitch markers
Optional: yarn bobbins; size D/3 [3.25 mm] crochet
hook; 3 buttons, about 1/2" diameter

GAUGE
22 sts and 30 rows = 4" [10 cm] in St st on size 6 [4mm]
needles. *Adjust needle size as necessary to
obtain correct gauge.*

Inc 1 st each side every 8th (8th, 8th, 10th) row 1 (7, 8, 3) time(s)—58 (60, 68, 70) sts. Work even until sleeve measures 10–1/2 (12, 14, 15–1/2)" or desired length from CO.

Begin raglan shaping:
BO 6 sts beg of next 2 rows—46 (48, 56, 58) sts.
Beg with RS row, dec 1 st each side—44 (46, 54, 56) sts
Next row (WS): Work even.
Rep last 2 rows 16 (17, 21, 21) times—12 (12, 12, 14) sts.
Dec 1 st each side every 4th row 3 (3, 3, 4) times—6 sts.
BO 6 sts.
Work second sleeve the same.

Block all pieces and allow to dry completely. Sew sleeves to raglan yoke. Sew sleeve seams and side seams tog with mattress st (see Glossary). Weave in ends to WS.

Neck Ribbing
With smaller circular needle, MC, and RS facing, pick up and knit 70 (80, 84, 84) sts around neckline. Join sts into rnd, and work k1, p1 rib for 1". BO loosely in rib patt. *Note:* If you prefer to have a back neck opening, join only the lower 4 (4–1/2, 5, 5–1/2)" of back left raglan, leaving the rem seam open. Beg at back opening, work neck rib flat, back and forth. After BO neck rib, with crochet hook work 1 row sc (see Glossary) along both edges of opening and neck rib. Work a second row, making 3 buttonhole loops evenly spaced on one side. Sew 3 buttons on other side, aligning them with buttonhole loops.

FINISHING
Weave in loose ends to WS to secure. Using press cloth, lightly press seams to flatten and lightly press intarsia work to smooth sts.

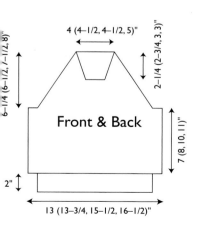

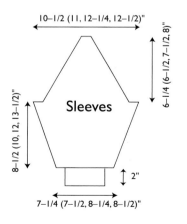

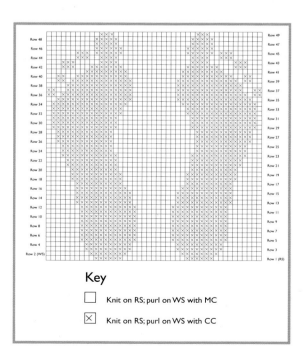

Key

☐ Knit on RS; purl on WS with MC

☒ Knit on RS; purl on WS with CC

Leg Warmers,
published by Hayfield, 1970s

Yes, these probably are your grandmother's leg warmers. None of that "ankle to below the knee nonsense" for Granny with these bay-bees! These are serious leg warmers, the style you need for sub-zero weather!

LEG WARMERS

With larger needles and MC, CO 60 sts.
Row 1: Sl 1, k2, *p2, k2; rep from * to last st, k1.
Row 2: Sl 1, *p2, k2; rep from * to last 3 sts, p2, k1.
These 2 rows form the rib patt. Rep rows 1 and 2 another 20 times.

Begin increases:
Maintaining rib patt (throughout), inc 1 st each end of next row, then every foll 6th row until 108 sts rem. Work extra sts into rib patt when possible.
Work even without incs until leg warmer measures about 30" from CO, ending with RS row completed.
Next row (WS): Sl 1, [k2, p2] twice, k2, [p2tog, k2, p2, k2] 4 times, p2tog, [k2, p2] twice, k2, [p2tog, k2, p2, k2] 6 times, p2, k3—97 sts.
Next row (RS): Sl 1, knit to end.
Next row: Sl 1, purl to end.
Work 2 rows in St st.
Join color B, work 2 rows in St st. Pick up MC and work 2 rows in St st.
Joining colors B and C as necessary, work rows 1–20 from chart B. The odd-numbered rows are knit and the even-numbered rows are purl.
After completing chart B, join MC.
Rows 1, 2, 5, and 6: With MC, work in St st.
Rows 3 and 4: Join B, work in St st.
With MC, change to smaller needles and work as foll:
Row 1: Sl 1, knit to end of row.
Rep row 1 another 4 times. BO all sts.
Work second leg warmer the same.

FINISHING

Lightly block, taking care not to flatten rib. Weave in all loose ends to WS. With threaded tapestry needle, weave leg seam tog with mattress st (see Glossary). Fold top cuff to RS. Fold first 3" at lower edge to RS.

FINISHED MEASUREMENTS

Length when worn: About 27", with top and lower
   edges folded over to right side of work
Circumference at widest section of rib: About 19–1/2"
   unstretched

MATERIALS

Yarn—CYCA #3 Light, 100% wool or blend: About 1100
yds main color (MC); about 100 yds each of colors
   B and C
Size 3 [3.25 mm]; size 6 [4 mm] knitting needles
Tapestry needle

GAUGE

22 sts and 28 rows = 4" [10 cm] in St st on size 6
   [4 mm] needles. *Adjust needle size as necessary to
   obtain correct gauge.*

Chart B

Row 20	O	O	O				O				O	O	O
Row 19	O	O				O	O	O				O	O
Row 18	O	O				O	O	O				O	O
Row 17	O				O	O	O	O	O				O
Row 16	O				O	O	O	O	O				O
Row 15				O	O	O		O	O	O			
Row 14				O	O	O		O	O	O			
Row 13			O	O	O				O	O	O		
Row 12			O	O	O				O	O	O		
Row 11		O	O	O						O	O	O	
Row 10	X	O	O	O	X	X	X	X	X	O	O	O	X
Row 9	X	X	O	O	O	X	X	X	O	O	O	X	X
Row 8	X	X	O	O	O	X	X	X	O	O	O	X	X
Row 7	X	X	X	O	O	O	X	O	O	O	X	X	X
Row 6	X	X	X	O	O	O	X	O	O	O	X	X	X
Row 5	O	X	X	X	O	O	O	O	O	X	X	X	O
Row 4	O	X	X	X	O	O	O	O	O	X	X	X	O
Row 3	O	O	X	X	X	O	O	O	X	X	X	O	O
Row 2 (WS)	O	O	X	X	X	O	O	O	X	X	X	O	O
Row 1 (RS)	O	O	O	X	X	X	O	X	X	X	O	O	O

Work the 12 sts between
markers 8 times total.

Key

☐ Knit on RS; purl on WS with main color (MC)

☒ Knit on RS; purl on WS with color B

⊙ Knit on RS; purl on WS with color C

☐ Pattern repeat frame

Paris Look Sweaters à la Mode, published by Patons, 1970s

Long-lined and boldly patterned, these sweaters were designed in France. This two-color design uses stranded knitting. The trick to success with this method is to resist the urge to pull the yarn that is not in use too tightly when stranding across the stitches.

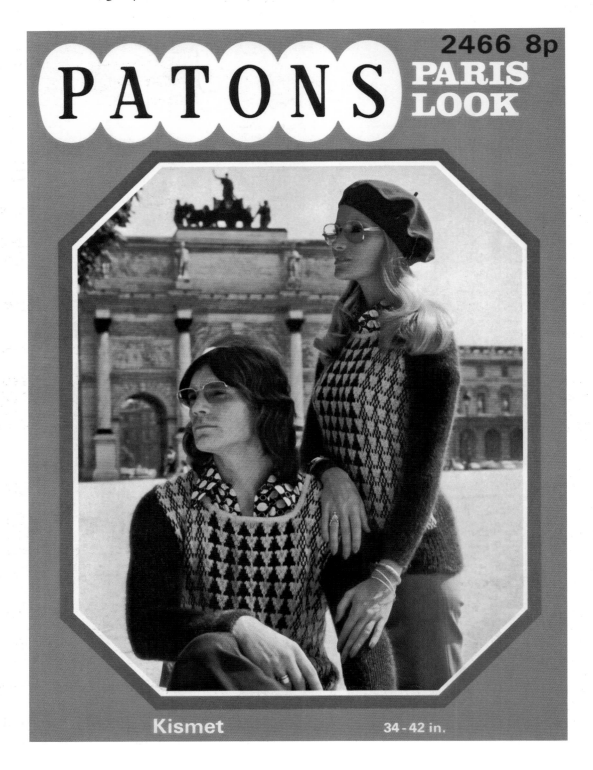

SIZE
34 (36, 38, 40, 42)"

FINISHED MEASUREMENTS
Front width at underarm: 17–1/4 (18–1/2, 19–1/2, 20–3/4, 21–3/4)"
Back width at underarm (unstretched): 15 (15–3/4, 16–3/4, 17–1/2, 18–1/2)"
Length: 23–1/2 (24, 25, 26, 26 1/2)"
Sleeve length to underarm: 17 (17–1/2, 18, 18–1/2, 19)"
Note: Back is worked in ribbing and is easily expanded to match front width measurement.

MATERIALS
Yarn—CYCA #2 Fine: About 1000 (1000, 1200, 1200, 1400) yds dark color (D); about 200 yds light contrast color (L)
Size 3 [3.25 mm] knitting needles, and 16" circular needle; size 5 [3.75 mm] knitting needles
Tapestry needle
Stitch holders

GAUGE
28 sts and 28 rows = 4" [10 cm] in St st on size 5 [3.75 mm] in 2-color stranded patt. *Adjust needle size as necessary to obtain correct gauge.*

FRONT

With D and smaller needles, CO 99 (107, 115, 123, 131) sts.
Row 1 (RS): K2, *p1, k1; rep from * to last st, k1
Row 2: P2, *k1, p1; rep from * to last st, p1.
Rep last 2 rows 18 (19, 20, 21, 22) times more, then work row 1 again.
Next row (WS): Rib 7 (11, 5, 9, 2), *inc in next st, rib 3 (3, 4, 4, 5); rep from * 20 times more, inc in next st, rib to end—121 (129, 137, 145, 153) sts.
Change to larger needles, join L, and work in patt as foll:

Main pattern:

Row 1 (RS): [K1L, k1D] 20 (20, 24, 24, 24) times, k1L, [k7D, k1L] 5 (6, 5, 6, 7) times, [k1D, k1L] 20 (20, 24, 24, 24) times.
Row 2 and all WS rows: Purl, using same colors as previous row.
Row 3: *K2L, [1D, 1L] 3 times; rep from * 4 (4, 5, 5, 5) times more, [2L, 5D, 1L] 5 (6, 5, 6, 7) times, 1L, **[1L, 1D] 3 times, 2L; rep from ** to end.
Row 5: [K3L, 1D, 1L, 1D, 2L] 5 (5, 6, 6, 6] times, [3L, 3D, 2L] 5 (6, 5, 6, 7) times, [3L, 1D, 1L, 1D, 2L] 5 (5, 6, 6, 6) times, 1L.
Row 7: *K4L, 1D, 3L; rep from * to last st, 1L.
Row 8: Same as row 2.
These 8 rows form patt.
Work even in patt until front measures 16 (16, 16, 16–1/2, 16–1/2)", ending with WS row completed.

Underarm shaping:

Keeping continuity of patt, BO 6 (7, 7, 8, 8) sts at beg of next 2 rows—113 (119, 127, 135, 143) sts.
Dec 1 st at each end of next 5 (5, 7, 7, 7) rows—103 (109, 113, 121, 129) sts.
Dec 1 st each end every other row 7 (7, 6, 7, 8) times—89 (95, 101, 107, 113) sts.
Work even until front measures about 19 (19–1/4, 20, 20–3/4, 21)", ending with 8th patt row completed.

Neck shaping:

Row 1: Work in patt across 28 (30, 31, 32, 33) sts, turn work and sl rem sts on st holder. Cont in patt on these 28 (30, 31, 32, 33) sts as foll:
Dec 1 st at neck edge every row until 25 (26, 28, 29, 30) sts rem.
Work even in patt until front measures about 23 (23–1/2, 24–1/2, 25–1/2, 26)", ending at armhole edge.

Shoulder shaping:

Next row: BO 8 (9, 9, 10, 10) sts, work in est patt to end of row.
Next row: Work even in patt.
Rep last 2 rows once more—9 (8, 10, 9, 10) sts.
BO rem 9 (8, 10, 9, 10) sts.
With RS facing, sl center 33 (35, 39, 43, 47) sts to st holder for front neck. Rejoin yarns to rem 28 (30, 31, 32, 33) sts at neck edge, work in est patt to end of row. Complete neck and shoulder shaping the same as first half.

BACK

With smaller needles and D, CO 105 (111, 117, 123, 129) sts.
Rep first 2 rows of rib the same as front 20 (21, 22, 23, 24) times. Change to larger needles and cont in rib patt until back matches front at side edge to armhole beginning, ending with WS row completed.

Underarm shaping:

Cont rib patt, BO 6 (7, 7, 8, 8) sts at beg of next 2 rows—93 (97, 103, 107, 113) sts.
Next row: Dec 1 st at each end of row—91 (95, 101, 105, 111) sts.
Next row: Work even.
Rep last 2 rows 12 (12, 14, 12, 12) times—79 (83, 87, 93, 99) sts.
Work even in rib patt until back matches front at armhole edge to shoulder shaping.

Shoulder shaping:
BO 8 (8, 8, 9, 9) sts at beg of next 4 rows—47 (51, 55, 57, 63) sts.
BO 7 (8, 8, 8, 9) sts at beg of next 2 rows—33 (35, 39, 41, 45) sts.
Sl these sts to st holder for back neck.

SLEEVES
With smaller needles and D, CO 47 (49, 51, 53, 55) sts, and work in rib same as front for 2."

Sleeve shaping:
Next row (incs): Change to larger needles. Cont in rib, inc 1 st at each end of row—49 (51, 53, 55, 57) sts. Gradually working new sts into rib patt, work the inc row every 6th (6th, 6th, 4th, 4th) row 3 (8, 7, 6, 12) times—55 (67, 67, 67, 81) sts. Then inc every 8th (8th, 6th, 6th, 6th) row 12 (9, 13, 17, 13) times—79 (85, 93, 101, 107) sts.
Work even until sleeve measures 17 (17–1/2, 18, 18–1/2, 19)" from CO, ending with WS row completed.

Underarm shaping:
BO 6 (7, 7, 8, 8) sts at beg of next 2 rows—67 (71, 79, 85, 91) sts.
Next row: Dec 1 st at each end of row—65 (69, 77, 83, 89) sts.
Next row: Work even.

Rep last 2 rows 17 (17, 20, 21, 22) times—31 (35, 37, 41, 45) sts.
Work dec row only 3 (5, 3, 5, 5) times—25 (25, 31, 31, 35) sts.
BO all sts.
Work second sleeve the same.

NECKBAND AND FINISHING
Pin front and back shoulders tog, easing in any extra fabric. With tapestry needle threaded with D, backstitch (see Glossary) shoulders tog. Remove pins. With RS facing, smaller circular needle and L, pick up and knit 30 (32, 33, 35, 37) sts along left side of neck, knit across the front neck sts, dec 4 sts evenly spaced—29 (31, 35, 39, 43) front neck sts after decs.
Pick up and knit 30 (32, 33, 35, 37) sts along right side of neck, knit across 33 (35, 39, 41, 45) back neck sts from holder—122 (130, 140, 150, 162) sts.
Join sts in circle, knit 4 rnds.
Next rnd: Purl, forming the turning ridge.
Next 3 rnds: Knit.
BO all sts loosely.
Fold neckband at turning ridge to WS of work. With threaded tapestry needle, whipstitch (see Glossary) the CO edge loosely to WS of knitting. Join sides and sleeve seams tog with backstitch. Sew sleeve caps into armholes with backstitch. Weave in loose ends to WS.

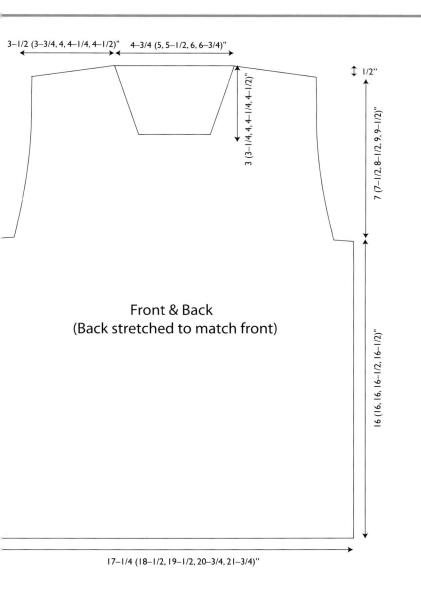

3–1/2 (3–3/4, 4, 4–1/4, 4–1/2)"   4–3/4 (5, 5–1/2, 6, 6–3/4)"

1/2"

3 (3–1/4, 4, 4–1/4, 4–1/2)"

7 (7–1/2, 8–1/2, 9, 9–1/2)"

Front & Back
(Back stretched to match front)

16 (16, 16, 16–1/2, 16–1/2)"

17–1/4 (18–1/2, 19–1/2, 20–3/4, 21–3/4)"

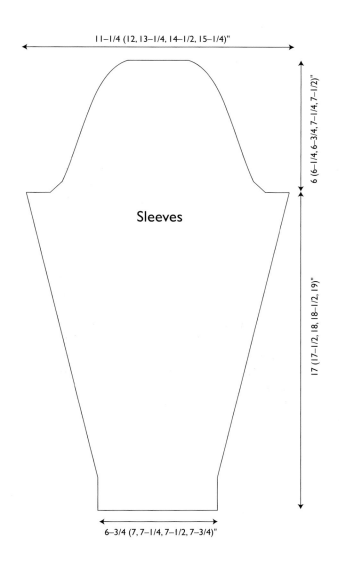

11–1/4 (12, 13–1/4, 14–1/2, 15–1/4)"

6 (6–1/4, 6–3/4, 7–1/4, 7–1/2)"

Sleeves

17 (17–1/2, 18, 18–1/2, 19)"

6–3/4 (7, 7–1/4, 7–1/2, 7–3/4)"

147

Women's Folk Cardigan, published by Craft, 1975

This simple, Tyrolean-style cropped cardigan in stockinette stitch, with seed-stitch borders and embroidery embellishments, is finished with four front metal closures.

Tyrolean-style cropped cardigan, left.

BACK

With MC and smaller needles, CO 75 (81, 85) sts.
Work in St st (knit 1 row, purl 1 row) for 9 rows, ending with RS row completed.
Next row (WS): Knit. This will be the turning ridge row for hemline.
Change to larger needles. Working a RS knit row, cont in St st until back measures 12 (12–1/2, 13)" from hemline turning row.

Underarm shaping:
BO 4 (5, 5) sts beg of next 2 rows—67 (71, 75) sts.
Dec 1 st each side every other row 4 (5, 5) times—59 (61, 65) sts.
Work even until armhole measures about 7 (7–1/2, 8)" from first BO row, ending with RS row completed.

Shoulder shaping:
BO 6 (6, 7) sts at beg of next 4 rows—35 (37, 37) sts.
BO 6 (7, 6) at beg of next 2 rows—23 (23, 25) sts.
Place rem 23 (23, 25) sts on holder for back neck.

LEFT FRONT (AS WORN)

With MC and smaller needles, CO 32 (37, 39) sts. Work in St st for 9 rows; CO 6 sts at end of last row—38 (43, 45) sts.

SIZE
32 (34, 36)"

FINISHED MEASUREMENTS
Back width at underarm: 16–1/2 (18, 19)"
Each front width at underarm, including border:
    8–1/2 (9–1/2, 10)"
Length: 18–1/2 (20, 21)"
Sleeve length to underarm: 16–1/2 (17, 17–1/2)"

MATERIALS
Yarn—CYCA #4 Medium: About 1000 (1180, 1350) yds main color (MC); about 20 yds contrast color (CC) for embroidery
Size 6 [4 mm]; size 8 [5 mm] knitting needles
Tapestry needle
Stitch holders
Four front metal clasps

GAUGE
18 sts and 24 rows = 4" [10 cm] in St st on size 8 [5 mm] needles. *Adjust needle size as necessary to obtain correct gauge.*

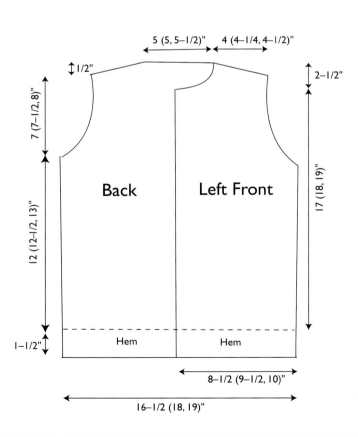

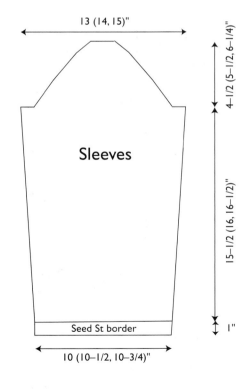

Next row (WS): [K1, p1] 3 times for seed st border, knit rem sts for hemline turning ridge.
Next row (RS): Change to larger needles. Knit to last 6 sts, [p1, k1] 3 times for seed st border sts.
Row 2: [K1, p1] 3 times for border, purl to end of row.
Rep last 2 rows until same length as back to underarm, ending with WS row completed.

Underarm shaping:
Next row (RS): At armhole edge, BO 4 (5, 5) sts. Knit to last 6 sts, work in est seed st for border—34 (38, 40) sts.
Next row (WS): Work even in patt.
Next row (RS): Dec 1 st at armhole edge, work in est patt to end—33 (37, 39) sts.
Rep last 2 rows 3 (4, 4) times more—30 (33, 35) sts.
Work even until front measures 5 (5–1/2, 6)" above underarm BO, ending at front edge with RS row completed.

Neck and shoulder shaping:
Next row (RS): Work 6 seed sts and place on holder, knit to end of row.
Next 6 (8, 9) rows: Dec 1 st at neck edge only every row, work in est patt for remainder of row—18 (19, 20) sts. Work even (if necessary) on these sts until armhole measures same as back, ending with WS row completed.
Next row (RS): At armhole edge, BO 6 (6, 7) sts, work in est patt to end of row—12 (13, 13) sts.
Next row (WS): Work even in patt.
Rep last 2 rows once more—6 (7, 6) sts.
Next row (RS): BO rem 6 (7, 6) sts.

RIGHT FRONT (AS WORN)
Work same as left front through first 8 rows of hem.
Row 9 (RS): Knit.
Next row (WS): Knit across row to form hemline ridge, CO 6 sts at end.
Foll left front instructions, reversing all shaping as follows: Beg underarm and shoulder shaping on WS rows.

SLEEVES
With MC and smaller needles, CO 45 (47, 49) sts.
Row 1 (RS): K1, *p1, k1; rep from * across. Rep this row for seed st cuff 7 times more.

Sleeve shaping:
Next row (WS): Change to larger needles and work in St st, beg with purl row; inc 1 st each side on this row—47 (49, 51) sts.
Inc 1 st each side every 12th (10th, 10th) row 6 (7, 8) times—59 (63, 67) sts.
Work even until sleeve measures 16–1/2 (17, 17–1/2)".

Cap shaping:
BO 4 (5, 5) sts at beg of next 2 rows—51 (53, 57) sts.
Dec 1 st each side every other row 7 (12, 14) times—37 (29, 29) sts.
Dec 1 st each side every row 8 (4, 4) times—21 sts.
BO 2 sts at beg of next 4 rows—13 sts.
BO 13 sts.
Work second sleeve the same.

EMBROIDERY
Beg with right front and RS facing, use a threaded sewing needle to mark the position for the stem and flower spray along fronts, inside seed st border. Each square on the diagram represents 1" on the cardigan. Once you have position marked, thread a double strand of CC on tapestry needle and embroider design, foll diagrams and st key. Work left the front same, reversing position of design.

FINISHING
Sew shoulder seams then sleeves in place with backstitch (see Glossary). Sew underarm and sleeve seams with mattress st (see Glossary). Fold lower hems to WS at turning rows and whipstitch (see Glossary) in place. Weave in loose ends to WS. Align center fronts and attach the metal closures, leaving about 3" at top and bottom open, or positioned as you prefer.

NECKBAND
With MC and larger needles, work seed sts across 6 right front border sts from holder, pick up and knit 15 (16, 17) sts along right front neck edge to shoulder, knit across back neck sts from holder, pick up and knit 15 (16, 17) along left front neck, work 6 seed sts across left front border sts from holder—65 (67, 71) sts. Work in seed st for 7 rows. BO in seed st.

Diagram of flowers

Diagram for placement of flowers.

Inside edge of Front Border

Bottom edge

Key
1: Lazy Daisy Stitch
2: Stem Stitch
3: Straight Stitch

Hooded Cape,
published by Craft, 1975

We love this cape. It's a super project for reducing your stash. If you don't have enough yarns in the same weight, consider using two or three finer yarns held together as one. As long as the yarn combo obtains the correct gauge, you're good to go!

Note: The project is worked flat, in pieces. Because of the number of sts worked in chunky yarn, you should plan to use a circular needle to work back and forth.

LEFT HALF (AS WORN)
With B, CO 27 sts.
Row 1 (WS): Knit

Row 2 (RS): K1f&b (see Glossary), knit to last st, k1f&b—29 sts.
Row 3: Knit
Row 4: Rep row 2—31 sts.
Cont to rep rows 3 and 2 in foll colors:
*6 rows C; 4 rows B; 6 rows A; 6 rows B; 2 rows A; 6 rows E; 2 rows A; 6 rows F; 6 rows A, 4 rows B; rep from * until there are 115 sts (88 rows).

The hooded cape, at rest or in flight, is elegantly primitive and incredibly dramatic. It is knitted in two parts and sewn together in back. One half is ombred; the other, more uniformly striped. Wool yarn is from Berga/Ullman. Turn to page 107.

SIZE
One size fits most

FINISHED MEASUREMENTS (UNSTRETCHED)
Shoulder to lower edge: 26–1/2", measured at center
  of pieces
Length along center back seam: 40–1/2"
Note: The weight of the yarn will lengthen the cape
  when worn.

MATERIALS
Yarn—CYCA #5 Chunky, 100% wool or wool blend with
  higher percentage of wool—Choose yarns that have
plenty of natural elasticity: About 2400 yds total, 550
yds each of colors A and B; 325 yds each of colors C,
D, E, and F
Size 10–1/2 [6.5 mm] 36" circular needle
Size K/10–1/2 [6.5 mm] crochet hook
5 buttons about 1–1/8" diameter.
Tapestry needle

GAUGE
12 sts and 24 rows = 4" [10 cm] in garter st (knit every
  row). *Adjust needle size as necessary to obtain
  correct gauge.*

Make arm opening (about 14–3/4" from CO):
Next row (WS): Cont color sequence and starting at
center back, k63, BO next 20 sts, knit to end of row.
Next row: K32 to BO sts, CO 20 sts over the BO sts,
k63 to end of row.
Cont in colors and inc until there are 185 sts. BO all sts.

RIGHT HALF (AS WORN)
Work to correspond to left half in foll colors and
reversing position of arm opening:
With A, CO 27 sts. Work *6 rows A; 4 rows D, 3 rows F;
2 rows E; 3 rows F; 4 rows D; 6 rows A; 4 rows C; 3
rows B; 4 rows A; rep from * for colors.

HOOD—RIGHT HALF
Starting at neck edge with A, CO 27 sts.
Row 1 (WS): Knit.
Row 2 (RS): Knit across to last st, k1f&b for center
back—28 sts.
Rows 3 and 4: Knit.
Rep these 4 rows in foll colors: *4 rows B; 4 rows C; 4
rows D; 4 rows F; 4 rows E; and 4 rows A; rep from *
until there are 36 sts (row 31). Work even in color
sequence without incs until piece measures about 9"
from CO. On next row dec 1 st at back edge, then every
other row until 24 sts. BO all sts.

HOOD—LEFT HALF
Work same as right half, reversing all shaping.

FINISHING
Seam center back of cape and hood using invisible
weaving for garter st (see Glossary). Sew hood to cape,
matching center back seam and front edges.

Border
On right side, starting at lower right front edge, with
crochet hook and C work in sc (see Glossary) up front
edge, across face edge of hood, and to lower left front.
Turn.
Row 2: Ch 1, sc in each sc to joining of hood and cape.
Turn.
Row 3: Ch 1, sc in each sc to lower edge. Fasten off.
Mark position of 5 buttons on border sts with first m at
neck edge and other 4 ms spaced 5" apart. Join C to
right front at joining of cape and hood. Sc in each of 2
sc, *ch 2, sk 2 sc, sc in each sc to next m; rep from * 4
times more, sc to end of row. Turn.
Row 4: Ch 1, sc in each sc and each ch-2 sp across row.
Fasten off.

Make armhole openings:
With RS facing and using same colors, work 1 row sc
around each armhole opening.

Fringe
Cut about 660 strands of C and 132 strands of A, each
strand about 22" long. The final number of strands will
depend on how you decide to space the fringes, so make
sure you have some C and A rem, or plan to add lengths
of other colors into fringes. Fold 3 strands of C in half,
insert crochet hook on WS in center back seam, draw a
loop of fringe through, insert both ends through the loop,
pull on both ends to tighten. Make next fringe using 2
strands of C and 1 strand of A, attach to lower edge of
cape same as previous fringe. Alternate these 2 colors of
fringes, spacing about 1" apart, around to center front
edge. Work other lower edge of cape the same, beginning
about 1" from center back seam. Trim fringes evenly.

GLOSSARY OF KNITTING TERMS

INVISIBLE WEAVING (OR GRAFTING) FOR GARTER STITCH

Arrange the stitches to be grafted onto 2 needles. Align needles so that one needle lies in front of (or below) the second needle. The stitches on the front needle must be purl stitches and the stitches on the back needle must be knit stitches. Thread tapestry needle with appropriate yarn color for the grafting.

1: Working from right to left, insert threaded needle purlwise through the first stitch on *front* needle. Leave stitch on needle and pull yarn through.

2: Insert needle purlwise through first stitch on *back* needle. Leave stitch on needle and pull yarn through.

3: Insert needle knitwise into the first stitch on *front* needle, pull yarn through, drop stitch from needle. Insert needle purlwise through next stitch on *front* needle, leave stitch on needle, pull yarn through.

4: Insert needle knitwise through first stitch on *back* needle, pull yarn through, drop stitch from needle. Insert needle purlwise through next stitch on *back* needle, leave stitch on needle, pull yarn through.

Rep steps 3 through 4 as many times as there are stitches to be joined.

KITCHENER STITCH (OR GRAFTING) FOR STOCKINETTE STITCH

Arrange the same number of stitches on 2 needles. With RS facing outward, align needles together, or one above the other. Thread tapestry needle with appropriate yarn color for grafting.

1: Working from right to left, insert threaded needle purlwise through first stitch on *front* needle. Leave stitch on needle and pull yarn through.

2: Insert needle knitwise through first stitch on *back* needle. Leave stitch on needle, pull yarn through.

3: Insert yarn knitwise through first stitch on *front* needle, pull yarn through, drop stitch from needle. Insert needle purlwise through next stitch on *front* needle, leave stitch on needle, pull yarn through.

4: Insert yarn purlwise through first stitch on *back* needle, pull yarn through, drop stitch from needle. Insert needle knitwise through next stitch on *back* needle. Leave stitch on needle, pull yarn through. Repeat steps 3 and 4 as many times as there are stitches to be joined.

MATTRESS STITCH—half stitch seams

Block individual pieces first for easier seaming and allow them to air-dry completely. Thread tapestry needle with yarn appropriate for seaming.

1: Place the pieces with right side facing and side by side on a flat surface.

2: Working through the centers of both edges of the stitches (see below for seaming one whole stitch each side), insert threaded needle under 1 or 2 stitches.

3: Move needle to second piece and insert under 1 or 2 adjacent stitches. The number of stitches worked should be the same on each side.

4: Return to first side, insert needle into the same place it came out of, and working upward, insert under 1 or 2 stitches.

5: Return to second piece and work same as step 4. Repeat steps 4 and 5 as needed, stopping occasionally to gently pull the yarn and close the stitches together.

Mattress Stitches—whole stitch seams

Work as above, except insert the needle between the first and second stitches of each piece and under the running thread between those stitches.

CROCHET CHAIN CAST-ON (provisional and permanent cast-on)

While there are several crochet cast-on methods, the following technique is suggested for projects worked in one piece from back to front, where the cast-on and bind-off edges will meet at side seams.

a) Permanent chain cast-on

1: Using the main yarn, make a slipknot and place slipknot on crochet hook.

2: Hold hook in right hand and knitting needle in left hand. Place the hook on top of the needle.

3: Take the working end of the yarn under the needle and over (yarn over) the hook, draw a loop

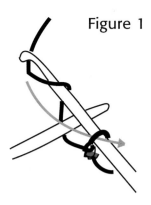

Figure 1

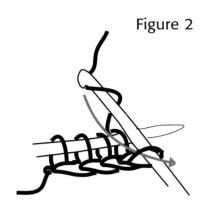

Figure 2

through the slipknot, bring yarn over the top of needle and form a stitch. (see Figure 1, above).

4: Bring yarn under needle again.

5: Yarn over hook, draw up a loop over the needle and through the stitch on the hook, creating a new stitch on the needle. (see Figure 2).

Repeat steps 4 and 5 until one stitch fewer than required number of stitches. Relocate last loop from hook onto needle to form the last stitch.

Work first row of pattern into stitches on needle.

b) Provisional (temporary) cast-on

To make a temporary cast-on, simply follow the same steps as above, using a smooth waste cotton yarn. When cast-on is finished, join main yarn to work first row. Later, remove the temporary cast-on by removing waste yarn, then place stitches in main yarn on needle, then follow instructions to complete project.

THREE-NEEDLE BIND-OFF

Place same number of stitches on two needles (it's easier to work this using circular needles or double-point needles) with right side of work together.

1: [Knit 2 stitches together, using one stitch from front needle and one stitch from back needle] twice, there will be 2 new stitches on right needle.

2: Bind off one stitch using standard bind-off.

3: Knit 2 stitches together, using 1 stitch from front and 1 stitch from back needle (2 stitches on needle).

4: Bind off one stitch using standard bind-off.

Rep steps 3 and 4 until all stitches are bound off. Cut yarn and thread through remaining stitch to fasten off.

The right side of the work is smooth and both pieces are joined together.

Note: The method can also be worked with the wrong side of the work held together, which produces a sporty, ridged seam on the right side of the fabric and a smooth seam on the wrong side.

BACKSTITCH SEAM

Pin both pieces right side together. With threaded tapestry needle, and working one stitch in from the seam edges, bring needle up 2 stitches from lower edge, reinsert back 2 stitches, then come up again 4 stitches ahead. This should anchor beginning of seam.

1: Reinsert back 2 stitches, then come up 4 stitches ahead, this will be about half the distance ahead of where the yarn emerged (see Figure 3, below). Continue in this manner, moving back 2 stitches, then ahead 4 stitches until seam is finished. Secure seam by working over the last 2 stitches once or twice more.

Figure 3

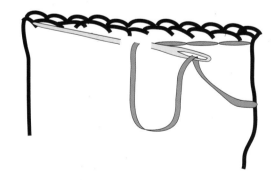

WHIPSTITCH

*Working at right angles, insert threaded needle under one stitch loop on one piece, then under one stitch loop of the adjacent stitch on second piece. Draw yarn through both stitch loops, and repeat from * until pieces are joined together (see Figure 4, below).

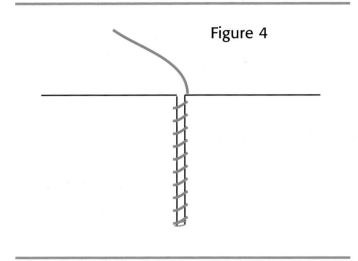

Figure 4

SINGLE CROCHET CHAIN
(worked in knitting)

Insert hook from front to back where designated, yarn over hook, pull up loop (chain 1 made). Insert hook into same stitch, yarn over hook, pull loop through (2 loops on hook), yarn over hook, pull through both loops.

Half Double Crochet (worked in knitting)

Make 1 chain same as above, yarn over hook, pull through loop on hook (chain 2 made). Yarn over hook, insert hook into same knitting stitch as first chain, pull up loop (3 loops on hook), yarn over hook, pull through all 3 loops.

Double Crochet (worked in knitting)

Work 2 chains same as above (a double crochet usually has 3 chains to match its height, but when applying crochet to knitting, many crafters find that 2 chains is enough, and 3 is too loose). Yarn over hook, insert hook into same knitting stitch as first chain, yarn over, pull up a loop (3 chains on hook), yarn over hook, pull through first 2 loops, yarn over hook, pull through remaining 2 loops.

TASSEL

Wind yarn around cardboard rectangle cut to the desired length of tassel about 20 times (more for thinner yarn, or thicker tassel). Cut 18″ strand yarn and thread tapestry needle. Insert needle under all wraps at one end, pull strand through leaving a 6″ end and a 12″ end. Tie both strands into a knot to secure wraps. Cut wraps at other end of rectangle. Wrap the long end of strand around the upper end of wraps several times, about 1/2″ down from top, then thread the yarn up through the top. Use this strand to secure tassel to project.

POM-POM

Cut 2 circles of cardboard about 1/4″ larger than the desired circumference of pom-pom (or use a commercial pom-pom maker). Cut narrow opening into both circles about halfway, then cut small circles in the center of both pieces of cardboard (see Figure 5). Place both circles together with narrow and inner openings aligned. Wind yarn around the cardboard circles until they are completely covered, and fully packed—the more wraps, the fuller the pom-pom (see Figure 6, below). Cut around outside edge of all the yarn wraps; do not remove cardboard circles. Cut a strand of yarn, about 18″ in length, and insert between both cardboard circles; pull both ends of strand until they are equal length. Tie strand into a tight knot to secure all the yarn wraps. Remove cardboard circles and fluff out yarn wraps. Trim yarn wraps if necessary. Use the ends of long strand to secure pom-pom to project.

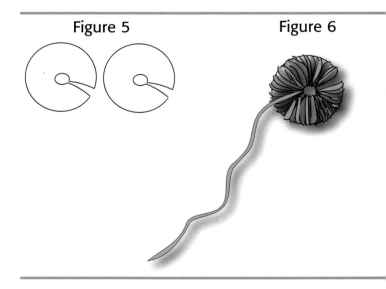

Figure 5   Figure 6

REVERSE SINGLE CROCHET (CRAB STITCH)

Work one row/round of single crochet After last stitch is completed, work from left to right as follows: Chain 1, *insert hook into single crochet of previous row, yarn over hook and draw loop through the stitch and *under* the loop on hook, yarn over hook and draw through both loops on hook*. Insert hook into next stitch to the right and repeat from * to * as indicated in project.

BUTTONHOLE STITCH (longer version often called blanket stitch)

Cut a length of yarn about 5 or 6 times longer than the section to be edged. With right side of work facing and working from left to right, insert a threaded needle from back to front at edge, leaving a 4″ tail on wrong side of work to weave in later. *Holding the working yarn under the needle and along the section to be edged, move the needle to the right about 1/4–1/2″ (step 1, Figure 7, below), then insert the needle from front to back about 1/2″ up from edge (step 2, Figure 7), then exit to front again at lower edge (step 3, Figure 7)*; repeat from * as necessary.

BACKWARD LOOP CAST-ON (also useful to make single increases)

Loop yarn around a thumb or forefinger so the yarn is crossed. Insert right needle tip under the outside strand as shown (see Figure 8, below) and slip new stitch on needle so that it doesn't unwind.

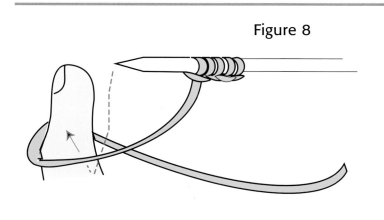

Figure 8

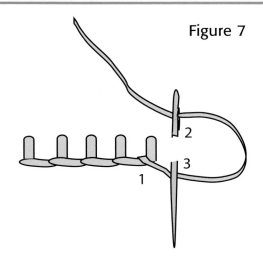

Figure 7

ABBREVIATIONS

beg	begin, beginning, begins
BO	bind off
CC	contrast color
cm	centimeter(s)
CO	cast on
cont	continue, continuing
dec(s)	decrease, decreasing, decreases
dpn	double pointed needle(s)
est	establish, established
foll	follow(s), following
inc(s)	increase(s), increasing
k	knit
k1f&b	knit into front then back of same st (increase)
k1f,b,&f	knitting into front, back, then front again of same st (increase 2 sts)
k1tbl	knit 1 st through back loop
k2tog	knit 2 sts together (decrease)
kwise	knitwise (as if to knit)
m(s)	marker(s)
MC	main color
mm	millimeter(s)
m1	make 1 (increase)
m1k	make 1 knitwise
m1p	make 1 purlwise
pat(s)	pattern(s)
p	purl
p1f&b	purl into front then back of same st (increase)
p1tbl	purl 1 st through back loop
p2tog	purl 2 sts together (decrease)
pm(s)	place marker(s)
psso	pass slip st(s) over
pwise	purlwise (as if to purl)
rem	remain(s), remaining

rep(s)	repeat(s), repeated, repeating
rib	ribbing
rnd(s)	round(s)
RS	right side (of work)
rev sc	reverse single crochet (crab st)
sc	single crochet
sl	slip, slipped, slipping
sl st	slip stitch (sl 1 st pwise unless otherwise indicated)
ssk	[slip 1 st knitwise] twice from left needle to right needle, insert left needle tip into fronts of both slipped sts, knit both sts together from this position (decrease)
ssp	[slip 1 st knitwise] twice from left needle to right needle, return both sts to left needle and purl both together through back loops
st(s)	stitch(es)
St st	stockinette stitch
tbl	through back loop
tog	together
w&t	wrap next stitch then turn work (often used in short rows)
WS	wrong side (of work)
Wyib	with yarn in back
Wyif	with yarn in front
yb	yarn back
yf	yarn forward
yo	yarn over
*	repeat instructions from *
( )	alternate measurements and/or instructions
[ ]	instructions to be worked as a group a specified number of times

INDEX